URBAN LEGENDS OF PRO WRESTLING

ANDREW KHELLAH

For permissions or media inquiries:

Screentimed Media LLC

436 Main Street, Ste 11, Spotswood, New Jersey 08884 · www.screentimed.com

First Edition: 2026 Printed in the United States of America

CONTENTS

FOREWORD BY CONRAD THOMPSON

Look, I'm just a mortgage guy who fell in love with wrestling watching WrestleMania IV. I've been lucky enough over the years to ask the questions fans want to know and dig deeper on our podcasts. *"Alright... chat me up... what happened when?"* What you see on TV is only half the story. That's the stuff you hear sitting around Starrcast weekend, or watching our Q&A live panels, or hanging out at Top Guy Weekend. That's where the stories live. The ones that get passed around and debated.

What I really like about this book is that Andrew doesn't just repeat those stories—he goes to the sources and tries to uncover the stuff that hasn't been fully told or expanded on before. That's kind of our style at RingClassics.

And if you're holding this book, chances are—you're one of us. You get it. So buckle up, because you're about to hear some stories you thought you knew the whole deal and a few you definitely didn't. Roll Tide.

— Conrad

PREFACE

I remember vividly the night Hulk Hogan was *"getting the life choked out of him,"* as Jesse Ventura said on commentary by Andre the Giant on Saturday Night's Main Event in 1987. All the babyfaces gathered from the locker room to try and get the Giant off our hero.

My Father did not break kayfabe even while I was in tears. He let me believe Hogan was going to die, and my six-year-old brain nearly exploded.

Fast forward to 1997: I am on America Online, tying up the landline telephone all night, every night, convincing people in chat rooms I never spoke to or met at age 14 to subscribe to my free wrestling newsletter.

Looking back, that would not have been the wisest or safest option. What began with a dozen or so subscribers grew to 27,000+ by the end of 1998. As I graduated from high school, I bid farewell to the newsletter and prepared for college life during the Attitude Era. I stopped writing at the time, but never stopped being a fan.

Years later, I found that truth and fiction weren't enemies in wrestling — they were tag partners. Some were confirmed, some contradicted, and some could never be proven.

I have interviewed hundreds of wrestlers from long-form "shoot interviews" to short clips on YouTube and throughout social media. This book is built from some of my interviews, many as recent as 2026, personal recollections with talent, and my own first-hand accounts.

Some research was based on archived tapes, production notes, fan testimonies, public and private sources, and other interviews, all of which are credited throughout the relevant chapters.

The intention is not to spread unverified gossip or scandal for shock value.

This project became more than a book. It became a bridge between eras — between the fans like myself who grew up believing and the wrestlers who made us believe.

DEDICATION

In loving memory of my Father, Fayez Khellah, who introduced me to my first love—professional wrestling.

For each show you took us to, every pay-per-view buy, and every piece of merchandise from Bret Hart's shades to foam fingers, fan club, and magazine subscriptions…

Thank you, Dad. *I was too young to understand your sacrifices.*

To my wife, **Elizabeth**—I will always have love for you for the greatest gift you've given me, our daughter, Ava.

To my sister **Mary**, and my brothers **Johnny** and **John**—one by blood and one by marriage—I love you all very much. I carry your love and support with me in everything I do.

To my nephew **Anthony**, whose contagious laugh lights up my heart. Uncle Andy loves you more than these words can express.

Keith Carlsen—you carry yourself in a way that would make our parents proud every single day. You've proven that blood doesn't define family, loyalty, or respect.

Adam Zied—Thank you for sharing the same love for wrestling and for all the road trips, long drives, and memories made. Those moments mean more than you know.

Mark, Monica, Alex & Lena - Your faith and love for God are an inspiration.

Joseph Segreti, a Bronx original, whom I am proud to call a dear friend, witnessed my tears after meeting Vince McMahon. It wouldn't have been possible without you.

Michael James Hall, Bryan Kelley, and Danny Dec — thank you for years of collecting/trading, but more importantly, your friendship and memories.

Varun, George, Bharat, Jay, Sunny, Al, Sleepy, and Swami —my friends and poker buddies, as George calls us. What we have goes far beyond flopping the nuts. It's built on years of laughs, stories, loyalty, and moments that will last a lifetime.

Med, Ernie, and Eli ("the dukes"), no matter the distance or where life has taken us, our bond will never be broken.

To **Conrad Thompson, Dave Silva, Mike Dockins, Evan Polisher, Dave Hancock, Kris McDonald, and John Hoopingarner** — thank you for the doors you've opened, the opportunities you've given me, and the support you've shared. But more importantly, I thank you for your friendship and kindness.

And special thanks to my friend, **Steve Keirn**. I am humbled and honored to be part of your circle.

To my daughter, Ava,

I see myself in you every time you watch wrestling with the same passion and fire I had growing up. Your laughter during entrances, the way your eyes widen in awe at surprises, and the little gasps you make at every near-fall remind me that the magic I once felt is still alive, and now it lives in you. Protect that spark and passion inside you and follow your heart. Stand up for what you love. And, never settle for less than you deserve. No matter where life takes you, my love walks beside you.

My pride in you is endless, and my spirit lives with you always.

Forever yours, pumpkin.

Love,
Daddy

CHAPTER 1
THE ROAD MOM

URBAN LEGENDS in professional wrestling usually begin with something loud—a riot, a betrayal, a body, something that forces its way into memory whether you want it to or not. This one doesn't begin that way. This one begins quietly, almost gently, with something small enough to hold in your hands. It begins with boots.

The building had already emptied itself of noise. It was August 3, 1997. SummerSlam. East Rutherford, New Jersey—my backyard.

Nearly 20,000 people inside that building had just watched Steve Austin take a piledriver from Owen Hart that would change wrestling history. But in the moment, nobody knew that. She wasn't backstage when it happened. She was in the crowd.

. . .

"YOU WERE THERE TOO, RIGHT?" she asked me later. We were just in different sections. Up in Section 106, there was no commentary in our ears, no replay to guide our understanding, no close-up to tell us what we were supposed to feel. From her seat, she watched the moment just a little too long. *"Stop, Owen. What are you doing?"* she thought.

At first, she assumed it was part of the show. Owen had always known how to stretch a moment and hold a crowd. But this felt different. As the match continued, Austin rolled Owen up. The bell rang. And then the night moved on.

Hours later, when the building had emptied, and the show had already become something else, she was still there near the loading dock. When the ambulance doors opened, a paramedic stepped down and handed her a pair of boots.

"He can carry his own boots," she said instinctively.

The paramedic looked at her calmly.

"He can't. He broke his neck."

There were no cameras to capture that moment. No announcers to frame it. No music swelling in the background.

Just boots in her hands. That was the road, and that was what happened after everything else stopped. Before guaranteed contracts, private buses, and charter jets, there were highways.

HER NAME WAS DAWN GUNDRUM, and it sounded like it could have belonged on a wrestling poster. But she was never the character; she was just the constant.

Often at the crack of Dawn—pun intended—she was already awake, already driving, already making sure someone else got where they needed to go.

DAWN GREW UP IN FRITZTOWN, Pennsylvania, about fifty miles from the Allentown television tapings that defined an era. As a child, she sat beside her father watching Bruno Sammartino and Pedro Morales, not just watching but learning. Her father didn't treat wrestling like background noise. He pointed things out. He explained holds, pacing, and why something worked. Those nights became something more than television—they became a connection.

As she got older, she didn't drift away from it. She leaned into it. She and her girlfriends would pile into cars every few weeks and drive to shows in Allentown or Hamburg, sitting in the same section every time. Close enough to feel the ring, far enough to see everything.

That consistency caught the attention of SD Jones, and eventually, conversations started. One night, Tony Atlas needed a ride.

She said yes.

And that yes became something much bigger than she could have understood at the time.

She drove Atlas. Then Rocky Johnson. Then Greg Valentine. One ride turned into another, and then another, until it wasn't something she thought about anymore. It was just what she did.

If Dawn could save them money and miles, she did. If they were hungry, she fed them. If their gear needed cleaning, she washed it as she did for Bret Hart many times.

She set a rule early and never broke it. *"If you want a friend, here I am. If you're looking for a bed partner, move on."*

That line defined everything. It gave her respect in a place where respect wasn't always easy to come by.

The road wasn't always serious. Sometimes it was ridiculous.

Jacques Rougeau once convinced her that her brand-new Subaru had transmission problems by knocking it out of gear at every stoplight. She blamed the car until Raymond, his brother and tag team partner, made him move to the back seat.

POLICE ONCE PULLED her over while Davey Boy Smith and Dustin Rhodes followed behind. An officer made Dustin say the alphabet backward. *"I couldn't even do that sober,"* she thought, watching him struggle. During the Attitude Era, she had Val Venis in the back seat and Test up front when Val's phone kept ringing. *"No, I don't have Pepper,"* Val kept saying. Al Snow had put his telephone number on television. Fans were calling nonstop. Andrew Martin (Test) laughed the entire ride.

THERE WERE moments under the lights, too. At Hershey Park Arena in 1989, she stepped into Rick Rude's "Rude Awakening." She agreed only because she knew how it would end. *"If there had been kissing involved, I would have refused."* Bobby Heenan stood in the ring with Rude, telling her she smelled like chocolate, which was a dig as they were in Hershey Park.

Rude insulted her. *"You couldn't even do my laundry."*

Dawn knew the truth behind it. The whole thing was improvised. She walked out exactly as she walked in. Later, a drunk fan tried to confront her. Mel Phillips removed him. He tried to sue. It went nowhere.

DAWN CAME HOME from work one afternoon, keys still in her hand, and saw it immediately — one message waiting on her answering machine. She pressed play and listened.

> *"Dawn, this is Davey Boy. I left my effing belt in your car, and I need it for TV."*

She walked back outside and opened the door. There it was, resting where it had been left, gold plates catching the daylight in a way that made it feel completely out of place. Before she overnighted it for almost $500, which WWF reimbursed  her for, she paused. She wrapped it around her waist once, to feel it, just to mark the moment, then took it off and placed it carefully into the box. She drove to FedEx, filled out the form, and handed it over the counter like it was just another package.

ONE NIGHT, Dawn was out listening to country music at a bar with Kerry Von Erich, and it didn't take long for attention to find him. It always did. Kerry had that kind of presence.

A woman approached Dawn directly, confident and direct, as if she had already decided what was going to happen. The Texas Tornado was no match for the Road Mom.

"This is my fiancée," they told the girl. That's what the road required sometimes.

.   .   .

AND THEN THERE WAS CHICAGO. WrestleMania 13 weekend didn't feel like a show. It felt like the entire business gathered in one place. Dawn was sitting with Owen's mother-in-law when Dwayne Johnson walked over—not yet the global icon, just Rocky Johnson's son finding his way. He hugged her immediately. As Rock introduced her, he joked, *"Yeah, she used to do my dad—"*

Dawn cut him off midway and smacked him, shouting, *"Dwayne!"*

Rock laughed. *"No, no—she used to **drive** my dad."*

Months later, that same sense of recognition would show itself again, but Penn State in October didn't feel anything like Chicago. Dawn had her van parked near the curb, engine running lightly to keep the chill out. She had already been driving people back and forth—staff, wrestlers, whoever needed to get across campus without fighting through crowds.

That trust hadn't started at Penn State. It had started years earlier, in quiet places—airport pickups, hotel lobbies, long drives between towns—watching how she moved, how she handled things, how she showed up.

Dawn with The Rock and Kama (aka The Godfather)

And the in-between is where everything real happens. The Virginia trip was one of those in-between moments. It almost didn't happen.

When the call came, it was Martha first. Her voice was calm, steady, not demanding. *"Can you take him to Virginia?"* she asked. Dawn already knew what that meant. *"That's seven hours each way,"* she said honestly. *"I have to work. It's just too*

long." Martha didn't push. *"I understand,"* she said quietly. But then the tone shifted. A different voice came through the line.

"Are you going to drive Daddy home?"

The drive was still fourteen hours. But children don't measure things in miles. They measure them in their presence. She looked over at Owen. *"Yes,"* she quietly said to Oje. *"I'll drive him."*

Eventually, Owen started talking about the house. They were moving in that weekend. Boxes everywhere. Then he told Dawn, *"1999 is my last year. I am done."*

Later in the drive, during a stretch of road where the conversation had thinned out again, he said something else. *"I'm not wrestling."*

She smiled, assuming it was one of his jokes. *"Okay,"* she said. *"Blue Blazer?"* He didn't smile. *"He's not wrestling either."*

They made Virginia. Fourteen hours total. Dawn pulled up to the curb. Owen grabbed his bag from the trunk. She hugged him. *"Tell your family I love them."*

Owen smiled and hugged her, *"Okay."* He turned and walked toward the terminal. She watched him go.

After Owen tragically passed, Dawn started calling airlines, and the prices didn't make sense. Every number she heard felt wrong — two thousand or more. But she remembered how the boys would cancel their hotel reservations and entrust the task to Dawn because she saved them money.

The airline asked her the same question over and over.

"Are you a family member?" There was a pause.

"Yes," she said. The price dropped.

Seven hundred dollars round-trip. She hung up the phone and sat there for a moment, holding it, staring at nothing.

Then she picked it back up and called Bret Hart. She didn't want it to feel like she had taken something she didn't deserve. When he answered, she didn't ease into it.

"I have to tell you something," she said.

Bret waited. She told him what she had said to the airline. That she had told them she was family. Then Bret asked her a simple question. *"What do the kids call you?"*

She didn't hesitate.

"Aunt Dawn."

Another pause. Then Bret answered. *"There you go."* It was validation and confirmation. Dawn was part of the family.

When she arrived in Calgary, nothing felt like a show anymore. She was inside the Hart home — the Dungeon — not as a visitor, not as someone standing outside looking in, but as someone who belonged there in that moment. Dawn stayed through the service, through the quiet moments afterward, through the conversations that didn't have clear endings. At one point, she found herself around the children, moving naturally into the role she had always taken on — steady, present, someone who didn't need to say the right thing, just needed to be there.

When she left Calgary, nothing felt resolved. The flight home felt longer than the flight there. And the road she had driven so many times before didn't feel the same anymore.

CHAPTER 2
THE CHAMP
AND THE KING

"I thought you were going to shoot me." -
Hulk Hogan.

BY THE EARLY 1980S, professional wrestling was in the middle of a civil war. On one side stood the territorial system — a network of regional promoters who ruled their cities and protected their markets. On the other stood Vince McMahon and the World Wrestling Federation, expanding nationally with television, merchandising, and a new kind of superstar at the center of that collision was Hulk Hogan. With his blond hair, red-and-yellow gear, and superhero persona, he was built for television and mass appeal. He wasn't just a wrestler — he was the face of Vince McMahon's national takeover. Hogan's rise and popularity in the Rock n' Wrestling era signaled the end of the old territorial system.

BUT ONE MAN embodied that old system more than anyone else—an eight-time NWA World Heavyweight Champion.

Harley Race wasn't just respected — he was feared. Kansas City was his city, his territory, his kingdom. And Hogan was coming for it, or at least how Harley saw it.

———

TENSIONS EXPLODED ON JUNE 6, 1986, when the WWF (already expanding into Kansas City two years earlier) ran local promotional segments in Kansas City for eight straight weeks, which, according to Hogan himself, heavily advertised his arrival as the WWF Champion to take on King Kong Bundy.

To Harley Race, this was war. In a 2000 interview conducted by RF Video, Race recalled:

"They (WWF) were in Kansas City, and I had a show running at Municipal Auditorium, right across the river. I walked up into the dressing room area, and it was like deathly silence. Terry (Hulk Hogan) was standing there talking to the two Funks, and they're looking at me, 'Oh my God —what's he here for?' I open-handed slapped Hogan—not in the face, but in the ribcage. If you've ever been hit there, you know it stings, and it knocks the wind right out of you. [Hogan] spun around, saw [me], and just fell back into a chair. Hogan said to Harley, 'I thought the first time I saw you, you'd have a machine gun—a Tommy gun.'

*Harley replied: "Well, I have one—but it's not **that** big. "*

Gorilla Monsoon and others rushed in to break it up.

Race explained, *"Hogan was working in my city as Vince McMahon's new head honcho."* The territorial king was watching his empire crumble in real time.

That Friday evening in 1986 was the breaking point for Harley. According to Hogan, things had escalated over the past year or two. Hogan wrestled in Kansas City in 1984 against Big John Studd and again in 1985 against Brutus Beefcake. On The Joe Rogan Experience, Hogan says that when he flew into Kansas City and arrived at the arena around two in the afternoon, members of the ring crew warned him that Harley Race had already been there and had tried to set the ring on fire. Hogan was told that Race had arrived with a gun and had said that when Hogan showed up, he intended to kill him.

Earlier that evening, Hogan had eaten at Rusty Scupper, a restaurant near the arena. He began feeling sick shortly after arriving at the building and went to the restroom hours before the show began. While Hogan was inside, Davey Boy Smith ran in, shouting that Race had arrived. Remembering the warning from the ring crew, Hogan rushed to get out of the bathroom as fast as he could.

According to Hogan, when he came around the corner into the hallway, Harley Race was waiting for him. Race allegedly pulled out a handgun and pointed it directly at Hogan's face. He told Hogan that he should kill him for coming into Kansas City and declaring himself world champion in Race's territory. Then, moments later, Race lowered the gun and said he needed a job. Hogan said he shook Race's hand, told him he had always been a fan, and the confrontation ended without violence. Hogan would keep his word and encourage Vince McMahon to hire Harley Race immediately.

The tension was building before 1986, when the WWF expanded into Kansas City — a market that had long belonged to Race. On July 19, 1984, a planned WWF show in Kansas City was reportedly canceled, possibly due to direct competition from nearby, with Harley Race headlining a major NWA event against Ric Flair for the NWA Championship at Memorial Hall.

By 1985, Vince McMahon pushed forward anyway. On May 31st that year, the WWF ran Kansas City with Hulk Hogan in the main event against Brutus Beefcake. The crowd was estimated at 10,000 fans — a massive number for a fully developed territory with a dominant local promotion. Hogan drew. But when Hogan left, the business collapsed.

The following month, on June 29, 1985, *without* Hogan on the card, attendance dropped nearly 70%! Junkyard Dog and Greg Valentine for the Intercontinental Title was the main event. The following month, on August 25, Ricky Steamboat and Tito Santana faced Don Muraco and Mr. Fuji in front of approximately 3,600 fans. Then, WWF returned on September 30 with Roddy Piper wrestling Paul Orndorff to a double count-out in front of 3,000 people. Hogan did not work that show.

The company did not headline another major Kansas City event with Hogan until two weeks after Harley Race was crowned King of the Ring in Foxborough, MA, on July 14, 1986, in front of twelve thousand fans. Two weeks later, on July 31, 1986, Harley Race made his Kansas City debut under the WWF banner. Hogan was positioned against King Kong Bundy in a WrestleMania II rematch. And Harley Race was featured as "Kansas City's own." Race was presented as the WWF's new heel King.

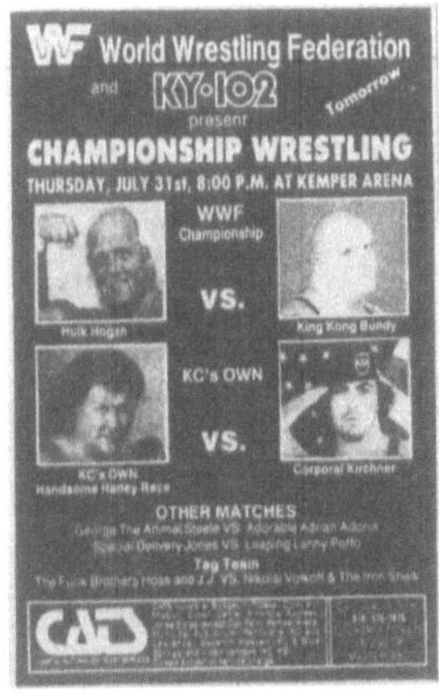

He had defended the Kansas territory and carried the NWA Championship. From that night on, he was their King under the WWF machine, except in one place.

They returned on September 28, 1986, with Hogan wrestling Orndorff while Harley wrestled Tito Santana. The following year, a Memphis court judge ruled that,

due to Jerry Lawler's lawsuit against the WWF for promoting Race as "the King of Wrestling," Race could not use the nickname or come to the ring in Tennessee wearing his crown and robe.

Then, on March 12, 1988, Hogan and Race had an intense, ahead-of-its-time hardcore style ECW match in which Race executed a piledriver on the concrete.

In an infamous spot, Race attempted a diving headbutt from the apron but missed and hit a table, resulting in a real-life hernia that shortened Race's career. Whether every detail occurred exactly as described or has grown over time, the legend remains one of wrestling's most chilling backstage stories in a Kansas City locker room, wrestling's past and future allegedly stood face to face — with a loaded gun *or* an open-hand slap with Gorilla Monsoon

CHAPTER 3
NOT EVERYTHING IS 20/20

"I'm an entertainer. But I promise you – I'm not fake." - 'Dr. D' David Schultz

THERE WAS a time in professional wrestling when kayfabe wasn't branding, nostalgia, or an inside joke. It was the job. It was how wrestlers protected their livelihoods, their families, and the audience's belief long enough to sell another ticket. When people talk about "protecting the business," this is what they mean. Not secrecy for its own sake, but survival.

The *20/20* incident involving David Schultz and reporter John Stossel didn't happen in isolation. It occurred at the intersection of pride, pressure, media intrusion, and an industry that had not yet learned how to coexist with open skepticism.

When I interviewed "Dr. D," David Schultz, he didn't deny what happened. He rejected the framing of why it happened.

. . .

SCHULTZ TOLD me there was one rule above all others in that era: *"You didn't go out and do an interview unless Vince [McMahon] told you to."*

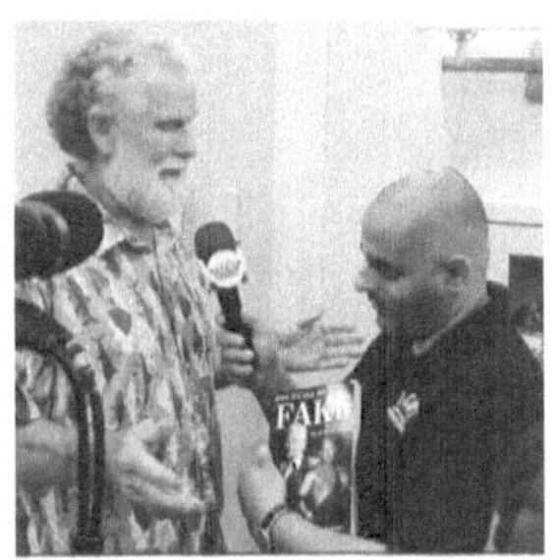

According to Schultz, Vince approved the interview and instructed him to stay in character. *"He told me to blast him. Tear his ass up. Stay in character—Dr. D."*

Schultz insists the situation escalated not because of a question, but because of a statement. *"He didn't ask me anything,"* Schultz said. *"He said, 'I think you're fake.'"* To Schultz, that wasn't journalism. It was an accusation delivered on national television inside a business that still treated the illusion as law.

When the slap came, Schultz didn't see it as losing control. He saw it as enforcement. *"I'm not fake,"* he said. *"I'm an exhibitionist. I'm a cartoon character. I'm an entertainer. But I promise you—I'm not fake."*

"Cowboy" Bob Orton remembers the moment as a cause-and-effect moment.

Fans loved him every time I booked him for public signings.

In March 2020, the night before a public signing I had booked with Orton and Rockin' Robin, the pandemic was just days away from shutting everything down. Over dinner, I asked Orton about the *20/20* incident because he had been sitting just feet away when it happened.

According to Orton, Schultz tried to set a boundary before the cameras rolled. *"David told him, 'You can ask me anything you want—just don't ask me if wrestling's fake.'"* Orton said Stossel agreed.

Then the cameras started. *"As soon as they rolled,"* Orton told me, *"the first thing he asked was, 'Is wrestling fake?'"*

ORTON DIDN'T HESITATE to describe what followed. *"David slapped that son of a b****. It sounded like a shotgun went off!"*

As I sat there stunned, Orton casually took another bite of his dinner, unfazed, while the Hall of Famer from St. Louis recalled John Stossel running down the hallway clutching his ear.

"[John Stossel] lied to him," Orton said.

———

JESSE VENTURA REMEMBERS the aftermath when asked about it during an RF Video shoot interview a decade ago:

"We drew even more," Ventura said. *"On the night 20/20 aired, the WWF ran in Pittsburgh and Detroit. Both sold out."*

Ventura was in Detroit and remembers the crowd more than the controversy. *"I'll never forget the banner,"* he said. *"'20/20 sucks.'"* To Ventura, the backlash wasn't just about Schultz. It was about the fans. *"They insulted the wrestling fan,"* Ventura said. *"Don't insult a wrestling fan. They're the most loyal fans on the planet."*

Ventura was also clear about one point. *"I was standing there. It was no work."* He acknowledged hearing Schultz later say Vince put him up to it, but stopped short of confirming that version. *"I don't know about that,"* Ventura said. *"But I was there when Stossel called Dave a fake and a fraud."*

Ventura also pointed out the contradiction that followed. "You call a guy fake and then sue him because he's a lethal weapon? *That's hypocrisy."*

———

BRET HART never celebrated the slap, but he also never dismissed why it happened. *"Back then, guys protected the business because it was their business,"* Hart said. *"Everything was predicated on the idea that this was real,"* Hart admitted. Schultz was aggressive, and the incident was unwise. *"Not a smart thing to do,"* he said. But Hart also believed Schultz acted out of pride. *"He took pride in the business. I think he thought he was doing it for the boys."*

Hart acknowledged Schultz's short fuse. *"When Dave got worked up enough, he could go off on anybody."* After watching the clip countless times, Hart added the uncomfortable truth. *"I have to admit—Stossel did deserve to get slapped."* He didn't say it triumphantly, only as cause and effect in a different era.

———

JUST TWO MONTHS after *20/20*, the tension between wrestling and television flared again on *Hot Properties*, when host Richard Belzer questioned Hulk Hogan and Mr. T about whether wrestling was fake, one week before the WWF was producing their biggest show to date.

CHAPTER 4
HOT PROPERTIES

" *I sued them all.*" - *Richard Belzer.*

ONLY THREE MONTHS after the infamous 20/20 confrontation in which David Schultz slapped John Stossel, and days away from their first WrestleMania on March 31, 1985, another outsider crossed over and made a mockery of professional wrestling.

It ended with a man unconscious on the floor, blood pooling beneath his head, and a lawsuit that was too bizarre. By the time this happened, the rules inside the wrestling business were already clear. Schultz had been fired.

The message had been sent: that kind of volatility would not be tolerated anymore—especially not on national television.

But one thing had also become clear in the aftermath. Hulk Hogan was now the meal ticket. If this had been almost anyone else—any lesser star, any expendable body—the consequences would likely have been immediate and absolute. Instead, the business bent around its biggest asset.

. . .

THE SETTING WAS *HOT PROPERTIES*, hosted by Richard Belzer.

Belzer later recounted the incident in detail during an interview with Bob Costas, still sounding amazed by how quickly things escalated. Belzer explained that before Hulk Hogan even appeared on the set, he had already interviewed Mr. T alone—and the tension started there.

According to Belzer, Mr. T came out hot. *"All the men in New York are wimps,"* Mr. T declared.

Belzer pushed back. *"All the men in New York?"*

Mr. T doubled down. He claimed he had been in Central Park that day and beaten up three muggers. Belzer, doing what talk-show hosts do, needled him verbally—using a word Mr. T didn't recognize. *"I don't know that word,"* Mr. T said. Belzer shot back that he didn't either—but that he'd learned it *"from the street."* The audience moaned, and Belzer sensed things heating up fast. Mr. T, as Belzer put it, was starting to "pump up," smoke metaphorically coming out of his ears. Belzer joked that Mr. T had begun "channeling Farrakhan," and he wisely cut to a commercial.

When they came back, Hulk Hogan joined the set. Immediately, Hogan addressed what he'd heard. *"I hear what you said about my man, Mr. T,"* Hogan said, accusing Belzer of giving him a hard time. Belzer described the atmosphere as thick with tension. Wanting to defuse it—and still believing wrestling was essentially a performance—he suggested a demonstration.

. . .

THAT ASSUMPTION WOULD PROVE CATASTROPHIC. Hogan applied a front chin lock. Belzer lost consciousness. Hogan released him. Belzer fell backward, his head striking the studio floor.

BLOOD IMMEDIATELY BEGAN POURING from the back of his head. *"I was unconscious for eleven seconds,"* Belzer told Costas. *"And I had a dream."* In those eleven seconds, Belzer dreamt he was late for Hot Properties—panicked that he'd missed his own show. Then he woke up to what he described as a surreal image: Hulk Hogan's massive, bleached-orange mustache hovering above him, dripping with blood.

Despite being in shock, despite actively hemorrhaging, Belzer's instincts kicked in. *"Hang on,"* he said on air. *"We'll be right back after this word from—you-know-who."* Hogan looked stunned. I do not believe Hogan dropped him to the floor on purpose, but I do feel he was trying to teach Belzer a lesson that went too far.

Belzer said his doctor later couldn't believe it. "You were in shock," the doctor told him. "You were losing blood. How did you do that?" Belzer's answer was simple: show business was in his blood. Literally, it was on his jacket. It was on the studio floor.

THAT NIGHT, from his hospital bed, Belzer flipped on the television. Every channel was running the clip.

Channel 2. Channel 4. Channel 5. Channel 7. Slow motion. Replay after replay. *"I got ten more stitches watching the damn thing,"* Belzer joked.

He even dreamed again that night—this time imagining his first show back, wondering if he'd have brain damage, his head "split open." Eventually, Belzer sued Hulk Hogan. The case never went to trial. Hogan settled out of court just before proceedings began.

Belzer summed it up with trademark dark humor. *"I have a lovely home in France called Chateau Hogan."* In his first book, Hogan recalls reading an article on an airplane in which Belzer calls it "Chez Hogan."

When Costas asked if it was a significant settlement, Belzer didn't hesitate. "It's all gone," he said. "But it was significant." What makes this episode resonate—especially placed so close to the Stossel incident—is how clearly it exposes the fault line between wrestling's internal logic and the outside world.

Inside wrestling, physical dominance was often treated as performative.

Outside it, a chin lock could still render a man unconscious and split his skull open on a studio floor.

WITHIN TWO MONTHS, two television personalities had learned the same lesson in different ways. Wrestling wasn't fake. And sometimes, it didn't care who was in on the joke.

WHEN RICHARD BELZER sat down with Roy Firestone in the early 1990s, he spoke less like a comedian and more like a witness still processing trauma. *"He came very close to killing me,"* Belzer says. He told Firestone that sports-medicine experts later explained to him just how narrow the margin had been. *"I was told that if I had fallen a few inches either way, I could have been crippled for life. I could have been dead. It's like a building coming up and hitting you in the head when you fall at dead weight like that."*

When the conversation turned to the lawsuit, Belzer was equally direct.

> *"I sued Mr. T. I sued Hulk Hogan. I sued Vince McMahon. I sued the World Wrestling Federation. I sued them all."*

What followed were years of depositions—days at a time, hours on end—during which lawyers asked questions that had nothing to do with the incident itself, according to Belzer.

> *"The trial was scheduled for January 2, 1990. On December 29, 1989—the final working day of the decade—both sides met. And they made an offer I couldn't refuse."*

Belzer sued for $5 million but ultimately settled for a reported $400,000 to $500,000. Placed beside the Stossel incident, the Schultz firing, and the consolidation of Hogan's power, the Belzer case marks a turning point.

The bizarreness of this urban tale isn't *just* that Belzer got knocked out on-air and then got paid.

It's what happened **after** the settlement—when the "good guys" on his side basically turned the whole thing into a second main event: **Belzer vs. his own lawyers.**

Once the case was settled, Belzer's attorneys went back to court. They applied for approval to take **50% of the recovery** instead of the standard one-third, dramatically claiming the case had cost them *"angst, aggravation, and life's blood."*

The story turns into a money brawl within Belzer's own team.

· · ·

HERE IS A DARKER TWIST.

Belzer had previously signed an affidavit praising the lawyers and appearing to support the bigger cut.

Then he reversed course and told the court he objected, claiming he only agreed because he felt pressured—saying they'd threatened to withdraw right before trial, when he felt emotionally wrecked and financially strained. He feared changing counsel could endanger the settlement.

And the judge didn't just deny it—he did it with the kind of language you rarely see in dry court writing.

The lawyers even branded Belzer "a paradigm of ingratitude," and the judge openly mocked the melodrama, dropping a Shakespeare reference while he was at it.

Then the court gets to the legal core. New York's contingency-fee rules in injury cases exist specifically to prevent lawyers from extracting what the courts view as unreasonable or unconscionable fees—even when a worn-down client appears to "agree."

Belzer had a one-third contingency arrangement, and the judge says (in substance) you don't get to rewrite the deal at the finish line just because you worked hard or the case got stressful. The request for 50% was denied, and the court held that any attempt to exceed the permitted percentage was void.

Richard Belzer died on February 19, 2023, from complications of respiratory disease at Chateau Hogan.

CHAPTER 5
WHO REALLY CREATED WRESTLEMANIA?

"To think that someone would take your idea, use it, and then not even make you a part of it —that's enough to break a man." - HTM (2000)

EVERY EMPIRE HAS A CREATION MYTH, and in professional wrestling, few myths are more fiercely contested than the origin of WrestleMania. The debate has never been about who promoted it or who financed it. We know it's Vince and Linda McMahon and their high-stakes gamble that could have gone to zero but succeeded, turning WWE into a billion-dollar company.

The real argument has always been about who first imagined it. Ask enough people who were around the WWF in the early 1980s, and you will not get a single answer. You will get several—each shaped by memory, proximity to power, and who was still around to tell the story once WrestleMania succeeded.

WrestleMania I was not just another wrestling show. It was a national gamble, a cultural crossover, and a near company-ending risk. Had it failed, the WWF likely would not have survived as a national promotion.

WrestleMania did not merely change wrestling—it rewrote legacy, power, and ownership of history.

One version of the legend begins with David Schultz, better known as "Dr. D." According to The Honky Tonk Man, in one of his earliest shoot interviews conducted by RF Video:

"...as we drove the highways in Pensacola and Tennessee and different places, David [Schultz] was always thinking about ways to draw the big crowd—the big show. Then Schultz picked up on an idea. Let's call it WrestleMania. Let's make a big event. Muhammad Ali. Mr. T—because Mr. T was really hot with The A-Team. Make a big, star-studded event. David talked about this big show for two years and called it WrestleMania. Then he gets over to Minneapolis. [Hulk] Hogan was living with David in the same apartment complex in Minneapolis. The whole WrestleMania thing—Mr. T, WrestleMania—it all started right there. Hogan gave it to McMahon. He and Schultz came to the WWF as a package against each other. But when it came time for WrestleMania, David had slapped John Stossel on McMahon's instructions. They thought David had too much heat. They didn't want to use him in the big event. There was heat between Hogan and Dr. D. It was all David Schultz's idea—the whole thing—to get Mr. T, to get Muhammad Ali, to get celebrities, and make this huge event. And to think that someone would take your idea, use it exactly the way you said it, and then not even make you a part of it—that's enough to break a man. And it broke David Schultz. Instead of using David Schultz and Roddy Piper, or David Schultz and Paul Orndorff, they used Piper and Orndorff against Hogan and Mr. T. That was David's spot. And he got bumped out of it."

Supporters argue that wrestlers were already thinking beyond territory shows and that the concept of a "wrestling Super Bowl" was circulating in locker rooms long before promoters formalized it. Critics counter with a blunt response that having an idea is not the same as building an empire.

What elevates Dr. D's claim beyond pure self-mythology is that it was later acknowledged—grudgingly and indirectly—by Hulk Hogan himself.

Speaking years later, Hogan recalled that WrestleMania had not yet been promoted and was still being actively thought through by Vince McMahon.

Hogan described how Schultz decided to shoot his own unsanctioned angle at the LA Forum, slapping Mr. T for real while Mr. T sat ringside. Police were called; Schultz was handcuffed and escorted out; and Hogan stated plainly that Vince McMahon was furious and that, after that incident, Schultz was *"pretty much done."*

Hogan then delivered the line that permanently anchors Dr. D to WrestleMania's origin story: the original idea for WrestleMania's main event was supposed to be Roddy Piper and Dr. D, because Schultz himself came up with the idea for the match.

The final main event became Hogan and Mr. T versus Piper and Paul Orndorff, but the architecture of Schultz's pitch—celebrity crossover, tag-team spectacle, mainstream appeal—remained intact.

SEVERAL ACCOUNTS CREDIT Howard Finkel with coming up with the name "WrestleMania," famously likening it to Beatlemania during a winter 1985 brainstorming session.

If Finkel did not create the event, he may have given it its identity, and names often outlive their creators. That version is complicated by firsthand testimony from George Scott, the WWF's head booker in the early 1980s. Scott recalled that the name WrestleMania emerged during a brainstorming meeting in Vince McMahon's office roughly six months before the event.

The official WWE version later placed the naming moment entirely on Howard Finkel and omitted the near-miss altogether. Brainstorming does not work the way folklore suggests.

Ideas surface repeatedly, names echo from different mouths, and history eventually chooses the cleanest story.

JIM BARNETT, adding yet another layer, was a longtime promoter who joined the WWF as Senior Vice President in 1983. Barnett recalled that the idea for WrestleMania emerged during a vacation—possibly to Martinique or St. Maarten—when WWF leadership discussed staging a massive, celebrity-driven show at Madison Square Garden.

Barnett did not claim to name WrestleMania. He claimed to help build it.

In later years, Barnett weas heavily involved in producing WrestleManias, particularly WrestleMania III in Pontiac, for which he received one of the largest bonuses.

Like George Scott, Barnett eventually left the company. And like Scott, his role faded once he was no longer present to assert it.

What unites all of these accounts is not contradiction, but context. WrestleMania was not a perfectly premeditated master plan. Backstage at WrestleMania, there was chaos. Roddy Piper recalled grabbing Vince McMahon by the shoulders and telling him to calm down because he was driving everyone crazy.

Celebrities flooded the building. Muhammad Ali, serving as a special referee, began shadowboxing in the ring and had to be calmed off-camera.

Both Piper and Scott later said WrestleMania was not as premeditated as people believe today.

Scott recalled Vince McMahon admitting afterward that if WrestleMania had failed, the company would not have survived.

That is the Urban Legend.

Depending on who you choose to believe, no one man invented WrestleMania in a single frame or moment.

"Dr. D" pitched the original celebrity-driven spectacle and, at least according to Hogan, the main-event concept featuring Mr. T.

In professional wrestling, execution earns credit, survival writes history, and everyone else becomes part of the legend.

Vince and Linda McMahon took the risk—and lived long enough to own the story.

CHAPTER 6
ONE PROMOTER VINCE MCMAHON FEARED

"Crockett wasn't the brightest branch on the tree."

- Vince McMahon

THERE WAS one territory during wrestling's national expansion that the industry's rising power treated differently.

While other regions were absorbed, outspent, or starved out, this one remained intact longer than anyone expected—not because it resisted, but its base wasn't built on spectacle. It was built on loyalty.

Entire states weren't just markets—they were communities. Television reached deep into living rooms, week after week, until the promotion felt less like a company and more like a shared ritual. Crowds weren't casual. They were invested. Wrestlers weren't brands or interchangeable parts; they were local heroes, known by name, rooted in place.

If you wrestled for him, got into a bar fight, and lost, you were fired. To his supporters, he was the last promoter who truly understood how powerful professional wrestling could be when it felt real. To his critics, Bill Watts was an inflexible tyrant obsessed with discipline and outdated notions of toughness. If you wrestled for him, got into a bar fight, and lost, you were fired.

Mid-South Wrestling, later the Universal Wrestling Federation, wasn't built on flash. Louisiana, Oklahoma, Arkansas, and Mississippi weren't just markets — they were communities, and Watts' television penetration was deep.

VINCE MCMAHON ADMITTED as much himself. Speaking on *The Steve Austin podcast a decade ago*, Vince singled out Bill Watts as the one promoter he did not want to compete with directly.

When McMahon mentioned Watts by name, there was a pause. He looked up and sighed—not in frustration or irritation, but in a way that suggested memory.

The sigh felt like acknowledgment, as if recalling a problem that couldn't simply be bulldozed.

It came across less as resentment and more as recognition—two operators who understood the same instincts and the same street-level realities of the business.

When Vince McMahon talks about the fall of the territorial system, he usually does so with indifference. In most tellings, promoters failed because they chose comfort over competition. They had money, resources, television, and infrastructure—and they declined to fight.

According to McMahon, they put *themselves* out of business.

But on The Steve Austin Show, his tone changed.

In Vince's telling, the territorial promoters weren't victims. *"They all had vast resources, far greater than mine,"* he explained. *"They just went like, 'Ooh, I've got my money. I'm not gonna compete.'* **Except one guy**—*Bill Watts of Oklahoma."*

McMahon continued: *"The first time we ran against Bill Watts,"* McMahon recalled, *"we loaded up the show."* This was standard procedure: stack the card, overwhelm the market, prove dominance. Watts responded differently. According to McMahon, rather than counter-booking inside the arena, Watts went outside it.

"Bill, in his infinite wisdom—because Bill was a street-smart guy," McMahon said, *"much like myself, but he's really street smart—he had, in the parking lot next door, this huge free event. 'Come see the boys work, come sign autographs,' all that kind of stuff."*

The timeline supports that admission. WWF's first Oklahoma incursion came on January 4, 1985, and it was anything but subtle. The show was headlined by Junkyard Dog, Bill Watts' top star and the emotional centerpiece of Mid-South. Junkyard Dog wasn't just over in the territory — he was the territory. That choice wasn't accidental.

McMahon understood that if you were going to test Watts' ground, you did it with a familiar hero in a new uniform. It was a controlled incursion, designed to prove WWF could draw there if it chose to. WWF returned just over a month later, on February 19, 1985, and that's when Bill Watts showed exactly why Vince hesitated. Vince responded by "loading the show," as he later described it.

The card featured Tito Santana defeating Intercontinental Champion Greg Valentine by disqualification, allowing

Valentine to retain the title. The main attraction saw Andre the Giant and The Junkyard Dog return to Oklahoma to face Big John Studd and Ken Patera. This marquee tag team bout ended in a double disqualification.

Instead of countering inside the arena, Watts countered outside of it. While WWF ran its show, Watts had his wrestlers in the parking lot next door, as Vince recalls, nearby signing free autographs, meeting fans, putting on a free wrestling show.

"Come see the boys work," as Vince says. It was grassroots warfare. Watts wasn't trying to outspend WWF — he was undermining the entire model. If fans could see their heroes up close for free, the spectacle inside the building mattered less.

An Illustration of Bill Watts running Vince out of Oklahoma, at least temporarily.

WWF would not return to Oklahoma again for more than two years.

Vince didn't retreat because of one stormy night — he retreated because Bill Watts made continued expansion costly in a way money couldn't easily solve.

"It was like... ooh. I don't want to compete with Bill." That single sentence is the heart of the story. Vince McMahon did not say he lost. He did not say Watts beat him. He said he didn't want to compete. And in a business defined by conquest, that admission is rare. Jim Crockett, in

McMahon's view, did not understand the business the way Watts did.

"Crockett wasn't the brightest branch on the tree," McMahon said. WWF's eventual return came in July 1987, headlined by Hulk Hogan defending the WWF Championship against Randy Savage. Two months earlier, in April 1987, Jim Crockett Promotions purchased Watts' UWF for roughly $9 million. That timing was not coincidental.

McMahon's posture shifted immediately. *"I said, 'Aha. I know where I'm going now,"* he recalled. With that sale, the territorial firewall disappeared. Crockett absorbed UWF's television and talent — including Sting — in an effort to challenge WWF nationally. Instead, the financial strain helped trigger Crockett's collapse and the eventual sale to Ted Turner, giving birth to World Championship Wrestling. Only after Watts was out of the picture did Vince return to the territory—and this time, it wasn't a test run, it was a full takeover.

And in professional wrestling, being the one man Vince McMahon chose to wait out may be the closest thing there ever was to winning. Every other promoter, in McMahon's words, *"gave up the ship."* They could have competed the same way Watts did, but they didn't. Watts did.

McMahon closed the thought the same way he closes most historical debates. *"You can say I put them out of business,"* he said. *"It's fine with me if you have that point of view. I really don't care. Nonetheless, it is what it is."*

But Bill Watts was the promoter who didn't blink. One promoter who understood the audience, the town, and the psychology of access well enough to counter power with presence. And for one moment—by Vince McMahon's own admission—that was enough to make him hesitate.

But Bill Watts didn't disappear quietly. In the immediate aftermath of WrestleMania I's success, Watts went on the air on his own programming and publicly ripped into McMahon, using his live television to attack another promoter at the height of Vince's momentum. Watts mocked the spectacle, questioned the substance, and refused to participate in the coronation.

WrestleMania had just worked, and McMahon was being hailed as a visionary. Watts went on television and said, this wasn't wrestling as he understood it — and he wasn't afraid to say so while he still had airtime. A decade later, the irony came full circle.

In 1995, Watts was briefly hired by WWF during a period of creative instability. Watts had always been the authority. In WWF, that role already belonged to Vince McMahon. Watts clashed with some executives and with the WWF Champion at the time, Kevin Nash, who wrestled as Diesel.

Ted DiBiase, one of Watts' most trusted stars, recalled that Watts told him that Vince had considered letting Watts run the company creatively, but couldn't follow through. The reason, as Watts framed it, was credit. If WWF improved under Watts' guidance, everyone would know why. Vince McMahon has always welcomed strong minds — but never shared authorship.

He may have been pushed aside because he was too capable.

And that unresolved history may explain why the Oklahoma chapter never truly closed. It didn't stay with Watts. It arguably transferred to the most visible Watts loyalist inside the WWF — Jim Ross. Watts didn't lose to Vince McMahon in a straight fight. He was waited out, outlasted, and remembered just enough to remain dangerous.

CHAPTER 7

PAUL BOSECH
RETIREMENT SHOW

"It felt like a funeral, but only after the final bell." - Steve Wagner.

ON OCTOBER 25, 1932, a young man stepped into a wrestling ring in Staten Island, New York. The country was in the depths of the Great Depression. More than fifty years later, Boesch recalled that night during a 1983 in-depth feature by The Eyes of Texas. *"I took the ferry over from lower Manhattan, got off, carried my bag, and walked away like I was going into the future. I didn't realize then that more than 50 years later, I'd still be involved in wrestling."* Wrestling took him across Canada, Australia, New Zealand, and the Philippines. It first brought Bosech to Houston in January 1942. Shortly after returning to New York, he entered the Army. He served three years, one month, and 27 days in the Infantry, was wounded twice in action, and returned as one of the most decorated wrestler-soldiers of World War II — earning the Purple Heart, Silver Star with Oak Leaf Cluster, Bronze Star, Combat Infantryman's Badge, and the French Croix de Guerre.

BOESCH PURCHASED the Houston promotion in 1966 and, over time, became Houston wrestling. If he advertised a wrestler, that wrestler appeared. If he promised a payoff, it was delivered. His word carried weight. By 1987, the territorial system was collapsing. Bill Watts sold the UWF to Jim Crockett Jr. without consulting Boesch. Years later, Bruce Prichard explained that both sides felt justified. *"Frankly, both sides were right in a lot of respects."* Boesch aligned with Vince McMahon. On April 11, 1987, he aired footage from WrestleMania III and announced Houston's transition to the WWF. But it felt different. *"It was night and day,"* longtime Houston fan Steve Wagner said. The national WWF presentation felt foreign. Boesch understood the old Houston wrestling would never be the same. So he chose to leave on his terms.

On August 28, 1987, twelve thousand fans filled the Sam Houston Coliseum. Thousands were turned away. At the time, Vice President George H. W. Bush sent a telegram honoring 55 years. The card featured Hulk Hogan vs. One Man Gang, Ted DiBiase vs. Jim Duggan, and Mil Máscaras closing the show.

"It didn't feel like it was about the wrestling," Wagner said. *"It was about Paul [Bosech]."*

Ringside seats once ran $10–$12. That night, floor seats reportedly ran $20–$25 and sold out instantly. Steve remembers getting to the local ticket office early and getting third-row mezzanine seats. Steve Wagner's connection began long before 1987. In 1974, at six years old, he stood at a urinal in the Sam Houston Coliseum next to

Blackjack Lanza — in full gear, about to wrestle. *"I looked up and up and up,"* Steve said. *"And I was horrified,"* Blackjack Lanza growled. Steve froze. In his mind, the villain was real. Lanza finished, walked out, shook Steve's father's hand, thanked him for coming, and went to wrestle.

Steve Wagner, who attended many Houston shows, proudly holds his commemorative program from the 1987 Paul Boesch retirement show—one of the sought-after collector's items in wrestling memorabilia.

Behind the scenes, negotiations over the gate turned tense. Bruce Prichard told the full story on Episode 31 of Something to Wrestle with Conrad Thompson — one of my favorite and most underrated episodes of that podcast. According to Prichard, Vince McMahon was all in on Paul Boesch's retirement show. WWF flew talent to Houston on a Learjet. Vince put everyone up at the Hyatt Regency downtown and covered every expense—building rental, security, travel, production, and catering. McMahon even organized an after-party for Boesch that rivaled a WrestleMania celebration, with an open bar, a live band, and elaborate food and drink.

The standing arrangement between WWF and Houston had been a 70/30 split — WWF keeping 70% of the profit after covering expenses, Houston receiving 30%. That was already better than the standard 80/20 split most other promoters received. On the day of the retirement show, Vince and Bruce went to meet with Boesch's representatives to finalize the financial arrangement. Paul was reportedly not there, but left after waiting for Vince, who was late to the meeting. When the subject of finances came up, Vince made a 50/50 offer, a more favorable split than the original 70/30 split. However, the response Vince and Bruce received was not what they expected. Houston's representative argued that, because it was Paul's final show and had "drawn the house," Houston should keep 100% of the live gate, while WWF absorbed all expenses and had taken all the risk.

WWF had paid all costs. WWF had brought in the talent. WWF had funded production. But the cash from ticket sales was physically in Houston's hands. And they wanted it all. According to Bruce, Vince stood up and made it clear they were being taken advantage of. He told Bruce, *"Let's go,"* and walked out. They got into a stretch limousine outside.

Bruce remembers Vince sitting silently in the back, holding a copy of USA Today, which was still a relatively new newspaper at the time. The car was quiet. Then suddenly, the wooden glass holder mounted inside the limousine went flying, and the crystal shattered against the window. The newspaper hit the floor. Bruce apologized, saying he didn't know this would happen.

Vince snapped — then immediately recalibrated. *"How would you know?"* he said. *"You didn't know they were going to do this."* Then came the directive: *"Do not tell Terry (Hulk Hogan)."* If Hogan believed Vince was being taken advantage of, he would refuse to work. If the locker room sensed weakness, the show could unravel. Bruce said it was the first time he truly witnessed Vince's philosophy firsthand—never sell it. Earlier in the dressing room, Boesch's nephew, Peter Birkholz, had handed him an envelope reminding him that he still owed $11,000 on a car loan. The show went on.

Afterward, back at the Hyatt Regency, the massive celebration for Paul Boesch continued. When Vince called Bruce to check on him, Bruce told him he didn't want to see anyone. Vince told Bruce to go downstairs and have a good time. *"You're going to thank Boesch. You're going to thank the nephew. You're going to smile. You're going to have a drink.* ***And you're not going to let anyone know they got to you."***

Bruce followed McMahon's advice. He went down to the party Vince paid for and smiled. He shook hands. Vince refused to go and stayed in his room. Later, when Bruce told Vince that the car loan had been called in, Vince asked one question. *"How much?"* Bruce told him $11,000, and Vince cut a check for that amount. Not a loan. He paid it off for Bruce, who had only been working for the WWF for three months at this point.

Bruce has often said that while Vince can be ruthless in business negotiations, he has also been personally loyal and generous. When people criticize Vince, Bruce remembers Houston. He remembers the 50/50 offer, even though Vince didn't have to make one.

WHEN STEVE WAGNER sat in that building on August 28, 1987, for Paul Bosech's retirement show and bid farewell, he wasn't thinking about corporate negotiations. He was thinking about the Friday TVs and Paul Bosech's voice. It was about realizing something woven into their childhood was gone. When the lights dimmed inside the Sam Houston Coliseum, Paul Boesch walked away with dignity. And for those who were there, like Steve, it wasn't just the end of Houston wrestling. *"When the final bell rang that night, it hit me like a ton of bricks,"* Wagner said. *"There is no next week. It felt like a funeral. But only after the final bell."*

CHAPTER 8

LOCH NESS MONSTER

"My pleasure." - Giant Haystacks

THE 20/20 slap was not the only time a reporter crossed a line and paid for it. Years earlier, a 600-lb wrestler, Martin Austin Ruane, who wrestled as Giant Haystacks, was involved in a separate confrontation with a reporter who pushed too far into wrestling's space. Accounts vary in detail, but the outcome is the same: the reporter was physically slammed. Like "Dr. D" David Schultz, Ruane was an old-school worker who believed the business survived only as long as it was treated with respect. No lawsuit followed. Haystacks impressed Hulk Hogan and Kevin Sullivan enough that they recommended to Eric Bischoff that they hire him, and he came in as the Loch Ness Monster.

Professional wrestling has always walked a fine line between illusion and reality. But every so often, that line disappears completely—especially when the action spills out of the ring and onto live television. Before he became one of the most physically imposing figures in wrestling history, Martin Ruane lived a far more ordinary life—working as a laborer and later as a nightclub bouncer. A friend encouraged him to try professional wrestling, setting him on a path that would take him around the world.

Ruane eventually made his way to Calgary, Alberta, Canada, where he competed in Stu Hart's Stampede Wrestling as The Loch Ness Monster—a character he took genuine pride in. Unlike many gimmicks handed down in wrestling, Ruane embraced the role, leaning into the mystery and spectacle of the name. To him, it wasn't just a persona—it was an extension of the larger-than-life presence he carried both inside and outside the ring. But in the United Kingdom, he was better known by another name: Giant Haystacks.

In January 1980, Haystacks appeared on the live UTV program Good Evening Ulster, filmed at Belfast's Havelock House studios. What was meant to be a routine interview quickly turned into one of the most infamous moments in television history.

Sports reporter Jackie Fullerton openly questioned whether professional wrestling was "fake," prompting Haystacks to respond in a way no one expected. When asked to demonstrate a move, Haystacks lifted the 175-pound presenter into position—reportedly only meant to simulate a powerslam. Instead, he followed through. With a sickening thud, Fullerton was driven into the hard studio floor. There was no padding. No safety net. No illusion. Fullerton suffered multiple broken ribs. Yet in a moment that made the incident even more surreal, he attempted to continue the interview while writhing in pain.

Trying to remain professional, he even thanked Haystacks— who coldly replied: *"My pleasure."*

The clip became legendary—a rare, undeniable moment where wrestling stopped being performance and became painfully real. But Haystacks' story wasn't the only time television hosts learned that lesson the hard way.

MORE THAN A DECADE LATER, in 1993, WCW star Sting appeared on the British breakfast show GMTV. This time, the tone was lighter. Presenter Martin Frizell agreed to take part in a demonstration, lying on the studio floor as Sting prepared to apply his signature hold—the Scorpion Deathlock. Unlike Haystacks' infamous slam, this was controlled. A "shoot" in the sense that the hold was real—but carefully applied. Even so, the effect was immediate.

AS STING LOCKED in the hold and applied pressure, Frizell's reaction shifted from playful to genuine discomfort. He flinched, laughed nervously, and struggled under the torque, while those around him joked about the situation. The moment became a perfect example of 1990s television— where wrestling and mainstream media collided in unpredictable ways. Because even when done safely... it still hurts. And then there are the moments when things go completely off script.

IN 1997, during a promotional appearance in Kuwait, Vader found himself in a situation eerily similar to the one Haystacks had faced years earlier. A television host began questioning the legitimacy of professional wrestling, pushing the conversation beyond entertainment and into confrontation.

Vader didn't take it lightly. In a shocking escalation, he grabbed the host and physically attacked him on live television. The segment descended into chaos, with stunned viewers watching as the situation turned from interview to real altercation in seconds.

THE FALLOUT WAS IMMEDIATE—AND serious. Three different decades. Three different wrestlers. One consistent lesson. Wrestling may be scripted—but the money and the miles are real. And so are the sacrifices, long-term injuries, and pain, physically and mentally suffered.

And sometimes, when the cameras are rolling, someone asks the wrong question, wants a move put on to demonstrate how phony our business is, there are no second takes. No rehearsals. No safe landings. Just reality. And as Martin Ruane —the man who once proudly became the Loch Ness Monster —proved better than anyone else.

SOMETIMES THE MONSTER isn't part of the act.

IT'S what happens when the act gets tested.

CHAPTER 9

GLASS HALF FULLER

*"I thought that if I started my own territory,
he was a guy I wanted." - Ron Fuller*

HE WAS BORN INTO IT, raised inside it, and shaped by it long before he ever stepped into a ring.

The Fuller and Welch families represent one of the deepest and oldest lineages in professional wrestling, a dynasty that stretches back to the early twentieth century and includes dozens of wrestlers, referees, and promoters who helped build the territorial system across the American South.

As Ron Fuller often explains, wrestling was not simply an occupation in his family—it was their way of life. *"I come from the oldest, largest wrestling family in the world,"* Fuller said. *"It wasn't just my dad, my brother, and me. I'm actually a third-generation wrestler."*

The roots of that dynasty began with his grandfather, Roy Welch, who entered professional wrestling during the early 1920s when the sport was still evolving from legitimate contests into the organized entertainment business that would later define the territorial era. Welch began his career in the Amarillo, Texas area and was trained by a tough old-school shooter named Dutch Mantell—one of the legitimate wrestlers of the time.

"My granddad was trained by a guy named Dutch Mantell— not the Dutch Mantell people know today," Fuller recalled. *"The original Dutch Mantell was an old shooter, and he taught my granddad how to wrestle."* After learning the fundamentals of the craft, Welch traveled north to Ohio, which already had two wrestling territories operating in the 1920s. There, he learned not only how to wrestle but also the business side of the sport, gaining experience in booking and promotion that would later define his career. *"He went to Ohio and learned how to wrestle and learned how to book a little bit,"* Fuller said. *"Then he left there and went to Tennessee and started probably one of the biggest territories in the history of wrestling."* From that foundation, the Welch family's influence grew across the southeastern United States. Over the decades, dozens of relatives became involved in wrestling in one form or another. Some wrestled, others refereed, and many helped promote events in cities and towns across the region.

"I had about thirty-five people in my family associated with wrestling or refereeing," Fuller explained, a number that illustrates just how deeply the business ran in the family bloodline. That legacy was significant enough that wrestling historians later devoted extensive research to documenting it. Fuller recalled a podcast series hosted by Jerry Brisco and John Latham that explored the Welch family's place in wrestling history. "Once they started talking about Roy and the Welch family, they ended up doing ten episodes on it," Fuller said. *"It covers everything from the early 1900s all the way up to the*

present time." Growing up in that environment meant wrestling was always present in Ron Fuller's life.

HIS FATHER, Buddy Fuller, continued the tradition as both a wrestler and a promoter, learning the business directly from Roy Welch and eventually building a reputation of his own in the sport. *"My father was a wrestler and a promoter,"* Fuller said. *"I grew up watching how he ran his businesses and how hard he worked."*

Buddy Fuller became known in the wrestling industry for presenting matches that felt realistic and for treating wrestlers fairly when it came time to pay them. *"He made his matches as realistic as he possibly could, and he had a good reputation for paying wrestlers,"* Fuller recalled.

IN 1954, Roy Welch sent Buddy Fuller south to Mobile, Alabama, where he began building what eventually became known as the Gulf Coast territory. At the time, Roy Welch was controlling a vast region of the country. *"My grandfather sent my father to Mobile when he was about twenty-three years old,"* Fuller said. *"Roy was running territory basically from Kentucky all the way down to the Gulf Coast."* Before moving to Mobile, Buddy Fuller had already begun learning the promotional side of the business by running smaller towns in Tennessee. *"He had my dad promoting Kingsport, Tennessee,"* Fuller explained. *"He wasn't booking yet, but he was learning how promotion worked."* Once he arrived in Mobile, Buddy Fuller distinguished himself by aggressively advertising events—something that many promoters of that era did not prioritize. *"My dad believed in advertising way beyond what anybody else did,"* Fuller said.

That philosophy paid off when Buddy Fuller promoted a massive event against the notoriously rough Mario Galento at Ladd Memorial Stadium in Mobile. The match drew an enormous crowd. *"They drew somewhere between twenty and thirty thousand people,"* Fuller recalled.

The match itself was brief and brutal. *"It only lasted about seven minutes, and both of them busted each other the hard way." The* aftermath became part of wrestling lore. "My dad put forty-seven stitches in Galento's face," Fuller said. "They basically just had a fight." In those days, such realism was rare in professional wrestling. "Nobody was doing that kind of stuff back then," Fuller added. Growing up hearing stories like that made wrestling almost inevitable for Ron Fuller, but his path into the business was not immediate. Instead, he first pursued athletics through basketball, using his towering six-foot-nine frame to compete at the collegiate level. "I played basketball at Clemson University my freshman year and then at the University of Miami for three years," Fuller said. Despite his success on the court, wrestling remained the goal he had carried since childhood.

"I always wanted to be a wrestler," Fuller explained. *"Not just a wrestler—I wanted to be a promoter like my grandfather and my father."*

In 1970, he left college and entered the wrestling business, beginning his career in the Georgia territory. *"I started wrestling in Georgia in May of 1970,"* Fuller said. The following year, Ron moved to Florida, one of the premier territories in professional wrestling at the time. *"In October of 1971, I went into the Florida territory and stayed there four years."*

Florida wrestling was widely respected for its production quality, strong talent roster, and the legendary commentary of Gordon Solie. While working there, Fuller received an opportunity that dramatically accelerated his education in the business. *"They opened a new building in West Palm Beach and asked me if I wanted to go down there and become the local promoter,"* Fuller recalled. He accepted the offer while still wrestling on the shows himself. *"I was basically the local promoter and a wrestler on the card."* Promoting a town required far more than simply organizing matches. Fuller found himself responsible for almost every detail involved in presenting the event. *"I handled televisions,"* he said. *"I made sure the TV stations got their tapes on time and that they were happy with the show."*

Advertising required constant attention as well. *"I went to the newspapers to make sure the ads were run,"* Fuller explained. *"I took the ads myself and made sure they were printed."* The experience provided a crash course in how wrestling territories functioned. *"That's where I really started learning the business."* Although he was trusted with promotion duties, he was not yet allowed to book matches. *"They didn't let me book anything, obviously,"* Fuller said. Even so, his wrestling career advanced rapidly. In most territories, it took several years before a wrestler could headline events. *"Normally, it takes about five years before a wrestler can work main events,"* Fuller explained. Fuller reached that level much sooner. *"Because I grew up around the business and had seen thousands of matches, I was working on top in about two years."* During that time, he also captured the Georgia Heavyweight Championship. *"I won the Georgia Heavyweight Championship after two years in the ring,"* he said.

After proving himself as both a wrestler and promoter in Florida, Fuller began running additional towns around West

Palm Beach, including Vero Beach, where he set a financial milestone for the territory. *"Vero Beach had never drawn a big house before,"* Fuller said. *"It became the first house in Florida history to draw over ten thousand dollars."* By 1974, Fuller had gained enough experience to recognize an opportunity when he saw one. While vacationing in the Smoky Mountains, he watched a wrestling television program in Knoxville, Tennessee. What he saw stunned him. *"It was the worst wrestling television show I had ever seen,"* Fuller said. Coming from Florida's polished production, the difference was dramatic. *"Florida had a great show with Gordon Solie and great wrestlers. It was a first-class operation."* The Knoxville promotion, owned by John Kazana, was running only a limited schedule. *"The only town he really ran was Knoxville, and one spot show about forty miles away,"* Fuller said. But Fuller noticed something important: the television signal reached nearly 150 miles beyond Knoxville. *"I knew right away there was more there than just one town."*

HE APPROACHED Kazana with an offer to purchase the operation. *"I paid twenty-five thousand down and five hundred dollars a week for five years,"* Fuller said. The total purchase price was $150,000. Many veteran promoters believed he had made a disastrous mistake. *"They said it was the worst deal ever,"* Fuller recalled. *"They said the kid would never make it happen."* Fuller ignored the criticism and focused on building the territory. In the beginning, attendance was extremely low. *"The first month I took over, we were drawing less than a thousand people,"* Fuller said. Within eighteen months, that number quadrupled. *"Eighteen months later, we were drawing four thousand."* Much of that growth came from the strong roster Fuller assembled, which included family members like Jimmy Golden and Roy Lee Welch as well as trusted performers from other territories such as Ronnie Garvin.

"I wrestled Ronnie Garvin more times than anybody when I was in Florida," Fuller said. When Garvin joined the territory, Fuller offered him something rare in the wrestling business at the time. *"Back then, there were really no guarantees,"* Fuller said. Garvin received one of the few guaranteed contracts in the territory. *"I always thought that if I ever started my own territory, he was a guy I wanted."*

ANOTHER WRESTLER who received guaranteed money was the Mongolian Stomper. *"Stomper was worth every penny of it,"* Fuller said. By 1977, the Knoxville territory was booming, drawing thousands of fans to the Coliseum for major shows. *"We were selling out the coliseum with six or seven thousand people,"* Fuller said. NWA World Champion Harley Race appeared frequently, and Fuller often wrestled him in the main event. *"I wrestled Harley Race a lot,"* Fuller said. *"Every time we wrestled, we sold out."*

YET WHILE THE territory appeared strong on the surface, trouble was quietly forming behind the scenes.

A WRESTLER NAMED BOB ROOP—AN accomplished amateur competitor and former Olympian— would eventually play a central role in what became known as the Knoxville Five. Roop had previously served as a booker for promoter Roy Shire in San Francisco, something Fuller did not know when he hired him.

· · ·

"IF I HAD KNOWN *that story, he would have never booked for me,"* Fuller said.

Roop had reportedly attempted to persuade wrestlers in California to take control of Shire's promotion. *"So it wasn't Roop's first time trying to steal a territory."* At the time, Fuller trusted him enough to give him the booking job—one of the most sensitive positions in any wrestling territory. *"When you make someone the booker in your territory, that's a very serious job,"* Fuller said. Around that same time, Fuller purchased his father's old Gulf Coast territory and spent much of his time rebuilding it alongside legendary wrestler Bob Armstrong. *"Bob Armstrong and I went down there to start that territory,"* Fuller said. During Fuller's absence, Roop gained influence with several wrestlers living in the same apartment complex, including Ronnie Garvin. *"He was living in the same apartment complex with Ronnie and Orton and Malenko,"* Fuller recalled. Fuller believes Roop gradually convinced a small group of wrestlers to turn against him. *"It was like throwing one rotten apple into a barrel."*

Most of the locker room remained loyal. *"I had fifteen or sixteen guys working for me, and most of them stayed with me,"* Fuller said. But four wrestlers joined Roop in a plan that would shake the territory. At the time, Fuller had no idea what was happening behind the scenes. The truth would only emerge later—and when it did, it would involve a missing championship belt, a boat that carried it away, and a legal battle that would threaten the entire territory. The story of what Ronnie Garvin did with that belt—and how Ron Fuller responded—was about to become one of the most unusual chapters in the history of territorial wrestling.

CHAPTER 10

THE BETRAYAL OF THE KNOXVILLE FIVE

"Looking back, I should have never done it." -
Ron Garvin.

BY THE LATE 1970S, Southeastern Championship Wrestling in Knoxville, Tennessee, was one of the hottest territories in the South. The promotion, run by Ron Fuller—known to fans as The Tennessee Stud—had grown from a struggling television show into a thriving regional wrestling powerhouse. Crowds were strong, the towns were steady, and the roster was stacked with talented workers who could deliver both spectacle and believable fights in the ring. Among the most important pieces of the operation was Ronnie Garvin.

Their relationship stretched back years, to the Florida territory where Garvin had worked for Fuller's father, Buddy Fuller. They had drawn together strong houses and built programs that grew week after week. There was real respect between them, and when Fuller heard Garvin might be leaving another territory, he made sure to reach out.

"I think I was in North Carolina when Ron called me," Garvin later recalled. *"I had given notice where I was working, and he heard about it. He wanted me to work for him. He gave me a guarantee money-wise, and I decided I was gonna go."*

In the territorial era, guarantees were extremely rare. Most wrestlers were paid strictly on a percentage of the gate, meaning their income depended entirely on how many fans showed up. Fuller's offering of guaranteed money to Garvin showed the level of trust he placed in him as a performer and as a draw. Garvin already knew the Fuller family well. *"His dad, Buddy Fuller, liked me,"* Garvin remembered. *"Every time I worked with Ron back then, his dad would come into the dressing room and say, 'I want you to beat the hell out of him.' That's the honest-to-God truth."*

That was the mentality of wrestling in the early 1970s, when realism mattered, and the line between fight and performance was intentionally blurred. *"Back then, promoters would give you fifty bucks just to get a black eye,"* Garvin said. *"Bust your eye up and go on television with your eye kicked out of your head. When they hit you, you hit."* By the time Garvin settled into Knoxville around 1976, he was far more than just another name on the card. He had influence and freedom to shape the direction of his matches and storylines. *"I pretty much did what I wanted,"* he said. *"Ron and Robert didn't interfere in the matches."* Garvin frequently suggested opponents and angles for himself.

"If I wanted to work with somebody, like Boris Malenko, I brought him in. I made money with him." It was during those matches with Malenko that Garvin developed one of his most recognizable trademarks—the Garvin Stomp. *"The Garvin Stomp started when I wrestled with Malenko,"* he explained. *"Malenko did a stomp, but he didn't go around the ring as I did*

and stomp the hell out of it." In wrestling, ideas are often borrowed and adapted, but there are unwritten rules about how far that borrowing goes. *"Everybody copies,"* Garvin said. *"But I never copied somebody who was still in the business."* After several years working as a villain, something interesting happened with the Knoxville crowds. The fans who once booed Garvin began cheering him. *"You make the best babyface when you've been a heel, and people hated you so much,"* he explained. *"Then you start kicking the ass of some bad guys, and it reverses."* To Garvin, though, the labels of hero and villain were never particularly meaningful. *"It was never babyface and heel to me,"* he said. *"I'm a wrestler. When you get in that ring, you fight."* That philosophy carried into his in-ring style. *"I laid in the punches, but I protected the guy,"* he said. *"I never crippled anybody. I took care of the guys. That's what you're supposed to do."*

The Knoxville territory thrived on that blend of believable wrestling and high-stakes spectacle. One of the most memorable angles was the Cadillac tournament, a week-long elimination series with a new car as the grand prize. Garvin remembers smashing a concrete ring post through the Cadillac's windshield during the buildup. *"I took that concrete post and stuck it right through the windshield,"* he said. *"The people were so mad. Oh my God."* The stunt worked perfectly, creating outrage among the fans and driving business higher.

Fuller remembers the moment clearly as well—but from a promoter's perspective. It wasn't spontaneous. It was planned. *"That was part of the finish,"* Fuller explained. *"He got out of the ring, walked over to the car, picked up the steel stanchion that had the ropes around it where fans couldn't touch the car, and threw it through the windshield. It was supposed to happen."*

The idea was simple: give the crowd something unforgettable. *"They see a great match, then they see that happen, and that's all they talk about when they go home,"* Fuller said. *"That's how you draw money."* After the Cadillac tournament was successful, the territory decided to expand the concept. Instead of a car, the next prize would be a boat. Garvin says the idea came from him. *"I told Fuller we could do a tournament for a boat,"* he recalled. *"We built it up for five, six, seven weeks. It wasn't just one match—it was a tournament."*

THE PRIZE WAS A 28-FOOT BAYLINER, and Garvin liked the concept because he already lived near the water. *"I lived on the lake,"* he said. *"I had a twenty-five-foot boat already. That's why I wanted the bigger one."* For decades afterward, Garvin insisted on one critical point: *"I bought the boat. The boat was in my name. It wasn't stolen."*

RON FULLER **strongly disputes that claim**. According to Fuller, the boat—like the Cadillac before it—was purchased by the promoter as part of the promotional contest. *"He never bought the boat,"* Fuller said plainly. *"I bought the boat,"* Fuller explains, noting that this practice dates back to promotions his father ran decades earlier. *"My dad had done those kinds of contests since the 1950s,"* Fuller said. *"The promoter bought the car or the boat."*

In some cases, the wrestler who "won" the prize might later arrange to pay part of the cost, but that had not even been discussed yet in Garvin's case. *"I hadn't even talked with Ronnie about what his part might be,"* Fuller said. At the time, Garvin had possession of the boat because Fuller allowed it.

"He had the boat and the keys," Fuller explained. *"I didn't mind. We weren't using it."*

THEN THE TERRITORY FRACTURED. The group, Fuller dubbed the "Knoxville Five," left Southeastern Championship Wrestling and attempted to start their own promotion. What had been one of the hottest territories in the country suddenly found itself in a war. Fuller understood immediately what that meant for business. *"When you have a war over a territory, it's the absolute worst thing that can happen to your company,"* he said. *"There's nothing worse than having a war."*

Wrestling history had shown the pattern before. *"You think about it, Andrew, now you've got two companies running. I run on Friday night. They run on Saturday night. It's a split audience,"* Fuller explained.

Some fans followed the Knoxville 5. Others stayed loyal to Fuller's territory. Many stopped attending wrestling altogether. *"There's never been a territory war where both companies did great,"* Fuller said. *"It always hurts business."* Garvin later admitted that the split was a mistake. *"Ron took very good care of me,"* he said. *"I had a guarantee. Many times, he gave me more money than I expected."* The territory he left had been one of the best situations a wrestler could hope for. *"I was treated like a king,"* Garvin admitted. *"I worked the angles I wanted. I worked with the guys I wanted."* He paused before acknowledging what might have been. *"I probably could have wrestled there fifteen or twenty years ago. It was a hell of a nice territory."*

But by then the damage had been done. The dispute between the two men eventually reached court over the boat.

According to Fuller, the legal battle reached a point where something even bigger was at stake than the boat itself.

"THE TRIAL CAME DOWN *to where we were going to have to get on the stand and say yes or no—was wrestling fake?"* Fuller said. For someone whose family had been in the wrestling business since the 1920s, publicly exposing the industry's secrets was unthinkable. *"Being from a wrestling family going back to my grandfather, I wasn't going to get on the stand and say wrestling wasn't real,"* Fuller said. So he made a decision. *"I decided just to let him keep the boat."*

THE BELT, however, was another matter entirely. To Fuller, the championship belt represented trust—the symbol of the territory's top star. When Garvin left with it and continued to present himself as the champion, it cut deeper than the boat's financial loss. *"He's going into the ring every week saying he's the Southeastern Champion,"* Fuller said. *"And he knew that belt wasn't his."*

Fuller eventually forgave the men involved, including Garvin, who would later admit the same thing. *"I should have never done it,"* he said. When I pressed Garvin — gently — asking what he meant about the regret, he didn't rush to fill the silence. Then he said two words. And in that moment, I realized we weren't talking about boats, championship belts, or payoffs anymore. We were reopening old wounds and another chapter in this story.

He gave a long pause.

THEN GARVIN SAID, *"PLAN B."*

CHAPTER 11

PLAN B

"It was the only time in my life I was a follower." - Ron Garvin

BOB ROOP, Ron Garvin, Bob Orton Jr., Boris Malenko, and Ron Wright broke away to form All-Star Championship Wrestling—informally known as "The Knoxville 5."

They ran opposition shows in Knoxville and surrounding East Tennessee cities like Morristown and the Tri-Cities. Fuller's group ran the Coliseum. The opposition ran the next night in other venues. As is typical in wrestling wars, both sides suffered, as Fuller said in the previous chapter. It forced fans to split and take sides. Attendance dipped, revenue split, and the momentum stalled. After roughly six months of fighting, Fuller sold the Knoxville office to Jim Barnett of Georgia Championship Wrestling and shifted his focus south.

But before the war concluded, something extraordinary and later infamous was captured on film.

It was called Plan B.

THE TAPE OPENS with Roop speaking calmly, methodically, almost academically. He introduces what he calls a "documentation." He lists his credentials: 1968 U.S. Olympic team member in Greco-Roman wrestling, college graduate, ten years in professional wrestling. He describes wrestling as a closed fraternity—a secret club. Then he says something that, in 1979, could have detonated the business in Knoxville. He says he has never had a real wrestling match. He explains that every match he has ever wrestled was arranged beforehand. Outcomes were decided in advance. The booker structures the matches. Television creates emotional investment. Wrestling, he says, is business—a billion-dollar industry reporting only a fraction of that revenue.

ONE BY ONE, the others corroborate him. Larry Simon (Boris Malenko - father of Dean Malenko) explains "gimmicks," demonstrating how a wrestler changes his voice, posture, and accent to create a persona. He says in 27 years he has never had a real wrestling match—every one was planned.

RON WRIGHT CONFIRMS THE SAME. In 25 years, he says, every match was worked out beforehand. The only real fights he ever had came from spectators. He recounts a night in Greenville, Tennessee, where enraged fans attacked him for his villainous performance, leaving him with 191 stitches in his back and 38 in his head. He turns to the camera and shows the scars. The danger, he implies, came not from opponents—but from belief.

RON GARVIN DESCRIBES himself as an actor. He explains how interviews required him to alter his eyes and facial expressions. He admits he has never had a real wrestling match. He adds that after cage matches and blood feuds, the same wrestlers often shared drinks. The rivalries were performance.

NEXT, shockingly, Bob Orton Jr. (Randy Orton's father) recounts discovering the illusion as a child. On the tape, Bob Orton recounts watching his father, Bob Orton Sr., seemingly mutilated in the ring by Freddie Blassie, and breaking down into hysterics. On the ride home, his father told him everything in the ring was a fabrication. Orton Jr., himself an accomplished amateur wrestler, says since turning pro, he has never had a real wrestling match. Injuries, he explains, are accidents—not competitive outcomes.

Each man repeats the same assertion: professional wrestling matches are pre-determined. Then Roop escalates. He outlines future segments. Plan C. Maybe D. He promises to reveal how blood is produced, how in-ring manipulation works, how money flows, how promoters resist unionization, how wrestlers have no pensions, no insurance, no protection. Roop references monopoly control, the IRS, political connections, drug abuse, and personal revelations about stars fans think they know.

AND THEN THE TAPE CUTS. Mid-sentence. It never aired. Decades later, when the footage resurfaced online, it stunned everyone involved. Fuller had never seen it until a fan sent it to him roughly thirty years later. Watching it, he was bewildered that it had not been broadcast during the war. He speculated that the tape might have been intended not just as insurance for Knoxville, but as leverage beyond it—possibly even as a tool to pressure other promoters.

I reached out to Bob Roop for this publication, but he was unresponsive. Garvin framed Plan B differently in our follow-up call after the boat and belt lawsuits. To him, Plan B was insurance. *"If we don't win this fight,"* he admitted, *"we'll kill the business."* He pointed to Vince McMahon, later publicly acknowledging wrestling's scripted nature to sidestep New Jersey's athletic commission regulations as evidence that wrestling will never die. Everyone said that would destroy wrestling. It didn't.

But in 1979, that wasn't obvious. The territorial system depended on local belief. Exposure in one market could poison it for years. Fuller believes Knoxville was dead for five years after the war. Barnett struggled to draw. Others tried and failed. It took time—and new strategies—to rebuild.

The war burned both sides. Television limitations hindered ASCW's reach. The tape remained buried. But what if it had aired? In 1979, before the national cable boom, before widespread public acknowledgment of scripted outcomes, Plan B could have triggered a domino effect. Sponsors might have pulled out. Instead, Plan B became something else: a relic of how close the business came to self-detonation from within. Five wrestlers. One camera. A coordinated confession in the middle of an active wrestling war. And perhaps that is why it remains so powerful. And in 1979, for a moment, the illusion was staring directly into a lens—ready to disappear.

Watching it decades later, Fuller was stunned. *"I couldn't believe they would even consider doing that,"* he said. To Fuller, exposing wrestling's secrets during an active territorial war would have been catastrophic. *"That would have killed wrestling nationwide,"* he said. *"There wouldn't have been any wrestling after that,"* Garvin remembers the moment differently. According to him, Plan B was born of desperation. *"We were fighting,"* Garvin explained. *"The NWA was big. They were sending Fuller talent regularly. They were helping them fight us."* The breakaway promotion simply did not have the same depth of roster. *"We only had so much talent,"* Garvin said. *"It was a losing battle."* Eventually, the group reached a drastic conclusion. *"We said, well, hell, let's kill it completely."*

Plan B became their nuclear option. *"If we don't win this fight, we'll expose everything."* The wrestlers went to a television station and recorded the tape together. *"Each one of us took turns,"* Garvin said. Looking back decades later, Garvin admits something he did not see at the time. *"It was the only time in my life I was a follower,"* he said quietly. *"I wasn't really being screwed,"* he admitted. In fact, he had one of the best deals in the territory. *"I had guaranteed money."*

THE TAPE WAS RECORDED. But something happened afterward. It disappeared. Fuller believes Ron Wright may have prevented it from ever airing. *"Ron Wright was a good guy,"* Fuller said. *"A good old, honest, hardworking redneck that I had a lot of respect for."* Fuller suspects Wright left the studio with the tape. *"My feeling is he took it, and they never saw it again."* Garvin himself isn't sure what happened to it. *"I don't know who had the tape,"* he said. *"But we did record it."*

Yet time has a way of softening even the hardest moments in wrestling. Ron Fuller eventually forgave many of the men involved. He ran into Bob Orton Jr. years later at a wrestling convention in Mobile, Alabama. The two men sat down and talked. *"He apologized,"* Fuller recalled. *"He said he was wrong.*

He said he did the wrong thing." Ron Wright eventually returned to work with Fuller as well when Fuller came back to Knoxville years later. *"Ron Wright was a good guy,"* Fuller said. *"I always had respect for him."* Even Ronnie Garvin, whose name had become tied to the belt, the boat, and the split, eventually admitted his regret. *"Ron didn't deserve that,"* Garvin said. *"It's a sad thing."* Looking back now, both men understood something that only time reveals. Southeastern Championship Wrestling in Knoxville was rare. It wasn't just another territory.

"Everybody wanted to come," Fuller remembered. *"My phone rang all the time with guys wanting to get into the territory."* Ironically, Knoxville had become known among wrestlers as a territory where the boys could actually enjoy their lives outside the ring.

The towns were close together, the lakes were everywhere, and many of the wrestlers who worked there eventually bought boats. In a strange twist of fate, the very object that became the center of the most famous dispute—the boat—was also symbolic of the life those wrestlers once shared. A territory where the pay was good. The drives were short. And the wrestlers could finish their matches, head out to the lake, and feel like they had found one of the best places in the wrestling business to work. For a few years in the late 1970s, Knoxville was exactly that. And like so many things in wrestling's territorial era, it disappeared faster than anyone expected.

The war ended. The tape never aired. The men eventually forgave each other. But the territory itself—the one wrestlers once called the best small territory in the world—never quite returned to what it once was. Like a boat drifting away from the dock, it slowly slipped beneath the surface of wrestling history.

CHAPTER 12

WRESTLERS UNION

"Now is our time to unionize." - Jesse Ventura.

FOR DECADES, professional wrestlers traveled constantly, worked while injured, and performed nightly, classified as independent contractors rather than employees.

They received no health insurance, no pension, and no long-term protection. When their careers ended, many were left without financial security.

By 1986, Jesse Ventura believed the system had reached a breaking point.

As WrestleMania 2 approached and the WWF expanded nationally under Vince McMahon, Ventura observed that wrestlers were generating unprecedented revenue from ticket sales, merchandising, and media exposure, yet lacked collective bargaining power.

Ventura believed that if wrestlers were treated as employees in practice, they should be protected as employees in law. If they were treated as entertainers, they should have the same rights as actors and athletes in other industries.

Ventura decided to raise the issue of unionization.

Years later, in an interview with Chris Van Vliet, Ventura described the moment. It occurred shortly before WrestleMania 2, in a locker room with no management present.

"We were all in the dressing room," Ventura said. *"There was nobody from the office."*

Ventura waited, then stood on a chair and addressed the room.

"NOW IS OUR TIME TO UNIONIZE," Ventura explained, noting that WrestleMania publicity had already been completed and that a collective refusal to perform would legally require management to negotiate. Ventura also believed that if wrestlers from the Charlotte territory joined them, the company could be forced into collective bargaining. *"And we can finally get a union,"* Ventura said.

"I GAVE MY IMPASSIONED SPEECH," he recalled. The following day, Ventura received a phone call from McMahon questioning the union effort. Ventura explained that he was paying approximately $5,000 per year for family healthcare and argued that a union could significantly reduce those costs. He also cited wrestlers who had spent decades in the business without retirement income.

"If we had a union," Ventura said, *"maybe they could retire with $500 a month."*

Ventura later explained that the idea had been reinforced by a chance encounter in Las Vegas with Gene Upshaw, then executive director of the NFL Players Association.

"He told me, 'You boys need a union,'" Ventura said.

Ventura left soon after to film Predator. When he returned, he informed McMahon that he would no longer speak publicly about unionization. By that time, Ventura had joined the Screen Actors Guild and obtained health and retirement benefits through his work in Hollywood. He later disclosed that he receives retirement income from both the Screen Actors Guild and AFTRA.

Years later, during Ventura's lawsuit against the WWF over unpaid royalties for videotape narration and voice-over work, the union issue resurfaced in sworn testimony. Ventura and his attorney deposed McMahon in Connecticut. Ventura remained silent, as required, but had previously asked his attorney to determine who had informed management about the locker-room speech.

DURING THE DEPOSITION, McMahon was asked whether wrestling had ever had a union. He answered no. When asked whether anyone had ever attempted to form one, McMahon responded that Jesse Ventura had discussed it years earlier. When asked how he knew, McMahon answered that Hulk Hogan had told him.

VENTURA LATER STATED that McMahon made the same acknowledgment publicly during an interview with Larry King.

Ventura reiterated these events in a separate interview with Graham Bensinger, noting that no agents or office personnel were present during the original locker-room meeting, making it clear that the information came from within the locker room.

"With no hesitation," Ventura said, *"Vince went, 'Hulk Hogan told me.'"*

Ventura stated that he understood Hogan's motivation after reviewing financial disclosures showing that Hogan earned more at WrestleMania 3 than the rest of the roster combined.

Ventura said he had no further communication with Hogan following the deposition. The only later contact came indirectly while Ventura was governor, when Hogan sought assurance that a book-signing appearance would not create legal issues.

Years later, Hogan addressed the matter himself in an interview with Chris Van Vliet. Hogan stated that he held no resentment toward those who criticized him.

When asked about Ventura's claim that Hogan informed

McMahon about the union attempt, Hogan did not dispute it. *"I did that,"* Hogan said.

Hogan explained that he was earning significant income at the time and did not support a system that would equalize pay. Hogan added, *"If I did it, I'll say I did it."*

There was no apology and no denial. Hogan admitted he was looking out for himself.

The union effort ended before it began. Ventura pursued opportunities outside wrestling and later entered politics. Hogan continued as the company's top star. McMahon retained control of the business structure.

THE INDUSTRY CONTINUED UNCHANGED.

Wrestlers remained classified as independent contractors.

No union. No pension. No collective bargaining.

The machine won.

Jesse Ventura identified the problem in 1986.

He attempted to address it. He failed. And the moment remains — one of professional wrestling's most significant what-ifs in not only professional wrestling, but the entertainment industry.

CHAPTER 13

SAMMARTINO & SHEIK
AS TOLD FROM MY UNRELEASED INTERVIEWS OF 2009

"..No one helped me but the Sheik." - Bruno

THERE ARE INTERVIEWS THAT AIR, and then there are interviews that disappear. In April 2009, I sat across from Bruno Sammartino with two cameras rolling. Two months later, in June, I sat across from The Iron Sheik. Two different cities. Two different rooms. Two separate conversations.

Neither interview was ever produced. Both still exist today on large, odd-format master cassette tapes that require specific playback decks and transfer equipment. I do not know how to properly connect or convert them.

They remain raw. Unedited.

Preserved exactly as they were shot. Nearly twenty years later, I don't need to replay them to remember what mattered, although I wish I could finally get these out.

. . .

TWO MONTHS APART — without coordination — both Bruno Sammartino and the Iron Sheik told me the same story.

THE DATE WAS JUNE 7, 1985. The WWF was in full expansion mode, running three shows in one night.

In Matsumoto, Japan, alongside New Japan Pro Wrestling, Antonio Inoki and Kenji Kimura defeated WWF Champion Hulk Hogan and Iron Mike Sharpe in a sold-out main event.

In East Rutherford, New Jersey, the Meadowlands hosted another full card featuring Paul Orndorff, Ricky Steamboat, and Jimmy Snuka against Greg Valentine, Bob Orton Jr., and Bobby Heenan.

AND IN PITTSBURGH, 7,000 fans filled the Civic Arena. The Pittsburgh card saw SD Jones battle Terry Gibbs to a time-limit draw. B. Brian Blair defeated Barry O with the sleeper hold. Tony Atlas pinned Matt Borne. Desiree Peterson defeated Judy Martin. Mike Rotundo and Barry Windham defeated WWF Tag Team Champions The Iron Sheik and Nikolai Volkoff via disqualification. Big John Studd pinned Swede Hanson. George Steele defeated Les Thornton.

And, in the main event, Bruno and his son, David Sammartino, defeated Brutus Beefcake and Johnny Valiant in a steel cage match when David escaped through the door.

Three cities and three rings, with the roster divided across continents. No surplus of bodies waiting backstage.

And in a hallway behind that Pittsburgh show, something unscripted happened.

.   .   .

SIX FOOTBALL PLAYERS wandered into a restricted backstage area. Among them was former Pittsburgh Steeler running back and later former CFL player Dave "Rooster" Fleming of the Hamilton Tiger-Cats.

Bruno approached calmly.

"At this time, I'm like 51 years old when this went on," he told me in 2009. In reality, he was 49 — but the lineup confirms the night. Bruno said, *"Hey, hi guys. What are you doing here? If security sees you, you might get in trouble. You're not supposed to be back here."*

Fleming extended his hand. Bruno accepted what he believed was a friendly handshake.

And the grip tightened.

Bruno told Fleming, *"Well, what do you think you're doing?"*

"You're nothing but a washed-up old man," Fleming replied.

"Not too washed up to take care of you," Bruno answered.

Fleming swung first, according to Bruno, and according to Sheik, who saw it as a sucker punch and sprinted from the showers.

"[Fleming] took a swing at me, I blocked it, and I nailed him, and he went down — and the others joined — and so I'm fighting all of them."

At 49 years old, Bruno found himself fighting six men in a narrow locker room. Even for someone who once held a world record in the bench press, numbers matter.

Then came the detail that never changed.

"The Sheik was taking a shower after his match, and he heard all of the commotion or saw him hit me," Bruno said. *"When he came out of the shower room, he saw just me fighting all these guys."*

"He came right out and joined next to me... and the two of us kind of cleaned house over there. That's a true story — and he was the only guy who came to help me."

The only guy.

Two months later, I asked Sheik about Pittsburgh in front of Eric Simms, his handler and super agent at the time. I always liked Eric. He gets a lot of heat, and honestly, I do not understand why. If he brought me a talent for an interview and said this was the deal or this was the location, he was as professional as anyone I can remember. Simms may be a bit too honest for some people's liking. But I always enjoyed Eric, his candor and honesty.

"Andrew, you go ask Bruno Sammartino in Pittsburgh who saved him from the football players. It was Iron Sheik," said Sheik.

I replied, *"I did several weeks ago. He said you helped him."*

"AMEN!" Sheik shouted. He described hearing the noise from the showers. *"I saw that. I run the hundred dash. Nobody else come save him. Bruno is the legend."*

He didn't name who froze or single anyone out. He simply said he ran in to help him.

Sheik had Olympic amateur credentials. Bruno had legitimate strength records. These were not ordinary men. That doesn't make memory immune to time. Details can shift. Angles can blur. And there is another version.

AFTER DAVE "ROOSTER" Fleming passed away on April 22, 2020, journalist Kevin Gorman revisited the story while covering Fleming's football legacy. Fleming's son disputed Bruno's account.

"I don't care what Iron Sheik says: I had seven dudes here last night telling me Rooster knocked Bruno out with seven left-handed punches," Fleming Jr. said. *"Bruno doesn't want to tell the real story. They said Bruno never got a punch in."*

For all the toughness attached to his name, Fleming was remembered as a devoted husband and father. He married his high school sweetheart, Susan, who battled multiple sclerosis for 45+ years and lived as a paraplegic for 35 years before her passing two years before him.

ON A NIGHT when the WWF stretched across continents — when Hogan headlined in Japan and another major card ran at the Meadowlands — Pittsburgh still had 7,000 fans in the building. The company was divided across time zones. The locker room wasn't overflowing with idle veterans waiting to intervene.

Bruno didn't leave. He later went out and wrestled a steel cage match, teaming with his son David in the main event. Whatever happened in that corridor, he walked back through the curtain and finished the night.

And here is what remains.

Bruno Sammartino and The Iron Sheik were unlikely partners in a bond. Different backgrounds. Different temperaments. Different public images. Yet beneath the characters and national rivalries was something older than storyline — respect.

That night in Pittsburgh didn't create that respect. It revealed it. Sheik didn't move because there were cameras. There was no angle to protect, no paycheck attached to the outcome. He moved because a fellow wrestler was in trouble.

The legacy of The Iron Sheik has grown into legend — toughness in the ring, toughness in life. But toughness is measured by instinct. By the one who runs toward the noise instead of away from it.

STANDING beside the Living Legend in that hallway — not as a heel, not as an opponent, but as an ally — may be one of the purest testaments to that toughness.

After the interview with Bruno in April, we went to dinner. Luigi opened his restaurant to us, and it was a wonderful evening.

Nick Cordasco was there as well. Nick had opened his home to us earlier that day so we could film the Bruno interview in front of a real fireplace — the kind of backdrop Bruno deserved. We had also filmed Nikolai Volkoff and Sgt. Slaughter interviews months earlier.

The unreleased Bruno Sammartino shoot interview, April 2009.

Nick was close to Hulk Hogan as a friend and booking agent with Darren Prince and the Prince Marketing Group. Nick currently has a great friendship and working relationship with Sylvester Stallone and many other stars across the movie, TV, and entertainment industries to this day. Nick is a great guy who gave me a lot of wonderful advice that I still carry today.

BRUNO GOT up from the dinner table to take a photo with a fan. As he walked back to our table, I gently touched his forearm to stop him for a moment before he went back to his seat.

We were hours removed from the interview and now at dinner. I simply asked, *"Who didn't help you?"*

Bruno knew exactly what I was referring to. He looked around first. Then he leaned in and whispered while staring me dead in the eye:

In between two legends, Bruno and my Dad.

"George Steele. Nikolai Volkoff. Brutus Beefcake and others. No one helped me but Sheik." Goosebumps ran across my arm. Then he sat back down and continued talking with my Dad, Luigi, and Nick as if nothing had just been said. I sat there quietly for a few moments, soaking in what he just told me.

THOSE TAPES DON'T JUST HOLD the Pittsburgh story. They hold history. The Bruno interview was raw and unfiltered. He went in-depth about Blackjack Mulligan being blackballed. He spoke about growing up and nearly dying before the age of ten. He talked about Vince McMahon Sr. and his legendary championship run, during which he sold out Madison Square Garden 213 times.

THE SHEIK INTERVIEW was the same. Both interviews still sit on separate master tapes. My relationship with Nick eventually soured partly because I never gave him a copy of the Bruno shoot filmed in his house, which I can understand. He opened his home to us. My Father, before he died, even told me to give Nick a copy, but the problem was never intent. It was technical.

The footage is on a larger master cassette tape, and I have no idea how to connect it, what wires are needed, or what equipment is required to properly convert it. The tape is still there, unconverted and unedited, but still unseen.

Inside those tapes isn't just wrestling history. It's Bruno in Nick's living room. It's later, the memory of my Dad, happy to see Bruno, and breaking bread with him. It's a whisper that gave me goosebumps and still does to this day as I write this. It's two men, two interviews, two months apart — telling the same story.

If anyone can assist with properly converting those master tapes so Nick — and the fans — can finally see those interviews as they happened, reach out. Lord knows I tried again to see if someone could assist me in opening the tape years in 2013, when Bruno was announced for the Hall of Fame and returned to the WWE, and converting it online. I have no intention of releasing an obsolete DVD.

Because some stories deserve to be seen. And some friendships — forged in a hallway without cameras — deserve to be remembered exactly as they were.

JIM DUGGAN AND IRON SHEIK ARRESTED

"Jim, what have you done to us?!" - Vince

THERE ARE moments in wrestling history when the illusion doesn't just crack — it splinters. May 26, 1987, was one of those nights. On television, Hacksaw Jim Duggan was portrayed as an American patriot. The flag-waving hero. The 2x4-carrying embodiment of red, white, and blue. Across from him, The Iron Sheik was the foreign villain. The sneering enemy of America. They were presented as mortal enemies — the kind that made arenas erupt, and kids wave foam fingers in fury.

OFF CAMERA, they were sharing St. Pauli Girl beer on the Garden State Parkway. And that was the night kayfabe cracked. That date lives differently for me.

IT WAS the night of my first wrestling show — a Tuesday night WWF C-show on the Asbury Park boardwalk, steps from my family's restaurant, named after my mother, Alice. That afternoon, Butch Reed stopped by our restaurant hours before bell time. He was wrestling Tito Santana that

night. I don't remember who won. I don't remember most of the matches. *As of this print, I'm still searching for the lineup sheet, a ticket stub, a program — **anything** from that May 26, 1987, event in Asbury Park.*

While I was discovering live wrestling for the first time, somewhere else, the illusion was breaking. The arrest that happened before bell time on Tuesday evening.

After flying into Newark for the Asbury Park house show, Duggan gave Sheik a ride down the Parkway. Sheik didn't have a credit card. They stopped for beer. Duggan, living in Louisiana at the time, didn't think much of drinking while driving. It was a different culture. They smoked marijuana. They passed a New Jersey State Trooper.

Duggan was holding a beer. They were pulled over.

When asked if there was anything the officer should know about, Duggan — the son of a police chief — didn't try to outsmart him. He admitted there was marijuana under his seat.

Then the troopers searched Sheik. Inside a purse were three separate grams of cocaine in three separate containers.

That wasn't a citation. That was a **felony**. Cars slowed down on the Parkway. People stared. There stood Hacksaw Jim Duggan and The Iron Sheik — on-screen enemies and opponents later that night — in handcuffs on the side of the road.

They were taken to the trooper barracks. Duggan received citations for drinking while driving and marijuana possession. Sheik faced felony charges. And somehow — incredibly — they still made the show that night in Asbury Park.

They performed. They told no one backstage. They assumed silence would protect them. It was 1987. No social media. No viral mugshots. By morning, it was everywhere.

Duggan laughs now, remembering the *New York Daily News* running his and Sheik's photos under the headline: *"Brawny Bozos."*

At 6:30 a.m., Duggan's wife, Deborah, called and told Jim, *"Everybody knows!"* Duggan called his father first. Then came the hardest call — to Vince McMahon.

"Never in my life have I gotten through so quickly to Vince McMahon," Duggan later said.

"Jim, what have you done to us?" Duggan admitted he was ashamed. The response was immediate. *"Turn in your tickets and go home,"* McMahon said before he hung up. In that era, wrestlers carried stacks of prepaid airline tickets for upcoming loops. Duggan turned them in and flew back to Louisiana, from the high of WrestleMania III to being fired within several weeks.

"I went off the deep end," he later admitted. Then McMahon called back weeks later. *"Keep your head low. We're gonna bring you back."* And they did — aided in part by Paul Boesch's retirement show discussed earlier. Sheik was not as fortunate. His return stalled until 1991.

But the arrest did more than derail careers. It exposed something bigger. On television, Duggan waved the American flag. Sheik denounced America. They were sold as bitter enemies. In 1987, kayfabe was still guarded fiercely in public. Sponsors mattered. Image mattered. The WWF was no longer a quiet territory — it was becoming a national corporate brand.

The Asbury Park arrest became a warning shot. The old territory road culture — beer in the car, drugs in the bag, blurred lines between character and reality — was colliding with a corporatizing industry.

When Sheik eventually returned in 1991, the company believed it could manage him. But the road culture had not disappeared.

In 2016, Marty Jannetty shared one of his favorite locker-room stories involving The Iron Sheik — a moment that perfectly captured the Sheik's unpredictable personality. According to Jannetty, Sheik was called in and informed that his urine test had come back positive for cocaine. *"Ahh, excellent!"* Sheik reportedly responded. Vince McMahon clarified: *"No, Sheik, that means you have cocaine in your system."* He allegedly began asking whether other wrestlers had tested positive. Each time, Vince's answer was no. With growing confusion, he asked Sheik why. Sheik's response, "I don't understand, *they were with me."* In trying to defend himself, he inadvertently implicated everyone else — a moment that, as Jannetty recalled, summed up the Sheik's larger-than-life absurdity perfectly.

Years later, on *Stories with Brisco and Bradshaw*, John Nord — The Berzerker — told a story that showed how thin the margin for error had become. Flying into Edmonton for a stadium show, Sheik told Nord he had placed "gimmick" in his bag. Customs agents were ten feet away. Nord opened his bag and found cocaine — three separate grams. The same substance that had nearly ended Sheik's career in 1987. Nord quietly removed it and discarded it before customs discovered it. Later, in the locker room, he went berserk (pun indeed intended), confronted Sheik, and WWF agents had to step in. They asked Sheik if it was true, and he admitted it. Iron Sheik was fired on the spot, Nord says. The WWF of 1991 was not the WWF of 1981. It was global now.

Sheik's second chance proved that wrestling could forgive. Canadian customs had made it clear it wouldn't forget if Nord had gotten caught. Iron Sheik was never just a gimmick, even though he used them 'A to Z,' as he liked to say. Sheik was volatile, loyal to a fault (as proven by Bruno Sammartino in the previous chapter), legitimately dangerous, and unintentionally hilarious. A former Iranian national hero. Trained by shooters like Billy Robinson and Verne Gagne alongside Ricky Steamboat. Shaped by exile, addiction, and a rigid personal code that never bent.

He was real. And reality is what cracked the illusion that night in 1987. While I sat in Asbury Park watching my first live wrestling show, believing in heroes and villains, somewhere on the New Jersey Parkway, the curtain slipped. May 26, 1987, was the night the balance shifted. And once the illusion cracks, even for a moment, you can never quite see it the same way again.

CHAPTER 15
WRESTLER STEALS MOM AT GUNPOINT

"If they didn't get out of his way, he'd cut a promo." - Vince McMahon.

NO FAMILY IN PROFESSIONAL WRESTLING—WHETHER bound by blood or by association—has ever had the reach, the influence, or the long shadow of the Grahams. And at the center of that dynasty stood one man: Dr. Jerry Graham.

Inside the ring, he was one of the most feared villains of the 1950s and 1960s. Outside of it, he was a man quietly losing a battle with alcoholism, depression, and severe mental illness. Fans believed Jerry Graham was legitimately insane. In truth, that wasn't far from reality. Jim Cornette would later summarize it bluntly on Dark Side of the Ring: he didn't know of any family in wrestling, real or professional, that had more impact than the Grahams.

. . .

ACCORDING TO CORNETTE, the dynasty began entirely with Jerry—bleached blond hair, movie-star posture, and a gift of gab that made every word sound dangerous. In 1958, the Graham Brothers—soon dubbed the Golden Grams—were born. The timing could not have been better. Wrestling in New York was already red hot, and television exposure was exploding.

Jerry played the unhinged doctor, diagnosing opponents with imaginary injuries. Eddie performed the "surgery" while Jerry looked on approvingly.

Cornette recalled that if you could sell out Madison Square Garden, you could sell out anywhere—and the Grahams did it repeatedly. By 1959, they were main-eventing the Garden and likely earning close to six figures per year, an astronomical sum for the era—well over millions of dollars annually in today's money.

With fame and money to burn—*literally*, Jerry Graham lived exactly the way fans imagined. To impress people, he lit cigars with hundred-dollar bills. Vince McMahon would later remember Jerry running red lights in Washington, D.C., blowing the horn, and watching traffic scatter. *"If they didn't get out of his way,"* McMahon said, *"he'd cut a promo."*

Long before he became the most powerful man in professional wrestling, Vincent K. McMahon was just a teenager in awe of a wrestling god. He dyed his hair blond, dressed like him, and followed him everywhere. The two rode around Washington together in Graham's blood-red Cadillac—the future king of wrestling sitting shotgun beside the most feared heel in the business.

Jerry Graham didn't just inspire Vince McMahon's vision of wrestling. That strut. That arrogance. Decades later, it would become the blueprint for the on-screen Mr. McMahon character. The famous McMahon strut was born in the 1950s, riding shotgun in a red Cadillac, breathing cigar smoke, which, ironically, he would later despise when others smoked cigarettes near him as WWE boss.

But while Jerry Graham's influence was growing, his personal life was collapsing.

GRAHAM STRUGGLED WITH SEVERE ALCOHOLISM, deep depression, emotional instability, and violent mood swings. Friends and promoters later admitted he had been unraveling for years. The breaking point came in August of 1969.

Graham learned that his mother, Mary J. Graham, had been hospitalized at Good Samaritan Hospital in Phoenix, Arizona, after suffering a heart attack. By the time he arrived, he was already intoxicated, emotionally unstable, and distraught when doctors informed him that his mother had passed away; something inside him shattered. He walked out to his car, opened the trunk, and retrieved a shotgun.

According to police reports and newspaper accounts, Graham re-entered the hospital carrying the weapon. He struck a nurse, threatened hospital staff, and fired a shot during the confrontation. Security guards attempted to restrain him, but at over six feet tall and more than 300 pounds, Graham overpowered them.

He then walked into his mother's room, lifted her body, placed her over his shoulder, and ran through the hospital corridors.

.   .   .

STAFF WATCHED in horror as the massive wrestler fled the building carrying his mother's corpse. Police were called immediately. Outside the hospital, Graham finally stopped and placed her body down before turning toward the approaching officers. He was arrested at the scene.

The following morning, Phoenix newspapers carried the headline: *"Wrestler Flees Hospital With Body."* It sounded like tabloid fiction, and for years, it was an urban legend. However, it was horrifyingly real.

GIVEN HIS MENTAL CONDITION, long history of alcoholism, and complete emotional collapse, Graham was committed to the Arizona State Mental Hospital. His wrestling career was effectively over. Promoters would not book him, and commissions would not license him, in an era when wrestling was not considered exhibition and wrestlers had to be licensed in the states where they performed. His reputation was destroyed overnight.

The man once billed as one of wrestling's most dangerous villains had become a tragic cautionary tale.

Jerry Graham never fully recovered, and his alcoholism worsened. His mental health deteriorated, and his personal life collapsed. The tragic irony is unavoidable: he inspired the man who would build the largest wrestling empire in history, yet he never lived to see it.

The hospital incident revealed Graham's unraveling, while the riot at Madison Square Garden in 1959 revealed the danger that had always been there — volatile and combustible. The Garden became a battleground not just inside the ring, but *in the stands*.

CHAPTER 16

MSG RIOT OF 1959

"A little red brings in the green." - Dr. Jerry Graham

THE DECEMBER 2, 1957, issue of *Life Magazine* is most remembered for its chilling coverage of Ed Gein—a name that would become synonymous with American horror and later inspire generations of fictional psychopaths. But buried within those same pages was another spectacle of chaos—this one not in rural Wisconsin, but in the heart of Madison Square Garden.

On November 19, 1957, professional wrestling once again proved it was more than mere entertainment—it was combustible theater.

That night, Argentine fan favorite Antonino Rocca was hoisted high onto the shoulders of ecstatic supporters as pandemonium erupted inside the Garden. The photograph, captured by Walter Kelleher of the *New York Daily News*, freezes a moment that, at first glance, feels almost triumphant.

Rocca, beloved and magnetic, floats above a sea of humanity. But the context was far more volatile.

The riot had been sparked by the theatrics—and provocations—of wrestling's flamboyant villain, Dr. Jerry Graham. Graham, draped in a $500 sequin-encrusted purple robe (a staggering sum in 1957), whipped the crowd into a frenzy. His brash persona, arrogance, and deliberate antagonism pushed the audience beyond the limits of suspension of disbelief.

An estimated 500 fans became actively involved in rioting. Nearly 300 chairs were smashed or thrown. Two police officers were injured as authorities struggled to restore order. Amid the disorder, Graham's extravagant robe—an essential part of his carefully constructed image—was stolen. Even more dramatically, Graham himself suffered a split-open head during the melee.

Professional wrestling in the 1950s operated in a delicate space between sport and spectacle. Kayfabe—the illusion that the drama was real—was fiercely protected. Audiences didn't just watch; they believed. And on that November night, belief turned physical.

The *Life Magazine* juxtaposition is striking: on one side of the issue, America confronting the horror of Ed Gein; on another, a wrestling riot in the nation's most famous arena. Both stories, in very different ways, reflected something deeper about the era's cultural temperature—violence, spectacle, and the thin line between fascination and frenzy.

The Rocca image remains one of the most haunting visual artifacts of wrestling's territorial era. Not because of the broken chairs or the stolen robe—but because it captures a moment when professional wrestling felt dangerous, immediate, and utterly uncontrollable.

In 1957, the Garden wasn't just hosting matches. It was hosting eruptions. The official attendance at Madison Square Garden that night was under 13,000 fans. It wasn't anywhere near a sellout or remembered for a record gate, although Graham was responsible for many sellouts and large gates.

Decades later, in a grainy 1980s interview that resurfaced online roughly eight years ago courtesy of the 6:05 Super Podcast, Dr. Jerry Graham reflected on November 19, 1957—not with regret, not with embarrassment—but with unmistakable pride.

"I knew the timing was right. The Puerto Rican people had never seen blood in Madison Square Garden. I hit him in the eye and split his eye — and they went insane." He described blood flowing "like water." His partner, Dick the Bruiser, was throwing fans "like a farmer picking up potatoes." Police reportedly carried out.

Dick the Bruiser remained suspended in New York. Jerry was fined $1,000 for inciting the riot, but returned to the Northeast. *"I paid my fine, and I'm still back in New York and New Jersey."*

For Jerry, the riot wasn't disgrace — it was validation. *"A little red brings in the green."*

On January 24, 1997, Graham died at the age of 75, due to complications from a stroke he suffered a month earlier. Graham was honored as a 2017 "Legacy Inductee" into the WWE Hall of Fame, although it would have been fitting for Vince McMahon to strut on stage and induct his favorite wrestler, and not in a video package, but with a memorable speech that was deserving of a man who was ahead of his time and inspired the most powerful man in wrestling history.

CHAPTER 17

A LITTLE ROCK RIOT

"You just lost your main event!" - HBK

NEARLY FOUR DECADES after the chaos of the Madison Square Garden riot of 1959—when fans in New York turned on the product and transformed a wrestling event into a full-blown disturbance—the industry once again found itself face-to-face with the unpredictable power of its audience.

The World Wrestling Federation was now a national powerhouse, and by 1997 it was entering the early stages of what would become the Attitude Era—edgier, louder, and more volatile than ever before. But one thing had not changed: when fans felt betrayed, disrespected, or misled, they could still turn on a show in an instant.

On December 15, 1997, that tension boiled over in Little Rock. What unfolded at Barton Coliseum that night would echo the same frustrations seen back in 1959—only now amplified by a new generation of fans who were louder, more cynical, and far less willing to accept anything less than what they paid to see. By late 1997, however, the WWF roster was dominated by heel characters and anti-heroes, and there were few traditional babyfaces positioned to calm an already agitated crowd.

Following the ceremony, D-Generation X entered the arena. Triple H came out accompanied by Shawn Michaels and Chyna. Almost immediately, fans began throwing crumpled paper, cans, and other objects into the ring.

Shawn Michaels then took the microphone and addressed the crowd. *"For all of you fans throwing s*** inside the ring... You just lost your main event!"*

D-Generation X exited the ring and headed backstage.

OBJECTS CONTINUED to rain down from the crowd. After several minutes of confusion, the arena announcer informed fans that the show was over. What followed was a full-scale riot.

According to eyewitness Ryan Henslee, who attended the show as a child with his family, trash, beer cans, and folding chairs were thrown from all directions.

Chairs landed in the ring and throughout the lower bowl—smoke-filled sections of the arena.

Henslee later stated that a security guard's shirt was ripped off and set on fire. Fights broke out among fans in the bleachers. Police were called in, and several attendees were arrested and escorted out in handcuffs.

Henslee described seeing multiple fans brawling in the aisles and falling over rows of chairs. He and his family remained frozen in their seats until the situation calmed. When the smoke cleared, they walked down the steps covered with discarded signs, spilled drinks, and debris.

Other fans in attendance shared similar accounts.

A Reddit user who claimed he was in attendance later recalled, "We realized we'd stayed too long when a roll of flaming toilet paper came from the second level."

Reader Shane Dixon wrote the night of the event, *"The line-up was not anything near what was advertised, and the matches lasted about three minutes each. At the end of the night, Hunter Helmsley was supposed to fight Dude Love. However, HBK was hit by a piece of paper and told the crowd that we had lost the main event. Everyone waited a couple of minutes to see if DX would return, but the announcer said the card was over. Chairs were hurled at the ring, and police were pelted with whiskey bottles. The cops used tear gas to stop the riot."*

Another fan at the show, Nick Nettles, recalled, *"Before the main event, Shawn Michaels made a presentation to Danny Hodge, but fans booed and threw things. When DX came out, they started throwing things again. Shawn got on the mic and asked them to stop. They didn't, so he said, 'You just lost your main event!' After that, I left."*

Reader Landon Wallace wrote, *"People made signs expecting Raw, so the crowd was angry from the start. It was a weak show, and as the night progressed, people got angrier and threw things in the ring."*

Jim Cornette later summed up the night bluntly, saying, *"Normal night in Little Rock for Mid-South Wrestling. Another case of Shawn Michaels causing s***."*

Police eventually regained control of the arena. Multiple fans were arrested. The ring was left covered in chairs, trash, and debris.

The December 15, 1997, Barton Coliseum riot remains one of the most infamous crowd incidents in professional wrestling history — a night when kayfabe broke down, tempers exploded, and a house show turned into chaos.

CHAPTER 18

THE OTHER PLANE RIDES FROM HELL

"You get in the back; I'll sit in the front." -
Johnny Valentine.

WHEN FANS TALK about the "Plane Ride From Hell," most think of the infamous 2002 charter flight from Europe.

But long before that nightmare, there was an earlier, far darker aviation curse that haunted the business — a year when the sky itself seemed to be hunting wrestlers.

TWO PLANE CRASHES in 1975 occurred less than eight months apart, leaving one wrestler dead, another paralyzed, a pilot killed, multiple careers ended, and a legend born that would follow Ric Flair for the rest of his life.

THE FIRST TRAGEDY struck on February 19, 1975, after a show at the Miami Convention Center. Gary Hart,

Bobby Shane, Buddy Colt, and Dennis McCord left the arena, grabbed food at Wolfie's, then headed to the airport to board Buddy Colt's single-engine Cessna 173 for the short flight home to Tampa.

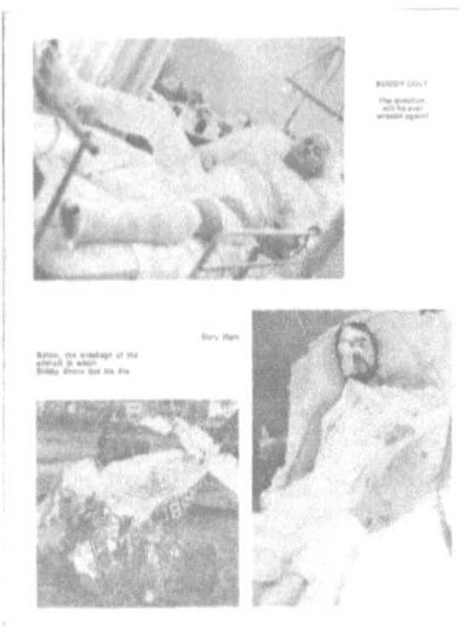

Colt was flying the plane, McCord sat beside him, Bobby Shane sat behind Colt, and Gary Hart sat behind McCord.

On the return flight, Hart asked to switch seats with Shane so he could stretch his legs. Shane agreed. The plane went down in the Everglades. Buddy Colt survived but was critically injured. Dennis McCord survived. Gary Hart survived. Bobby Shane did not.

The following night in Tampa, the crash was announced to the crowd — **and in one of the most chilling moments in wrestling history, fans cheered the deaths.** Shane had been a hated heel, and the audience believed villains deserved whatever fate found them.

Jack Brisco later recalled standing in the ring listening as the crowd celebrated the fact that wrestlers had died in a plane crash. Wrestling had conditioned its audience too well.

EIGHT MONTHS LATER, fate struck *again*.

ON OCTOBER 4TH, 1975, Jim Crockett Promotions chartered a tiny twin-engine Cessna 310 to fly from Charlotte, North Carolina, to Wilmington for an evening show at the sold-out outdoor Legion Stadium.

On board were Johnny Valentine, Ric Flair, Bob Bruggers, Tim Woods — wrestling under a mask as the original Mr. Wrestling — promoter David Crockett, and pilot Joseph Michael Farkas. Valentine was seated next to the pilot.

The following week, he was scheduled to challenge NWA World Heavyweight Champion Jack Brisco at the Greensboro Coliseum.

Earlier in the flight, Flair had been sitting up front but grew uneasy next to the cockpit. He complained repeatedly until Valentine finally said, *"You get in the back; I'll sit in the front."* They swapped seats.

Valentine turned to the others in the rear of the aircraft, smiled, and said, *"Guess what… we're out of fuel,"* then laughed, knowing the plane could technically fly on one engine.

The humor didn't last. The aircraft began losing altitude. Woods remembered a conversation he once had with Austin Idol, who survived a previous crash and told him the worst part wasn't the impact — it was the floor ripping the bottoms of his feet down to the bone because he wasn't wearing shoes.

Woods realized he didn't have his on either. He grabbed the pilot's briefcase full of flight manuals and shoved it under his feet as a shield.

David Crockett later said that if they had cleared the trees, they would have made the runway. Farkas deliberately slowed the aircraft, but it was still traveling between 85 and 100 miles per hour when it crashed.

Every seat broke loose, cascading forward like a domino effect. Crockett's head burst through the seat in front of him, breaking Woods' ribs.

His mouth was ripped open, and his shoulder was dislocated. Ric Flair, just 26 years old, suffered multiple deep lacerations and broke his back in two places.

Bob Bruggers, a former linebacker for the Miami Dolphins and San Diego Chargers, also broke his back.

Johnny Valentine remained conscious the entire time.

As his back was crushed, a bone fragment wedged into his spinal column. His spine would later have to be reattached with a clamp.

He was paralyzed from the waist down. Johnny Valentine's legendary career was over.

All six men were rushed to New Hanover County Hospital in Wilmington.

Pilot Joseph Farkas survived for two months before dying from his injuries.

Bruggers had a steel rod inserted into his spine and never wrestled again.

Crockett suffered head trauma and lingering injuries for more than six months.

Doctors told Ric Flair he would never wrestle again. But he returned within months, reinventing himself into the jet-flying, limousine-riding Nature Boy who would become the most traveled world champion the business had ever seen.

What turned the crash into legend, however, was the seat. For decades, wrestlers whispered that Flair had given up the front seat moments before impact — the seat that absorbed the worst of the crash.

Valentine's wife, Sharon, would later say, *"That's fate. Neither John nor I feels bad about the fact that had Ric still been sitting there, he'd be in this shape. John never showed any animosity about it."*

THOUGH SHE WOULD LATER DESCRIBE

Flair as "callous" and "cold," claiming her husband never heard from him again after the crash.

The front of StarNews on Oct. 5, 1975, about the plane crash that injured Ric Flair, paralyzed Johnny Valentine, and killed the pilot. The group was traveling from Charlotte to Wilmington for an event at Legion Stadium.

When newspapers reported the accident, they used Tim Woods' real name — George Woodin — to hide the fact that

Woods, a heel, had been traveling with his kayfabe mortal enemy Johnny Valentine.

EVEN IN THE HOSPITAL, kayfabe lived.

When Wahoo McDaniel arrived to visit Flair, hospital staff tried to restrain him and called the police, believing he had come to attack his storyline rival.

In locker rooms, wrestlers whispered that Flair never truly left that plane. They joked about it every time he boarded a jet. They warned promoters not to let him change seats. They believed death had missed him by inches — just like it had missed Gary Hart while claiming Bobby Shane eight months earlier.

Two crashes. Two seat swaps. One paralyzed legend.

One dead pilot. One survivor who went on to conquer the world.

TO THIS DAY, the seat-switching story has never been officially confirmed. Still, in wrestling, when a tale survives every locker room generation, it stops being a rumor and becomes folklore.

BECAUSE BEFORE THERE was a Plane Ride From Hell in 2002, there was the year the sky took a pilot, a star, a champion's legs, and injured many—two crashes within the year, and professional wrestling learned that even its toughest men were no match for fate at 10,000 feet.

CHAPTER 19

THE PAWNED WWF WORLD TITLE

"He walks out holding something wrapped in a New York Post." - Tom Burke.

FOR DECADES, one of the most persistent urban legends in professional wrestling surrounded the disappearance of Pedro Morales' original WWWF Championship belt.

The story most fans heard was simple and dramatic.

Morales claimed his championship belt had been stolen from him at a restaurant in New York City. The belt vanished, never to be recovered. Another priceless relic of wrestling history lost forever.

But as with many stories in wrestling, the truth lived somewhere else. Not in a police report. Not in a locker room. And not in a courtroom.

It lived quietly behind a counter on West 49th Street.

While researching this book, I reached out directly to wrestling historian and memorabilia expert Tom Burke to finally get his side of this long-circulated urban tale.

Burke is one of the most respected collectors in wrestling history and personally owned Pedro Morales' original WWWF Championship belt for more than three decades.

What he told me completely dismantles the "stolen belt" story.

In the mid-to-late 1970s, long before the internet, eBay, collector conventions, or wrestling memorabilia markets existed, hunting wrestling artifacts meant walking the streets.

It meant flipping through dusty boxes. It meant asking questions. And Tom Burke was one of the original hunters.

Wrestling Historian, Tom Burke and Andrew Khellah

"I would go into various back magazine stores and consignment stores in Times Square. It was a regular stop for me," Burke recalls.

One of those regular stops was a small consignment shop on West 49th Street between Broadway and 8th Avenue.

On one visit, Burke was digging through a box of old 8x10 wrestling photos from the 1950s when he casually asked the shop owner if he had anything else related to wrestling.

"The gentleman's wife said, 'Abe, we got that wrestling prop in the back,'" Burke recalled.

Moments later, the owner emerged, holding something wrapped in a New York Post.

"HE WALKS *out holding something wrapped in a New York Post. He opens it up and boom — the WWWF belt."*

Burke immediately knew what he was looking at.

The condition told its own story.

"The condition was very good. You could see the leather folding onto the metal from Pedro putting on some pounds," Burke said.

THE SHOP OWNER initially asked $200 for the belt.

"I asked him how much he wanted for the belt. As I recall, it was $200. I said $125."

The owner's wife explained they were closing the store in six weeks and moving to Florida. Burke left a $20 deposit and returned the next day with the remaining money—the final price: $125.

"I gave him a $20 deposit. The next day, I went back with the balance," Burke told me.

JUST LIKE THAT, one of the most important championship belts in wrestling history left a pawn shop and entered a private collection. Burke would go on to own Pedro Morales' championship belt for over 30 years.

BUT BURKE DIDN'T JUST BUY the belt. He asked questions. He was, and remains, considered one of the most respected and knowledgeable wrestling historians in the world.

"I asked him how he acquired the belt," Burke said.

The shop owner's answer was simple.

"He told me a big Puerto Rican came in with the belt."

There was no theft report. No robbery claim. No police involvement. Just a transaction. Burke later told me he had been informed that the man might have been Pete Sanchez or Manny Soto, both well-known figures in the New York wrestling scene at the time.

And among insiders, a consistent story circulated.

"Pedro liked the ponies," Burke said. *"He loved horse racing."*

The implication was clear. The belt wasn't stolen. It was sold to cover gambling losses.

For years, the story persisted that Pedro Morales's championship belt had been stolen from him at a restaurant. But collectors, historians, and those who knew the business quietly told a different version.

A champion down on his luck. A gambler chasing losses.

A belt was exchanged for cash.

Pedro Morales remains one of the greatest champions and a triple-crown champion in WWWF/WWF/WWE wrestling history.

One of the most beloved figures of the WWWF era.

———

ONE OF THE most unforgettable moments of his career came in September 1972, when Morales stepped into the ring against his close friend and former titleholder, Bruno Sammartino, in a historic showdown at Shea Stadium. More than 22,000 fans packed the venue, eager to see two titans of their era collide.

What followed was nothing short of epic. The match raged on for an astonishing 75 minutes. Ultimately, the bout was declared a draw because New York's state athletic curfew forced the match to be stopped at 11 p.m. Eastern time. There was no winner, yet the contest instantly became legendary, etched into wrestling lore by those fortunate enough to witness it live.

Morales' reign as World Champion lasted an incredible 1,027 days—nearly three years—making it one of the longest and most impressive title runs in history.

. . .

AFTER RETIRING FROM WRESTLING, Morales permanently settled in Woodbridge, New Jersey, less than fifteen miles from me. Over the years, I attempted numerous times to interview him and to book him for autograph signings. He declined every request.

Morales did only one known public signing in the early 2000s, appearing at a small event in Carteret, New Jersey, in either 2003 or 2004. By all accounts, he looked like he didn't want to be there. He signed quickly, avoided conversation, and left as soon as possible.

Pedro wanted distance from the business. Distance from the spotlight. Distance from the stories. And perhaps, distance from the truth.

Because the truth is simple.

Pedro Morales's championship belt was not stolen.

It was sold. And for $125, one of wrestling's greatest artifacts was rescued from disappearing forever.

In professional wrestling, some legends are born in the ring. Others are born in pawn shops. And sometimes, the truth sits quietly behind a counter, wrapped in yesterday's newspaper, waiting for someone who knows to ask the right question.

CHAPTER 20

UNDERTAKER
TRADEMARK SOLD

FEW CHARACTERS in professional wrestling history have achieved the cultural impact and longevity of The Undertaker. Debuting at the 1990 Survivor Series, the eerie, funeral-themed character portrayed by Mark Calaway quickly became one of the most recognizable figures in the wrestling business. Managed early on by Brother Love and later by the unforgettable Paul Bearer, the character evolved into a centerpiece of WWF and later WWE programming for more than three decades.

YET BEHIND ONE of wrestling's most legendary gimmicks lies a lesser-known story involving two independent wrestlers from the Northeastern wrestling scene who once used the name themselves.

THOSE WRESTLERS WERE Val Puccio and Tony Pucci, brothers who wrestled together as "The Undertakers."

THROUGHOUT THE LATE 1980s and early 1990s, the duo worked numerous independent shows along the East Coast, where regional wrestling promotions often relied on colorful gimmicks and memorable names to draw local crowds. Tony Pucci wrestled under the name Henchman, while his brother Val Puccio competed under the name Punisher.

Together, the team gained modest recognition on the independent circuit performing as The Undertakers, a dark and imposing tag team that stood out among the era's colorful characters. Around 1990, when the World Wrestling Federation 

was preparing to introduce a mysterious new character on national television, the company realized that the name "The Undertaker" was already being used in the wrestling world.

According to historical wrestling records and profiles compiled by Online World of Wrestling, Vince McMahon purchased the rights to the Undertaker name from Puccio and Pucci to ensure there would be no confusion between the independent tag team and the new WWF wrestler who would soon debut under the name. The deal reportedly amounted to $3,000, a one-time payment that secured the name for the company's new character.

At the time, the agreement likely seemed like a straightforward business decision. Independent wrestlers rarely saw significant financial opportunities, and there was no way to predict that the character WWF was preparing would become one of the most successful gimmicks in wrestling history.

Once the name was sold, the Puccio brothers changed their team name and began performing under a new identity: "Double Trouble." Rather than disappearing from the WWF scene entirely, the team soon found themselves working for the very company that had purchased their original name. In 1991, Double Trouble began appearing at WWF television tapings and live events, often wrestling in dark matches or house show bouts against established teams. Their early appearances included victories over preliminary opposition during television tapings in Wheeling, West Virginia, and Huntington, West Virginia, before they began a more consistent run on the WWF house show circuit in 1992.

That summer, Double Trouble faced a series of well-known WWF tag teams while touring the country. On June 19, 1992, in Long Island, New York, they faced the popular duo The Bushwhackers, who defeated them. The following nights saw similar results, as the Bushwhackers defeated Double Trouble again on June 20 in Philadelphia, June 21 in Springfield, Massachusetts, and June 22 in Providence, Rhode Island. Though victories were hard to come by, the matches placed the team in front of large WWF audiences across the Northeast. Later that year, the Puccio brothers faced the energetic tag team High Energy, consisting of Owen Hart and Koko B. Ware. On August 24, 1992, in Syracuse, New York, High Energy defeated Double Trouble, beginning another short series of house show encounters between the teams.

As the fall schedule continued, the brothers also found themselves stepping into the ring with the massive WWF Tag Team Champions The Natural Disasters, who defeated Double Trouble on September 13, 1992, in Johnstown,

Pennsylvania, and again the next night in Wheeling, West Virginia. Double Trouble continued working throughout the fall tour, again facing High Energy in matches held in Omaha, Nebraska; Tampa, Florida; East Rutherford, New Jersey; Boston, Massachusetts; and Baltimore, Maryland. Despite tough competition, the Puccio brothers finally secured a victory on October 2, 1992, in Poughkeepsie, New York, defeating Mark Thomas and Phil Apollo, a win that would be their lone recorded victory during that run.

Their schedule that month also included a series of unusual handicap matches against Road Warrior Animal, one-half of the legendary Legion of Doom. In Des Moines, Iowa, on four consecutive nights from October 8 through October 11, 1992, Animal defeated Double Trouble in handicap matches that highlighted the imposing strength of the Road Warriors' powerhouse. While their run in the WWF was relatively brief, the team also expanded their careers internationally.

The Puccio brothers completed two tours of Japan, appearing for All Japan Pro Wrestling and working events connected with the WAR promotion, giving them exposure to an entirely different wrestling style and audience. Outside the WWF, the brothers continued working for regional promotions, including Tony Rumble's Century Wrestling Alliance, a well-known New England promotion during the 1990s independent wrestling boom. During their time there, they captured the CWA Tag Team Championship, becoming the promotion's inaugural champions after defeating The Interns in September 1993.

Later in 1994, the brothers experimented with another version of their tag team persona, calling themselves "The Trouble Makers." During this run, Val Puccio wrestled under the name Chaos, while Tony Pucci competed as Mayhem. Their final recorded match together in the promotion took place on December 12, 1994, when they defeated Alex Shane and Cherokee Renegade in Elizabethton, Tennessee. By the mid-1990s, the team eventually split up. Val Puccio later appeared in ECW, while Tony Pucci continued working independently for promotions such as Northeast Wrestling and the Century Wrestling Alliance before retiring from active competition in 1997.

Outside the ring, Valentino Puccio faced well-documented health challenges related to severe obesity. His struggles were featured on the TLC documentary series Inside the Brookhaven Obesity Clinic, which chronicled patients seeking treatment for extreme weight conditions. Puccio passed away on January 7, 2011, at the age of 45, with his brother Tony announcing the news publicly. His death was believed to have been caused by complications related to obesity.

Today, the story of Val Puccio and Tony Pucci remains one of professional wrestling's most intriguing "what-if" tales. A name once used by a regional tag team was purchased for a relatively small sum and eventually became the identity of one of the most successful characters in wrestling history. The Undertaker would go on to win multiple world championships, headline countless WrestleMania events, and generate tens of millions of dollars in merchandise and ticket sales for the WWF and later WWE.

Meanwhile, the original Undertakers quietly moved on with their careers, their brief connection to the legendary name becoming a fascinating footnote in wrestling history. What began as a $3,000 business transaction would ultimately become one of the most iconic gimmicks ever created in professional wrestling.

CHAPTER 21

DEAD MAN WALKING

"Oh, brother, you got me!" - Hulk Hogan.

ON NOVEMBER 27, 1991, the night before Thanksgiving, Survivor Series came to Detroit, Michigan.

The WWF was in transition.

Hulk Hogan's golden era was fading. The New Generation was coming. Vince McMahon needed a new monster.

That monster was The Undertaker.

Only one year removed from his debut at Survivor Series 1990, The Undertaker stood across the ring from Hulk Hogan for the WWF Championship. Ric Flair had just arrived from WCW and inserted himself into the title picture, calling himself "The Real World's Champion."

The plan was bold. Flair would interfere.

Undertaker would win the title. A new era would begin.

During the match, Flair slid a steel chair into the ring. Undertaker struck Hogan with a Tombstone Piledriver onto the chair. The referee counted three.

Backstage, Hulk Hogan sold his neck so much that many believed it was career-ending. Initially, the Undertaker was genuinely concerned and second-guessed himself. He felt terrible that he may have injured the golden goose.

Hogan was lying on the floor in Vince McMahon's office, complaining that the Tombstone had jammed his neck. Some thought this was the end of Hulkamania. He insisted that even though his head never hit the mat, Undertaker's grip and the jolt of the move had done damage.

But there was a problem.

THE TAPE.

WHEN THE FOOTAGE WAS REVIEWED,

Hogan's head never came close to the mat. Undertaker's knees absorbed the impact exactly as the move is designed. The Tombstone was clean.

Ironically, a year prior, at the same event in his debut, Undertaker dropped Koko B. Ware with a tombstone, which made Koko angry backstage. The Dead Man apologized and acknowledged on his podcast that he hurt Koko in his debut.

To many in the locker room, it looked like Hogan had sold an injury that never happened.

For Undertaker, the fear was real.

He wasn't a ten-year veteran.

He wasn't untouchable. He wasn't a made man yet.

He had only been in the WWF for one year. And now the company's golden goose was claiming he had nearly been crippled.

In wrestling, hurting the top star — even accidentally — was unforgivable. Careers had ended for far less. Wrestlers had been buried for crossing Hogan. Undertaker truly believed he might be fired.

What happened was that a young champion, a year into his WWF run, was wondering if the most significant moment of his career was about to be taken away.

Six days later, on *Tuesday in Texas*, Hogan regained the WWF Championship. Undertaker's reign lasted six days.

Hogan's fourth WWF title reign lasted less than six days.

The title was held up until the Royal Rumble in January 1992, where the winner of the 30-man rumble match would be crowned champion.

Ric Flair, who drew #3, would be the winner, outlasting everyone for over an hour.

During the bizarre November weekend that produced two WWF pay-per-views with just days of one another, the Dead Man did something very brazen that many didn't normally do.

UNDERTAKER CONFRONTED Hogan face-to-face and said this on his *Six Feet Under* podcast:

"On my one-year anniversary with the company, I wrestled none other than the golden goose himself — the star, the moneymaker, the big dude. I'm going over.

*I'm winning the championship. I'm walking down the hall to my locker room, and he goes, 'Hey brother, can I talk to you?' He tells me he's really nervous about taking the Tombstone because he's got a bad neck. I tell him, 'Look, I promise you I'll take great care of you. Don't worry about it.' So we get into the match, and now it's time for the finish. The finish is me Tombstoning him on a chair. I've given my kids rougher bumps than I ever gave Hogan. I wrap him up, I've got him tight, the chair comes down — boom. As soon as my knees hit the mat, he goes, 'Oh brother, you got me.' My heart sinks. I'm thinking, 'Oh f***... I just crippled the golden goose. I just hurt Hogan.' I go backstage and ask where he is. He's laid out on the floor in Vince's office. I'm trying to check on him, apologize, do whatever I can. This is all before I ever saw the footage. And now there's a pay-per-view coming up — Tuesday in Texas —, and I'm thinking, 'Oh man, this is going to be punishment. They're going to take the title right back from me.' A few days later, I finally saw the tape. His head never touched the chair. Not even close. Terry comes to me and says, 'I watched the footage back. Your head never hit. But you had me so tight that when I came down, I didn't have any room to move, and it wrenched my neck.' And that right there told me everything I needed to know about who he was as a person."*

Hogan told him his head never hit the mat — but insisted the jolt hurt his neck. Undertaker listened. But he didn't buy it. The footage didn't lie. From that moment on, the trust was gone, and so was what changed in Undertaker's career.

The faith Vince McMahon had briefly placed in him was shaken the moment Hogan planted doubt.

Undertaker didn't touch world championship gold, or any title for that matter, again for more than six years.

The 6-day title reign for the Undertaker that bizarre Thanksgiving week turned into **six more years**, when the Undertaker, Mark Calloway, finally got his moment at WrestleMania 13 in Chicago.

Six long years.

He worked every house show. He protected every opponent while he was working through his injury, both mentally and physically. He helped carry the company through lean years, wrestling in high school gyms, not knowing what the future held, and turned down more money from WCW countless times.

He rebuilt trust with Vince McMahon one night at a time.

By the time he finally won the WWF Championship again at WrestleMania XIII in 1997, he was no longer a rookie.

The Dead Man became the untouchable cornerstone and locker room leader. But few remember how close it came to ending before it truly began.

Undertaker certainly did and never forgot that Thanksgiving weekend, nor did his resentment ever fade. It sat quietly beneath the surface for over a decade.

And when Hogan returned to the WWF in 2002, nearly ten years later, the power dynamic had flipped.

Hogan won the Undisputed Championship from Triple H, but the reign lasted only a month. At Judgment Day 2002, The Undertaker took the title from him.

The torch was not passed. It was taken.

. . .

THIS WAS NO LONGER Hogan's yard, and ironically, it would be the last time Hulk Hogan held a World title.

Twenty-plus years later, Hulk Hogan's final WWE appearance came on the Netflix debut of Monday Night Raw. January 6, 2025.

And he got booed. And it was not heel heat. It was go-away heat. The look of disappointment and shock on the icon's face was noticeable. Backstage, Undertaker watched it unfold. On his Six Feet Under podcast, before the interviewer could finish asking about it, Taker laughed.

"Here we go!"

When the host tried to soften it — "That was a pop, right?" — Taker replied: *"That was an ego pop."*

He saw Hogan no-sell the reaction and immediately start pushing his beer brand on camera. When asked if he felt bad for him, Undertaker said:

"No (short pause). *I got feelings for people. But sometimes in life, some things come back."*

Those comments came before Hogan's passing. When Hogan died, Undertaker paid tribute and honored his legacy — because that is who he is.

But he never forgot.

Thanksgiving Eve 1991 will forever be remembered as the night Hulk Hogan nearly ended The Undertaker — and unknowingly created the most powerful figure the business would ever know.

CHAPTER 22

TOUGH AS NAILZ

"I don't regret it." - Nailz

LONGTIME WRESTLING fans have heard the story for more than thirty years.

The day a wrestler snapped. The day Vince McMahon was allegedly attacked. The day a locker room rumor later turned into a federal court case.

The incident involving Nailz — real name Kevin Wacholz — remains one of the most controversial, disputed, and dangerous backstage confrontations in professional wrestling history.

And unlike most wrestling legends, this one ended up in court. The confrontation took place on December 14, 1992, during a WWF Superstars television taping at the Brown County Expo Center in Green Bay, Wisconsin.

The WWF was in town for a TV taping. Talent was in and out of Gorilla Position. Vince McMahon had his office set up backstage. Producers were moving between matches. Agents were handling finishes.

AND NAILZ HAD BEEN STEWING. According to multiple accounts, Wacholz was wound up by some of the boys, who believed he had been short-changed on his Summerslam 1992 payoff in London.

The Wrestling Observer Newsletter reported that Nailz and McMahon had been arguing over money. Nailz allegedly demanded more pay. McMahon refused.

According to Meltzer's reporting, Nailz then jumped across the room, grabbed McMahon by the throat, and threw him down.

WHAT HAPPENED NEXT DEPENDS on who you believe.

SGT. SLAUGHTER, during a live Q&A on Canada's Inside the Ropes, said that Nailz approached him to ask if he could go inside and talk to Vince.

Sarge checked with McMahon. Vince said to let him in.

Minutes later, Sarge heard furniture moving. He ran inside along with the other wrestlers.

According to Slaughter, he kicked Nailz off Vince and tried to restrain him, but Nailz broke free and choked McMahon a second time.

Sarge said the situation was out of control.

BRET HART DETAILED the incident in his autobiography.

"Vince had problems to deal with in Green Bay. For the past six months, he had been building Kevin Wacholz as a psycho killer ex-con named Nailz. Kevin cornered Vince in his office and screamed at him for fifteen minutes about all the lies he'd been told. His yelling got so loud I got goosebumps up my back as I listened from down the hall. Suddenly, there was a loud crash. Nailz had knocked Vince over his chair, choking him violently, until Slaughter and a swarm of agents teamed up to pull him off. Nailz walked out and immediately called the police and accused Vince of making a sexual advance toward him."

Bret added that some wrestlers actually admired Nailz for standing up to Vince.

————

JERRY SAGS of The Nasty Boys witnessed the incident.

According to Sags, Nailz demanded payment. Vince said no.

Nailz then lifted Vince by the neck and threw him on the floor. Sags remembers yelling to Slaughter: *"He's killing him in there."*

————

MEAN GENE OKERLUND recalled hearing part of the argument during a RF Video shoot interview: *"You give Big Boss Man twenty-five thousand, and you give me eight thousand? Take this check back."*

————

JOHN NORD (AKA The Berzerker) claimed Nailz told him beforehand that he intended to attack Vince.

According to Nord, Nailz asked him to sit outside the office and pretend to pull him off afterward.

Kevin Wacholz denies nearly every version of the story.

Speaking to Mike Johnson of PWInsider on Highspots TV, Wacholz said the fight was about money, not premeditation.

"Usually, a guy wouldn't quit or have a problem with ownership if he was happy with what he was getting paid. That sums it up right there."

He denied calling Vince beforehand or planning anything with Nord.

He did confirm he called the police and claimed he had been assaulted.

"I did go to the phone and call the police and said I had been assaulted," Wacholz said. He was not concerned about being arrested.

He also said many wrestlers privately thanked him for what he did: *"People said, 'That must have taken guts. I wish I could've done that years ago.'"*

No charges were filed.

AFTER BEING FIRED, Wacholz filed a wrongful termination lawsuit against WWF. He also accused McMahon of sexual assault.

WWF filed a countersuit. Both lawsuits were later dropped.

. . .

IN 1994, Wacholz testified against Vince McMahon in the federal steroid distribution trial.

His testimony became part of one of the most critical cases in wrestling history.

Speaking with Mike Johnson on Highspots TV, former **Nailz** offered a firsthand account of how he was pulled into the federal steroid trial involving Vince McMahon—a process he claims he tried repeatedly to avoid.

According to Nailz, he initially flat-out refused when contacted about testifying. *"I told them to get lost,"* he recalled.

"They called me up and said, 'We need you to testify against Vince McMahon in the steroid trial,' and I said, 'I'm through with that guy, I don't want to deal with anything.'"

That refusal, Nailz said, quickly escalated when the federal government became involved. A representative from the Department of Justice allegedly warned him, *"You're dealing with the Federal Government, we can make you do this."*

Nailz maintained his defiance—until the next morning. He claims that when he left for work around 7 a.m., his house was surrounded by FBI agents. They served him with a subpoena and informed him he was going to New York to testify.

After negotiating, Nailz agreed, saying, *"They basically paid me what I want to come out and do it."*

Nailz described being flown to New York, only for the trial schedule to change, forcing him to return home due to business obligations.

The following week, he was flown back again to finally take the stand.

Vince McMahon was ultimately found not guilty on July 23, 1994—a verdict that stunned Nailz. *"Yeah, I was shocked,"* he admitted. *"I was downstairs in a room, and they had boxes full of evidence."*

Court records later noted a critical moment from Nailz's testimony that has become part of wrestling legal lore.

Court sketch Kevin Wacholz (Nailz) from the Trial

Under oath, he initially stated that he had no animosity toward McMahon. Later, when asked directly whether he hated McMahon, Nailz answered yes—contradicting himself and underscoring the emotional volatility surrounding his testimony and the deep personal resentment that still lingered.

The episode remains one of the strangest intersections of wrestling, federal law, and personal vendetta.

McMahon was ultimately acquitted. He retired from wrestling in 2001 with no regrets.

"I'm fine with what happened. I don't regret it." - Nailz

CHAPTER 23

SECRET LIST FOR NEXT WWF CHAMPION

"I kept waiting for someone to say, 'Wait a minute — we changed our mind." - Bret Hart

BY LATE 1992, Vince McMahon wasn't building a future — he was trying to save his company. The steroid era had collapsed, the giants were disappearing, and the superhero blueprint that built the WWF empire had been wiped off the board almost overnight. The men who once defined what a champion was supposed to look like — Hulk Hogan, The Ultimate Warrior, Davey Boy Smith, and others, cut from the same massive mold — were suddenly liabilities.

Inside Titan Towers, uneasy conversations were happening behind closed doors. The question was no longer who looked the biggest, who sold the most merchandise, or who turned heads in airports. The only question that mattered was who could be trusted when everything else was falling apart. That's when the list was created. Five names. Five possible champions. Five different answers to the same desperate problem.

If not for the FBI steroid investigation, there is little debate that the next WWF Champion would have been The Ultimate Warrior. When Warrior returned at WrestleMania VIII, it wasn't nostalgia — it was positioning. He signed one of the most lucrative contracts in company history, complete with guaranteed championship reigns and multiple pay-per-view main events annually through WrestleMania X. Vince had already chosen him as Hogan's replacement — the new franchise, the next superhero. Then the investigation exploded. Wrestlers were subpoenaed. The media circled Titan Towers.

In a matter of months, the steroid-era prototype vanished.

RIC FLAIR WAS NEVER MEANT to be the long-term answer. He was on his way back to WCW in a matter of months. Flair brought prestige and legitimacy, a stabilizing presence while the company recalibrated; however, he quietly dropped the championship in Saskatoon in a match that later aired on Prime Time Wrestling, closing the curtain on the old guard. Randy Savage could have been a fallback, but after SummerSlam 1992, he lost the WWF Championship back to Flair at a house show with outside interference from Razor Ramon. The direction was clear — Savage was no longer being positioned as the future.

But Bret remembers that Vince sent Flair and Savage out to do the matches they had against each other when they walked in the curtain, the first time. The boss was not happy. Bret remembers them getting sent out and Flair and Savage doing the same match again. That's when Vince had made up his mind.

. . .

THE UNDERTAKER WAS PROTECTED and respected, but still seen as a special attraction whose character didn't require the belt. Shawn Michaels was electrifying in the ring, but not yet fully trusted as the company's face. The board was clearing fast, and the margin for error was shrinking.

THE IRONY IS that Vince had already found his champion years earlier without realizing it. In 1987, Bret Hart accidentally created an urban legend named Tom Magee. Magee looked like everything Vince loved: six-foot-five, sculpted physique, movie-star presence, explosive athleticism. The problem was that he couldn't wrestle. Bret pulled him aside before their match and said, *"Give me your best three moves, and I'll build the match around them."* Magee showed him a dropkick, a leapfrog, and a powerslam. Bret constructed the rest. He controlled the pace, fed him perfectly, sold every movement as if it were life-or-death, and made the audience believe they were witnessing the birth of a superstar. Backstage, Vince pointed at Magee and declared, *"That's my next champion!"*

Ted DiBiase had a strong outing with Magee as well, and for a moment, the illusion held. Once Magee worked on others, the reality surfaced. He faded away, and the tape of that match disappeared into the WWE vaults, whispered about for decades until it resurfaced publicly in 2019. When it finally played in front of an audience, it confirmed what the locker room had always known: Bret Hart could make anyone look like a star. Bret's own singles ascent had been repeatedly delayed. His push was scheduled for 1988, then postponed.

It was revisited in 1990, then pulled again. By the time momentum truly built in 1991, he had already endured years of near misses. *"It was like Charlie Brown with the football,"* Bret told me. *"They want me to kick it — and then they pull it away."* When WWF road agent, Chief Jay Strongbow, pulled him aside in 1992 and said there was a list of five names under consideration for WWF Champion and that Bret's name was on it, Bret didn't celebrate. *"I dismissed it as soon as he told me,"* he said. He had heard promises before. Even when the title match with Flair was set for Survivor Series 1992, Bret didn't know he was winning until the day of the show. *"I didn't find out till the day of,"* he told me. And even then, he couldn't fully accept it. *"I didn't believe it was gonna happen till it happened."* Walking to the ring, he was still bracing for disappointment. *"I kept waiting for someone to say, 'Wait a minute — we changed our mind."* He wasn't paranoid; he was conditioned. *"Vince was always pulling the rug out from underneath me,"* Bret said. *"I never had a lot of faith in anything they ever said — mostly because they always changed their mind."*

———

ANOTHER SERIOUS CONTENDER was Tito Santana. A consummate professional and respected locker-room leader, Tito had been repackaged as El Matador and was being tested in international markets. He defeated The Undertaker clean in Barcelona inside a sold-out Olympic venue, a clear attempt to rebuild his credibility. Tito told me that while he never knew a literal list existed, he felt something significant was brewing. When Warrior and Bulldog were on their way out, he sensed opportunity. After the Barcelona victory, he believed a major elevation was coming. But months later, Bret returned as the centerpiece, Tito was shifted back down the card, and the attendance told the story.

Later, Pat Patterson confided to him that it had come down to Bret and Tito. However, Tito laughed when recounting it to me, noting that by then he had been around long enough to understand how those conversations often shifted depending on who was being spoken to.

BOB BACKLUND WAS another choice on the shortlist of five—he was the only one who was a champion for a six-year reign —but his time had passed. The former long-reigning WWWF Champion. The believable standard-bearer.

By 1994, Backlund had reinvented himself as the unhinged Mr. Backlund and was getting real heat again. Vince trusted him.

He was seen as a possible bridge champion while the New Generation was being built. Two years later, that trust paid off when Backlund shocked the world by defeating Bret Hart for the WWF Championship in 1994. The reign lasted two days.

Backlund dropped the title to Diesel at Madison Square Garden.

He was never meant to be the future. He was meant to stabilize the transition.

TED DIBIASE REPRESENTED CONTROL. Elite on the mic. Elite in the ring. A master of psychology. A locker-room general. Years earlier, he had been positioned to become champion while Hogan filmed No Holds Barred. Plans shifted. Money Inc. was dependable. Had the team been broken up in 1992, DiBiase as champion would not have shocked anyone. But his role wasn't to lead the New Generation.

It was to hold the company together while it changed.

THE FIFTH NAME was never officially confirmed —
and that's why the legend lives.

Most believe it was Bam Bam Bigelow or Big Boss Man.

Both had the natural size and look Vince loved, and they could
work. Serious conversations happened. But conversations
don't save companies. Decisions do. Vince wasn't building an
empire in late 1992. He was rebuilding one. He didn't need
the biggest body.

He needed professionalism. Stability. Trust. International
appeal. A man who could wrestle anyone and make them look
like a million bucks. Vince finally picked the guy who had
fooled him once before.

The man who made Tom Magee look like a future champion.

The man Vince once declared was his "next champion" — not
realizing it wasn't Magee who made the magic happen.

It was Bret.

What ultimately separated Bret wasn't size or spectacle. It was
reliability. It was trust. It was the ability to wrestle anyone,
anywhere, and elevate them. And it broke a barrier that had
defined the company for nearly a decade. Bret told me that
Shawn Michaels was genuinely happy for him when he won
the championship.

According to Bret, Shawn told him his win opened the door,
allowing smaller, more athletic wrestlers to be taken seriously
as World champions. Shawn acknowledged that Bret breaking
that stigma made it possible for guys like him to ascend
realistically. The era of pure bodybuilder champions had

cracked. Bret didn't smash it down with flash; he broke it down through guts, conditioning, technical excellence, and an unwavering belief in his craft.

By the end of 1992, Vince wasn't choosing the loudest personality or the most imposing physique. He was choosing stability amid chaos. The list of five was never about building the next superhero; it was about survival.

When the steroid era imploded and the giants vanished, Vince selected the man who had quietly been holding everything together for years. The choice wasn't dramatic. It was practical. And in Saskatoon, when the moment finally arrived, and Bret Hart realized no one was coming to change the finish, the company's future shifted with it. The Hitman hadn't forced the door open with politics or size. He walked through it because, when everything else fell apart, he was the one Vince could trust and the champion, for years, that was right under his nose.

CHAPTER 24

BLACK EYE OVER CAESARS PALACE

"I never got into a fight with Randy." - Hulk Hogan

ON APRIL 4, 1993, WrestleMania IX arrived at Caesar's Palace in Las Vegas. The show itself was surreal — an outdoor Roman-themed arena, toga-clad extras, and even a real elephant escorting Lex Luger to the ring.

Then Hulk Hogan arrived. Wearing sunglasses.

WITH A MASSIVE BLACK EYE.

The biggest star in wrestling history had returned after nearly a year away — and he looked like he had just come out of a street fight. Wrestlers noticed immediately. And the locker room erupted with whispers.

On commentary, WWF attempted to fold the injury into the storyline. Hogan's opponents, Money Inc., were said to have hired goons to ambush him at a gym the night before.

THE EXPLANATION AIRED ONCE. Then it was never mentioned again. Hogan's return came at the worst possible time.

During his absence, real life had collapsed behind the scenes.

Randy Savage and Miss Elizabeth had gone through a bitter, public divorce. Savage blamed Hogan and Hogan's then-wife, Linda, for talking Elizabeth into leaving him. Later that year, Savage would go on Radio WWF and publicly blast Hogan — something unheard of at the time.

THE MEGAPOWERS WERE DEAD. The friendship was over, and the resentment was really intense

So when Hogan arrived bruised on the biggest weekend of the year, the story wrote itself.

Savage confronted and punched Hogan. Or so the story has been told and retold.

In a WWE-produced Peacock documentary on WrestleMania IX, Bruce Prichard confirmed that the explanation they [the office] were given was that Hogan had suffered a jet-ski accident days before WrestleMania.

Hogan himself has said he downplayed the severity of the injury to get cleared by doctors. He folded it into the storyline, blaming Money Inc.'s hired goons, as he and Brutus Beefcake, with Jimmy Hart turning babyface on their side, challenged the champion heels for the tag team titles. Hogan even wore an eyepatch while filming Thunder in Paradise, which was shot around the same time.

Many of the talent didn't believe the jet ski story.

BRET HART REMEMBERED SEEING Hogan and thinking it looked like a real shot. He asked him directly, *"What happened to you?"* and later recalled thinking it looked like a pretty good punch.

JIM CORNETTE HAS NEVER BELIEVED the jet ski explanation. He argues that if Hogan had truly suffered a serious water accident, Savage would never have made jokes about it on commentary. Cornette insists that no commission doctor would confuse a legitimate orbital injury with an angle.

To Cornette, the story reads like a wrestling script that wrote itself. He believes Randy Savage punched Hulk Hogan.

Cornette also commented that Hogan and Brutus Beefcake need to stay away from jet skis. The reference was that two years earlier, Beefcake nearly died in a serious boating accident, and Hogan helped save his life when he got a doctor on short notice and did his surgery.

Scott Steiner has never backed down from what he believes happened. Steiner traveled with Savage. He rode with Savage. He talked with Savage. Steiner is also widely known to despise Hulk Hogan for claims that Hulk Hogan tried to get him thrown in jail on a bogus assault charge. And according to Steiner, the story Savage told him was simple.

Savage punched Hogan.

Steiner says that was the version going around the locker room. That was the version Savage shared. And to this day, Steiner says he believes Randy.

. . .

WHEN HOGAN WAS SHOWN Steiner's comments on the WrestleMania IX documentary, Hogan smiled and replied:

"Interesting. I guess he bought the story Randy told him. I never got into a fight with Randy."

When Hogan arrived wearing sunglasses to hide the injury, even The Undertaker, whose heat with Hogan was covered in the previous chapter, couldn't resist.

With a smirk, the Dead Man said, *"Brother should have bobbed instead of weaved on that one. Everyone knows that Savage and Hogan didn't get along. It didn't take long for the rumors to start flying around,"* said Undertaker.

THAT SAME NIGHT, wrestling history was rewritten. For the first time, the WWF Championship changed hands twice in one night.

YOKOZUNA DEFEATED Bret Hart earlier in the show. Then Hogan walked out unannounced and challenged Yokozuna on the spot. Mr. Fuji accepted on behalf of Yokozuna, and then Hogan won the title in less than 30 seconds, becoming champion for a then-record-breaking five times. Ironically, Bret Hart would later become the second man at Summerslam 1997 to become a 5-time WWF champion.

Bret Hart has long maintained that Hogan maneuvered his way into the finish. Cornette believes the black eye, the sympathy, and the spectacle gave Hogan leverage with Vince McMahon.

• • •

WHAT ELEVATED the story from rumor to legend was that Savage himself seemed to lean into it. While calling the action at WrestleMania IX with Jim Ross, who made his debut wearing a toga that evening along with Bobby Heenan on commentary, Savage directly referenced Hogan's injury numerous times. His tone was dry, and his delivery was sharp. But the implication was unmistakable.

At one point, Savage quipped that Hogan *"must have been hit with a hell of a punch."* The line was never followed up on, nor was it explained or addressed. But fans, including myself, caught it. And once fans caught it, the story became immortal. We talked about it at school the next day, before the internet. It was folklore then in 1993.

Savage wasn't just any announcer. He was the man whose marriage had collapsed, blamed Hogan for it, and publicly buried Hogan on Radio WWF.

And now he was casually alluding to a mysterious black eye on the biggest stage in wrestling. By every account, Savage was in an unusually good mood that day.

Too good.

Undertaker later remembered Savage sounding amused — like a man enjoying an inside joke. Whether he threw the punch or not, Savage clearly enjoyed the rumors that said he did. In a company-produced WrestleMania IX documentary, The Undertaker and Scott Steiner are shown mentioning Hogan's black eye on camera.

The film never settles the story. It simply presents the question.

Then WWE replays Savage's commentary.

They could have buried the rumor. They didn't.

CHAPTER 25

BRET HART
JOINS THE KLIQ

"If they didn't like somebody, they'd get rid of them." - Bret Hart.

THERE'S a long-standing urban legend in wrestling: Bret Hart was invited to join The Kliq. And if he had said yes, the entire 1990s might have unfolded differently. So I asked him directly.

It happened in Germany.

Present were Kevin Nash and Scott Hall, and according to Bret, possibly Triple H and Sean Waltman (1-2-3 Kid) as well. At the time, Hall was the Intercontinental Champion, Nash was the WWF Champion, and Shawn was on the rise.

They pulled Bret aside and laid out a vision. *"They said they were taking over. They were gonna form a clique ("Kliq"), and we would all work with each other."* The idea wasn't subtle. Control the booking. Control the championships—control who got paid. *"Kevin would only drop the belt to whom he wanted. Shawn would only work with Kevin, Scott, 1-2-3 Kid...*

just the guys." Bret listened, and then he said something that defines his entire career: *"I don't really work like that."* He turned them down.

BRET DESCRIBED it as more than friendship. In his view, it was an attempt to take over creative influence — even circumvent Vince. *"They would pick who they wanted every week. If they didn't like somebody, they'd get rid of them."* He mentioned names like Savio Vega — wrestlers who, in his eyes, could be frozen out simply because they weren't in the circle. Bret hated that mindset. *"I hate people who think like that — that they can just decide who's a star."* Because Bret never operated that way. He never chose opponents. He never demanded insulation. *"If they wanted me to work with Bob Backlund — even if I thought it was a bad idea — I'd do it. It's your company."*

That tension showed itself again before WrestleMania XII — just days before Bret would lose the title. Bret remembers a conversation with Shawn Michaels where Shawn laid out his plans once he became champion. *"I'll work with Kevin. Then I'll work with Razor. Then I'll work with Triple H..."* Bret caught it immediately. *"So you're gonna work with all your friends first."* And then he explained the economics. When Bret was champion, whoever worked him in the main event got main-event pay — and Bret was the highest-paid guy at the time. So if Shawn only worked with his friends, his friends made the money. *"It's not fair to the rest of the wrestlers."* That wasn't jealousy. That was locker-room awareness. That was fairness.

. . .

OVER AND OVER in our conversation, Bret circled back to something simple: *"I was always a company guy."* He never refused to work with anyone. Ever. He took pride in being the champion who could wrestle anyone and elevate them. He told me about Mark Canterbury (Henry Godwin) being nervous before their match, *"He was biting his fingernails,"* and afterward nearly in tears because, *"You saved my job."* He brought up Jean-Pierre Lafitte, too — two matches, two different styles, no cookie-cutter repetition. *"I didn't wrestle like Ric Flair — doing the same match every night."* Bret took pride in giving each opponent the best match possible. That was his leverage. Not politics.

AT ONE POINT, Bret shifted from politics to something more personal — appreciation. *"I was always frustrated that they didn't appreciate that I was an artist."* Artist. That word matters. *"I painted a different picture."* Critics have said his comeback was predictable, that fans knew what was coming. Bret laughed at that. *"That's precisely the whole point."* He explained his psychology—a comeback isn't random. It's orchestration. *"I had about seven or eight moves I'd use on my comeback. They were similar — but you couldn't predict which one was coming next."* The backbreaker. The second-rope elbow. The suplex. The Sharpshooter setup. *"When I've got the guy at my mercy, I'm gonna use my best moves."* The crowd recognizing a pattern isn't a weakness. It's an investment.

Then he said something that reframes everything: *"I was always a really good wrestling fan."* Before he was Bret Hart, the champion, he was Bret Hart, the kid watching wrestling at 4 years old. *"I understood wrestling way before Ric Flair even thought about being a wrestler."* That wasn't arrogance. It was lineage. He grew up in it. He studied it. Where some wrestlers discovered wrestling later, Bret was raised inside the rhythm of it. That shapes pacing. It shapes psychology. It shapes respect for structure.

At one point, he put it as plainly as anyone ever could: *"To be a great wrestler, you need to be a great fan. And I was a good fan."* That sentence explains why he could never be Kliq material. Bret also described something that separates him from most champions of that era: control — and his willingness to give it away. With heels like Steve Keirn, Mike Rotunda, Ted DiBiase, Roddy Piper, he didn't dictate every beat. He deferred. *"You're the heel. You tell me what to do. Call the match."* That's almost unheard of for a top babyface champion. Most champions control everything. Bret trusted the heel to drive the story because, in his mind, that's what a good match requires. *"I trust you. You already know how to wrestle."* He wasn't protecting himself. He was building the match.

That's why the urban legend about Bret joining The Kliq has always been backward. The myth says he missed out on protection. What he rejected wasn't protection — it was control. The Kliq wanted to steer the ship. Bret wanted to sail wherever the company sent him and make it work.

And there's another twist that complicates the narrative. Bret remembers that in the early days, Shawn wasn't his enemy. When Bret defeated Ric Flair for the WWF Championship in 1992, Shawn came into the dressing room genuinely thrilled and told him, "The fact that they put the title on a guy like you opens the door for guys like me." Bret remembers it clearly. *"Shawn was one of my biggest supporters in the early days."* That's the part people forget. What came later wasn't born from hatred. It grew from ambition, ego, insecurity, and the slow drift of philosophy. By the time Shawn became champion in 1996, Bret felt something shift. Handpicking opponents. Working only with friends and narrowing the circle. To Bret, that violated a fundamental principle. *"You can't be a champion with an attitude like that. I told him that."*

IN BRET'S EYES, the champion doesn't choose comfort. The champion chooses the draw. The champion works with whoever elevates the business. *"Everybody deserves a chance. I worked with anyone and never had the same match. With Yoko (Yokozuna), it was a different match. With Bam Bam (Bigelow), it was a different match. I worked with Pierre, and he was proud of the matches he had before he left. He had problems with Nash and the Kliq. He [Pierre] knew he was on his way out, and it meant a lot to him to have great matches with me before he left the company."* That was Bret's worldview, whether the opponent was a world-class worker or a midcard talent trying to survive.

IN THE END, the story of Bret being invited into The Kliq isn't just a piece of backstage trivia. It's a fork in the road. It's two philosophies staring at each other in a hallway overseas: one built on positioning and protection, the other built on craft and obligation. Bret didn't just turn down a social group. He turned down a way of operating that he believed would poison the locker room and distort who got opportunities.

HE SAID it in one sentence, and it still echoes: *"I don't really work like that."* And if you want to understand the entire decade that followed — the resentment, the fractures, the politics, and eventually the breaking point — that's where it starts.

CHAPTER 26

HBK INHERITS $2.5 MILLION FROM A FAN

"No comment." - Shawn Michaels

BY THE MID-1990S, Shawn Michaels was not just the face of the WWF — he was its most powerful locker-room figure. He was the company's top star, its creative centerpiece, and the performer carrying WWF through one of the most turbulent periods in wrestling history.

But according to one of wrestling's most enduring urban legends, Michaels possessed a hidden source of power behind the scenes — one that may have quietly reshaped the balance of influence during the Monday Night Wars.

THE STORY GOES that in 1996, Shawn Michaels inherited a massive sum of money — most often cited as $2.5 million — from a devoted, extremely wealthy wrestling fan who had passed away and named Michaels in their will.

The fan's identity was never publicly revealed. According to legend, the fan had followed Michaels for years, attending events, traveling to shows, and forming a personal bond with the WWF superstar before leaving him a fortune upon the fan's death.

No will was ever produced, no estate records were ever made public, and no legal confirmation ever surfaced — yet the story spread rapidly through locker rooms and wrestling media circles.

THE TIMING of the rumor was explosive. It began circulating during Michaels' WWF Championship reign, his infamous "lost my smile" hiatus, his tense contract negotiations, and his growing creative influence backstage. Suddenly, the idea that Shawn Michaels might be financially independent changed everything. If true, it meant he did not need the WWF paycheck, could walk away at any time, could push back against Vince McMahon, and could demand creative control. To some insiders, it explained why Michaels seemed untouchable.

DAVE MELTZER of The Wrestling Observer wrote that the inheritance had happened months earlier, but only became public because word finally leaked despite Michaels' attempts to keep it quiet.

The report claimed the fan was unknown to Michaels personally, yet had named him as a beneficiary anyway, leaving him a multi-million-dollar payout. The outlet noted that Michaels planned to continue wrestling, although he could obviously retire immediately if he wanted to.

WHAT ELEVATED the rumor from locker-room whisper to full-blown legend was what happened next.

AT THE 1996 Royal Rumble press conference in Fresno, CA, Michaels was asked directly about the inheritance. Instead of laughing it off or denying it, he reportedly became visibly angry and shut down the question, telling reporters he did not want to be asked about it again, gave a blunt "no comment," and told the reporter never to bring it up again.

There was no denial. No clarification. Just silence.

Wrestling insiders were divided. Some claimed the inheritance was genuine and that Michaels' sudden financial independence gave him the leverage to challenge Vince McMahon and push back on creative decisions.

Others dismissed it as exaggerated locker-room gossip — a story inflated by jealousy, politics, and the myth-making culture of professional wrestling. Yet the rumor refused to die.

PERHAPS THE MOST fascinating part of the legend is not the money itself, but what Michaels never did with it. During the mid-to-late 1990s, WCW was throwing around money like never before. Guaranteed contracts. Fewer dates. Lighter schedules.

Top stars making millions while working a fraction of the WWF grind. Kevin Nash jumped. Scott Hall jumped. Bret Hart jumped. The entire industry followed the money — except Shawn Michaels.

· · ·

DESPITE HIS CLOSE ties to The Kliq and WCW's willingness to write blank checks, there was never a serious push from Michaels to leave. No contract drama. No public flirtation. No leverage plays. To many insiders, the inheritance story explained why.

Shawn had already secured his money. While WCW offered less work for more money, Shawn had done the opposite. He got the money and still worked harder than anyone.

Another $2.5 million a year would not have changed much if it meant less spotlight, less influence, less creative fulfillment, and fewer opportunities to steal the show every night. To Shawn, wrestling was not just business. It was art.

TENSIONS BETWEEN SHAWN MICHAELS and Bret Hart had reached a boiling point. In May 1997, at a WWF television taping in Hartford, Connecticut, the simmering hostility finally exploded into a real backstage confrontation.

What started as locker-room tension nearly turned into a full-blown fight with Michaels' hair pulled out.

In the aftermath, emotions were raw. Shawn, frustrated and exhausted from months of politics, pressure, and personal issues, reportedly went directly to Vince McMahon and told him he wanted out. He asked for his release and threatened to walk. For a brief moment, it looked like history might change.

VINCE MCMAHON REFUSED. According to those close to the situation, Vince told Shawn bluntly that WCW would not know what to do with him — that he was a WWF creation, a WWF champion, and a WWF cornerstone.

And Shawn stayed not for the money or the big guaranteed contract. But out of loyalty.

Despite WCW throwing guaranteed millions at everyone in sight, Shawn never made a serious push to leave. Even with The Kliq firmly entrenched in Atlanta and Turner money flowing freely, Shawn remained loyal to Vince McMahon and the WWF.

Many believe that if the inheritance story were true, money would never have been the deciding factor anyway. Shawn already had it.

Then came the cruel twist of fate. In early 1998, Shawn Michaels suffered a devastating back injury that forced him into retirement at just 32 years old. The timing could not have been worse.

The Attitude Era was exploding. Mike Tyson had just appeared at WrestleMania XIV. Stone Cold Steve Austin was becoming the face of a new generation. Wrestling was entering its hottest boom period since Hulkamania — and the man who had carried the company through its darkest years was suddenly gone.

The artist was forced to put down his brush just as the industry he helped save was catching fire in his absence.

Yet according to long-standing locker-room lore, Shawn never truly left the payroll.

DURING HIS FOUR-YEAR hiatus from 1998 to 2002, it was widely rumored that Vince McMahon continued paying Michaels while he was home recovering. The figure most often cited was $15,000 per week — nearly $800,000 a year. To many insiders, this was not charity. It was loyalty being repaid.

The WWF business had been down from 1995 through 1996. WCW was winning the war. And through it all, Shawn Michaels stayed. He carried the company as champion during Bret Hart's much-needed hiatus for the latter part of 1996.

By the time the industry reached its hottest peak, with Steve Austin leading the charge, Tyson bringing mainstream attention, and the WWF finally winning the war, Shawn was already gone.

THE NEW ERA was marching forward, and the man who carried the company through its darkest days was watching from home. And yet, behind the scenes, Vince McMahon had not forgotten.

WHETHER IT WAS $15,000 a week or simply a generous support contract, the message was the same.

Shawn Michaels had earned his place in company history long before the Attitude Era ever arrived.

To this day, the $2.5 million fan inheritance remains a widely unknown and unanswered urban tale of true windfall and perhaps exaggerated half-truth that was spoken of in the locker room and not really public until decades later.

Like many of wrestling's greatest urban legends, it exists in that perfect grey area where truth, rumor, and mythology collide. And as long as Shawn Michaels refuses to talk about it, the legend lives on.

CHAPTER 27

SHANE DOUGLAS' LAST NIGHT IN WWF

"I would never return if they called." - Shane Douglas

SHANE DOUGLAS never spoke to me like someone trying to reshape history. He spoke like a man explaining a decision that, for him, stopped being dramatic the moment it became unavoidable.

"This is how I make my living, Andrew," Shane Douglas told me. *"This is how I feed my kids—and yeah, how I lavished my ex-wife at the time. I don't do this as a hobby."*

By the mid-1990s, wrestling wasn't a childhood dream anymore. It was work. Douglas was on the road nearly twenty-eight days a month, away from his family, his friends, and any sense of normalcy. And like any job, the bills didn't pause just because creative direction was unclear.

Douglas told me he lived in a small town where everyone knew everyone's business. *"My mortgage payment at that time, Andrew, was $496 a month. If we didn't have enough money in* *the bank to make that mortgage payment, the rumors would've started immediately. Affairs. Drugs. A second family on the road. God knows what else."*

DOUGLAS TRIED to explain this reality to Vince McMahon. One conversation in particular, which Douglas remembers vividly, lasted over an hour. The setting was the Meadowlands. The message never changed.

"I promise it's going to get better. Just hang in there," McMahon would say, according to Douglas.

After hearing the same sentence repeated again and again, Douglas finally stopped him.

"Is that all you're going to say?" Vince said yes. That's when Douglas drew the line. *"I don't know what else to say, Vince. I can't afford to work anymore. I'm putting my notice in."*

Vince looked at him, Douglas recalled, like he'd grown a third eye. When it became clear Douglas was serious, the tone shifted. The volume went up. The intimidation started.

"I don't intimidate easily," Douglas told me. *"That screaming and yelling stuff does nothing to me. If anything, it stiffens my spine."* Vince insisted he had over a million dollars invested in the Dean Douglas character. Douglas laughed. *"Where?"* he asked. *"Because it sure as hell doesn't pay. And it sure as hell wasn't in that silly outfit."*

What followed was a surreal negotiation. Vince wanted Douglas to work four more months. Douglas said he couldn't afford it. Vince countered with three months. Douglas said two weeks. Vince said two months. Douglas said one week.

They settled on roughly four weeks. Those final weeks revealed everything.

DOUGLAS' last two in-ring appearances for the WWF came on consecutive nights on November 24, 1995, at the CoreStates Spectrum in Philadelphia, which is ironic when you realize he returns there at ECW weeks later, and then on November 25, 1995, at Madison Square Garden. On both cards, he was scheduled against Savio Vega in low-priority, throwaway "popcorn" matches as Douglas recalls.

PHILADELPHIA WAS the final night Shane Douglas physically wrestled for the WWF. The physical collapse had already begun earlier that week.

ON MONDAY NIGHT RAW, Douglas was scheduled to open the live portion of the show against Scott Hall. Minutes before airtime, Davey Boy Smith went to stomp in the ring—and his knees dropped straight through the mat. The ring collapsed. Crew members tore it apart and rebuilt it on the fly. There was no time to test it.

As pyro hit and cameras rolled, Douglas and Hall were sent to the ring anyway.

They worked a familiar sequence. On the third pass, Hall was supposed to clothesline Douglas over the top rope. Douglas knew the fulcrum point of the rope instinctively—but there was no give. He didn't clear it. Hall pushed him to protect him.

. . .

SOMETHING SNAPPED IN DOUGLAS' spine.

He hit the floor, knowing immediately something was wrong. He wasn't paralyzed—but his legs weren't responding correctly. When he told them to move one way, they went another.

A referee yelled at him to get back in the ring.

"My f***** legs aren't working," Douglas said.

Hall waved it off and called the match. Vince ordered the Razor's Edge. Hall resisted, then executed it as carefully as possible, laying Douglas down instead of spiking him.

"When I hit that mat," Douglas told me, *"it felt like I was going to s*** my kidneys out."*

HE COLLAPSED. Officials helped him to the curtain— then let go. Douglas crumpled to the floor and crawled on his elbows nearly a hundred yards through the arena.

NOT ONE PERSON checked on him, he recalls, except Dustin Rhodes, who wrestled as Goldust at the time.

An EMT examined him for ten minutes and diagnosed a muscle spasm. No X-ray. No MRI. Douglas went home believing it.

He was wrong. By Friday night in Philadelphia, he could barely move.

By Saturday, driving toward Madison Square Garden, every pothole on the New Jersey Turnpike felt like a knife in his back.

. . .

IN THE GARDEN DRESSING ROOM, a New York commission doctor—someone Douglas had never seen before—performed a full physical. Not the usual cursory clearance. A real exam.

At the end, the doctor said something Douglas had never heard in twenty-two years.

"YOU CAN'T WRESTLE TONIGHT."

When Douglas pushed back, the doctor stopped him cold.

"You could end up in a wheelchair for the rest of your life."

VINCE IMMEDIATELY CONFRONTED THE DOCTOR, stepping inches from his face.

"I don't understand all that medicalese," Vince said. *"So dumb it down for a dumb f*** like me."*

The doctor explained that Douglas presented with asymmetrical reflexes, indicative of either a ruptured disc or a broken back. Without diagnostics like an MRI or a CAT scan, he refused to clear him.

VINCE TURNED TO DOUGLAS, chest pressed against chest.

"Dean, do you agree with that diagnosis?"

Douglas couldn't even look him in the eye.

"I'm not qualified to agree with that," he said.

Vince spun, threw a tantrum, and deliberately shoulder-checked Douglas, nearly knocking him down. The doctor pulled Douglas into the hallway.

That's when Arnold Skaaland came to see Shane. He told him Vince wanted me to tell you to get your bags and leave the Garden. And that he doesn't need his services any longer, even though he had already quit. Skaaland whispered, *"If you ask me, Dean, you're doing the right thing. Take care of your back."*

Douglas whispered back, *"I always knew there was a reason I respected you, Arnie."*

AS DOUGLAS HEADED toward the elevator, Vince jammed his hands into the doors.

"Where are you going?" he demanded. *"You've got to at least appear tonight."*

Douglas repeated the verbatim message he'd been given—to get his bag and leave. Vince denied it, then pivoted.

"At least go make an appearance," he said. *"Why don't you do one of those shoot promos you're famous for?"*

What makes this account different from every other Shane Douglas interview is its completeness.

Shane has told pieces of this story before, but nowhere else does he walk through his WWF departure in this level of uninterrupted detail.

In the ring, he told the crowd that twenty-five thousand fans had been screwed because the only real wrestler on the card wasn't performing—and that Vince McMahon wanted him to wrestle against the advice of a world-renowned neurosurgeon who warned he could end up in a wheelchair.

"And I told them they could kiss my ass."

He dropped the microphone and walked out.

Backstage was empty. Douglas packed his bag and left Madison Square Garden.

"That," he told me, *"was the last day I worked for WWF."*

Technically, one brief appearance followed. In December 1995, Douglas appeared at In Your House from Hersheypark Arena, where he made an on-screen introduction. He did not wrestle. Buddy Landel filled in for him against Ahmed Johnson. That detail matters—because the booking that followed is even more revealing.

At the end of 1995, Douglas was scheduled on house-show loops opposite Ahmed Johnson, a wrestler widely regarded at the time as reckless, injury-prone, and carrying significant backstage heat. For someone already injured, it was an unsafe assignment.

When Douglas became unavailable, the loop didn't change. He was replaced by Louie Spicolli, working as Rad Radford.

The system didn't slow down. It just swapped the body.

Shane Douglas saw that clearly—and he didn't wait around.

There was no cooling-off period. He returned to ECW the very next week. That's where the urban legend becomes permanent.

Years later, when I asked him the question everyone eventually asks—what if they called?—his answer never wavered.

"I WOULD NEVER RETURN *to WWE if they called."*

CHAPTER 28

MCMAHON AND THE OKLAHOMA KID

*"As much grief as Vince gave me, I could look at my bank account and feel pretty good." -
Jim Ross*

THE RELATIONSHIP between Jim Ross and Vince McMahon remains one of the most uncomfortable and quietly debated dynamics in modern wrestling history.

Ross was the voice of WWE's most profitable era, yet an enduring Urban Legend suggests McMahon resented him—and expressed it through humiliations, and on numerous occasions, terminations.

The tension dates back to Vince's time on commentary. On Live Wire, fans openly praised Ross while mocking McMahon's predictable announcing style, even imitating him on air.

McMahon appeared visibly upset. Not long after, Vince removed himself from full-time play-by-play, handing the role to Ross following the Montreal Screwjob that led to the iconic Mr. McMahon heel run.

That resentment surfaced repeatedly on television.

Jim Ross was mocked for his Bell's palsy in a random backstage impression delivered by McMahon—no angle, no continuation, no payoff. It was aired and forgotten, except by those who felt it crossed a line.

Wrestling teaches fans to expect a reason. This had none.

Ross's battle with colon cancer was treated no differently. The infamous "Dr. Heiney" segment, in which Vince portrayed a grotesque doctor pulling objects from Ross's backside, served no storyline purpose. Ross later said he felt deeply disrespected. Fans agreed.

This didn't appear to many as heel heat; it was a mockery. It did not sell tickets with an eventual payoff.

When WWE came to Oklahoma—Ross's home—the humiliation turned personal. During the Kiss My Ass Club, Vince wore a cowboy hat, leaning into Ross's identity. The segment escalated when The Undertaker physically forced Ross into submission and turned heel in the process.

On his podcast with Conrad Thompson, "Grilling JR," Jim Ross joked that he didn't even get a t-shirt for joining the club. He knew that 20 miles from where he lived, something was coming.

"IF THE COACH CALLS A PLAY, *you damn sure better run it. And that's what I did. I ran the play."*

When Jim Ross was drafted from Monday Night Raw to

SmackDown, the cruelty wasn't the move—it was the camera. Jerry Lawler stayed on Raw. Ross did not.

Production held a tight, lingering close-up on Ross's face as he processed the demotion in real time.

For an announcer, SmackDown was objectively a step down.

This wasn't slapstick. It was career reality, televised.

Ross has also stated plainly that he was legitimately fired multiple times. One of the strangest involved hosting a WWE 2K panel—a low-risk corporate assignment.

He was fired anyway, even though Ric Flair was a bit intoxicated and spoke about other wrestling companies. The blame landed at Ross' doorstep.

Years earlier on television, WWE crossed a line that few broadcasters had ever experienced. Ross was fired on television by Linda McMahon, then hit with a low blow and a McMahon family celebration while he sold the pain.

Where did this happen? Oklahoma, of course.

Broadcasters don't need beatdowns to exit television. But dignity wasn't the goal. Dominance was.

TODD GRISHAM RECALLS another incident in Oklahoma (see a pattern here?) where Vince McMahon pulled him aside and instructed him to grab a microphone and head to the ring.

This was untelevised and after the show had ended. Ross was already addressing his home crowd. Vince handed Todd a list of questions and told him to interrupt—questions designed to antagonize Jim Ross in front of his hometown audience.

Todd followed the instructions. He entered the ring, cut off Ross mid-speech, and began asking the questions, implying that Ross was being fired because Vince didn't believe he was good enough.

Ross looked at Todd and asked for the microphone. Todd hesitated. He knew that handing it over could bring consequences. But he did it anyway.

The moment cut through the charade. The audience understood. The locker room understood. Ross had never blamed Grisham for the incident. Ross knew exactly where it came from—and who it was meant to serve.

Even years later, Ross remained a prop. During the Jerry Lawler vs. Michael Cole feud, Jack Swagger placed Ross in the Ankle Lock to sell the angle—another moment where Ross absorbed punishment for someone else's story.

One anecdote best captures the legend. Sean Waltman recalled Vince once saying, *"Sometimes you gotta eat shit and like the taste of it, right JR?"* Ross nodded. According to Waltman, he wasn't just shocked by the insult—he was surprised by how normal it seemed.

And that is why the question still lingers:

Does Vince McMahon hate Jim Ross? And, if so, why?

One date is often cited quietly by those who believe this wasn't random cruelty, but remembered resentment—the day Jim Ross was fired for the first time, of many times, after being diagnosed with Bell's palsy.

Ross later summed it up bluntly with a line that has echoed ever since: *"On February 11th, 1994, he fired my ass!"* The wording mattered. It wasn't about performance. It was about humiliation.

The subject surfaced publicly on Live Wire when Michael P.S. Hayes alluded to Ross's firing while questioning Vince McMahon on air. The implication—never stated outright, but unmistakable—was that Ross had been talking to dirt sheet writers.

From that point forward, the legend suggests, Ross became someone Vince could punish at will. Not fired permanently and not erased. But used and whipped when convenient.

A government mule—valuable, durable, and expendable. Vince paid Ross well. He leaned on him repeatedly. He eventually inducted him into the WWE Hall of Fame.

But the honors came with a cost.

Humiliation.

Public embarrassment whenever Vince felt like reminding Ross who was in control.

That context reframes everything that followed—not as isolated incidents, but as chapters in a long memory Vince never let go of.

Ross wasn't just an announcer. He was a reminder. And reminders, in Vince McMahon's world, were often punished long after the original sin was forgotten.

Which only deepens the legend.

Because if this wasn't cruelty for entertainment and it wasn't storytelling for payoff, then maybe it was something colder.

Jim Ross took pride in wearing many hats—far more than the signature black cowboy hat that became his "John Wayne" tribute on camera. He wasn't only the lead play-by-play voice of a generation; he was the architect behind the scenes, the second-in-command who hired, nurtured, and assembled the very team that would carry the company through the Attitude Era, topple the Monday Night Wars, and ultimately position WWE to go public.

Ross has never claimed sole credit for that transformation, and he's careful not to overstate his role—but history doesn't require permission.

You cannot tell the story without him. Mick Foley does not get hired without Jim Ross believing in him, advocating for him, and fighting for him first.

Which makes the moment linger even longer: Vince McMahon telling Ross, *"I'm going to hire him—so you know what it's like to get your heart broken."*

Jim Ross wasn't just an announcer. He was a reminder of trust given, of loyalty extended, of influence earned.

Humiliation didn't arrive as immediate punishment. It arrived later, dressed up as television, spaced out just enough to feel accidental.

That's what gives the story its chill. If this wasn't cruelty disguised as entertainment, and it wasn't storytelling with an endpoint, then it was something colder.

Perhaps a private ledger kept by only one man. A debt believed Jim Ross still owed to him—collected slowly, publicly, and without ever announcing when the balance would finally be zero.

CHAPTER 29

STORIES OF THE MISSING WALLETS

AS TOLD BY PAUL NEU (P.N. NEWS)

"For what it's worth, I hope you sell a million copies of this book." - P.N. News.

THERE'S an urban legend that followed me for years—that I stole wallets, that things went missing from guys' bags, that I was that guy in the locker room—and I'm telling you straight, that's not who I was.

I'VE MADE mistakes in my life like anybody else, but I never stole from the boys, and that's a line you don't cross in this business.

The way that story got attached to me says more about how the wrestling business works than it does about me. It's about timing, perception, politics—and what happens when nobody bothers to ask the person at the center of it.

. . .

RANDY COLLEY and I were in Germany, and we had been traveling together for months, and one night we were literally crammed into a phone booth—two big guys, him around 280, me pushing 400—calling Ole Anderson, who had the book for World Championship Wrestling at the time. Based on Randy's word alone, Ole wanted me in. That should have been the moment everything broke my way. But in wrestling, timing is everything—and mine was off.

Right as that opportunity came together, the power structure changed.

DUSTY RHODES WAS COMING IN, Ole was on the way out, and suddenly I wasn't walking into a job anymore —I was starting over. They sent me to do a dark match in Macon, Georgia. I went out there, did what I do, and the next day we watched the tape. Dusty liked it. He told me, *"Give me a little time, baby. I'm gonna bring you in."* So I waited. Weeks turned into months. Then came Pensacola, Florida.

They threw me in the opener against Brad Armstrong. I worked heel, exactly how I wanted, and we tore the house down. When I came back, Barry Windham had watched the whole match, and the word backstage was immediate: *"Just show up to Marietta for TV—we'll get you on, maybe even with Ric Flair."* That's when I knew I was finally breaking through. By March, I was in the office with Dusty and Magnum T.A., cutting a rap promo. They loved it.

NEXT THING I KNOW, I'm recording audio and shooting a video for The Great American Bash that looked like a full-blown rap music video. I was doing appearances, getting exposure—everything was happening fast. Too fast. Because the reality was, I wasn't even under contract yet.

THAT BECAME A PROBLEM INTERNALLY, especially with Jim Herd, because Turner didn't like the idea of someone being featured without being locked in. So they rushed to fix it. They brought in a group of us they saw potential in—Scott Hall, Steve Austin, Marc Mero, Del Wilkes, Chip Minton, Mark Hildreth—and handed us all the same deal: $75,000 the first year, $150,000 rollover the second.

EVERYONE SIGNED that day except me. Something didn't feel right. The contract was thick, complicated, and they gave you no time to read it. Just sign it. That never sat well with me. I took it home.

TWO HOURS LATER, my phone rings—Magnum T.A. telling me I was blowing my opportunity if I didn't sign immediately. Looking back, that should have told me everything. That was panic.

THEY NEEDED me to sign more than I needed to sign. But I didn't see it that way then. That Sunday, I was at the Omni Coliseum. I was supposed to do a rap, nothing more. The setup was a mess—no proper playback, delayed audio, and it threw me off completely. Before the show, I saw Dusty at the hotel and told him I wasn't sure about the contract. He told me not to worry, said we'd talk at the building.

· · ·

WHEN I GOT THERE, he pulled me into a VIP room and did what Dusty did best—he worked me. *"Baby, you're like my son. You're the first one I brought in."* He made me feel like I was the future. And I bought it. I signed the contract right there.

THAT SAME NIGHT, I drove home—and there was a message waiting: call Jay Strongbow. Vince McMahon loved the gimmick. They wanted me immediately. I called Pat Patterson the next morning, and when I told him I had just signed with WCW, he said, *"Then we can't do anything."* Just like that, one of the biggest opportunities of my life was gone. From there, things started shifting. I was getting what looked like a push, but it wasn't by design—matches were going long, and I was being told to go home in under a minute. It made me look like I was being pushed hard, which created heat among guys who thought I was being favored.

THEN CAME ENGLAND—THE turning point. We were in Sheffield when money went missing. Mine was gone. Terry Taylor was gone. As far as I knew, nobody else was hit. I immediately told Grizzly Smith to call the police and check the cameras—because England has cameras everywhere, and it would show exactly who went in and out of that dressing room. Nothing happened. No investigation. The next day, people were acting differently and looking at me differently. That's how it starts. Nobody asks you anything. Nobody confronts you. They start talking. And before you know it, you're the guy they're talking about.

. . .

THAT'S HOW THE "WALLET STORY" was born —not from proof, but from assumption and silence.

AROUND THAT SAME TIME, I had the incident with Rick Rude. We were at the hotel, had some drinks, and something flipped in him. He smashed a bottle over his own head and then hit me, blackening my eye instantly.

THE NEXT DAY, he told me I could hit him back. I didn't. I said, *"Let's make money with it."* We came up with a story—arm wrestling, table breaks, I fall, and hit my face. We stuck to it. Didn't matter. People still talked.

ONLY A FEW GUYS knew the truth—me, Rick Rude, Joey Maggs (who the girls called), Paul Heyman, and Curt Hennig. But once the narrative is out there, it doesn't matter who knows the truth. And that's how I got labeled.

THEN I GOT HURT at the BattleBowl pay-per-view against Ron Simmons—my foot caught the rope, my hip got pulled out. And when you're gone, the business keeps moving without you. I left WCW and went back to Europe. Started focusing on life. My wife was pregnant, and that changed everything.

I HAD another shot at the WWF when Sgt. Slaughter told me they had been looking for me for six months, and Yokozuna even put me over strong to Vince in person. But I chose to go back to Europe and work, because a family was coming. That was my second chance.

THE THIRD CAME years later at a WWE SmackDown taping. I was in shape, ready, backed by Fit Finlay and Dean Malenko. John Laurinaitis liked what he saw and talked about bringing us in as heels. Everything was moving forward. Then it stopped. Politics again. Old perceptions. Same story.

YEARS LATER, I was riding with Scott Hall, Shawn Michaels, and Kevin Nash, and Nash was the only one who ever apologized to me about that time in WCW. Said he didn't know the truth. That meant something. And there were guys like Brad Armstrong who never believed it in the first place.

I'VE WRESTLED in 55 countries—over 5,000 matches. My body's broken. I've had opportunities in film with Miloš Forman, music deals tied to Keith Sweat and Boyz II Men—all of it happening during that same window when this rumor was spreading. That's the irony. But the truth is simple: the "wallet story" was never proven because it never happened. It was an urban legend built on timing, jealousy, and silence.

AND IN WRESTLING, if a story gets repeated enough, people stop questioning it. I know who I was. And that's enough. I appreciate you, Andrew, for allowing me the chance in this urban legends book to tell everyone something I've been wanting to address properly once and for all. And for what it's worth, I hope you sell a million copies of this book.

· · ·

I APPRECIATE Andrew being honest with me about what he was doing. Most people don't do that. They write whatever they want and put it out there. Wrestling history rarely allows for that kind of certainty.

WHAT IT PRESENTS INSTEAD ARE the accounts that exist—firsthand testimony, personal suspicion, locker-room hearsay, and direct rebuttal—clearly labeled and placed side by side. But for the first time, the record includes the voices of those involved—speaking plainly, on the record, after more than thirty years. Urban legends don't disappear because they're false. They disappear when the truth—and the uncertainty—finally has a place to stand.

I APPRECIATE THE FANS—THE ones who loved me and the ones who hated me—because without them, none of this exists. I forgive the people who believed it or pushed it, because I won't let it define me. I'd do it all again—maybe smarter, maybe for more money—but I'd still do it because this is my story. And now you've heard it from me.

CHAPTER 30

THE MANY TALES OF NELSON FRAZIER

"It never made it on TV, and it's more of a trophy that was made for me." - King Mabel

IN THE YEARS following WWF's 1995 King of the Ring tournament, a mysterious championship belt began quietly circulating among wrestling insiders and smart fans. The photographs showed Nelson Frazier Jr. — better known to the world as Mabel — posing with a massive gold championship belt that looked official at first glance, yet had never appeared on WWF television. I know this belt was genuine because he showed it to me. He shared personal photos with me and allowed me to display them publicly during our first shoot interview together in 2009.

When we met, we formed a real friendship. His wife, Cassandra, even mentions me in her book about Nelson and our connection. He trusted me with his story, and I will always be grateful for that. Nelson had quietly turned down countless shoot interview offers over the years after leaving the WWF as Mabel, Viscera, and later Big Daddy V.

At first glance, the King of the Ring belt looked legitimate. But the more fans studied the photos, the more questions surfaced. The WWF logo was not in the company's trademark block font. The country flags on the strap appeared inaccurate. Most suspicious of all, the belt had never been seen on WWF programming.

Some fans believed the WWF had quietly created a King of the Ring championship that was never introduced. Others thought the belt had been stolen, hidden, or pulled before it could debut. That mystery was finally answered during our shoot interview. *"It never made it on TV, and it's more of a trophy that was made for me,"* he said. Nelson contacted legendary belt maker Reggie Parks, who coordinated with Dave Millican to craft the title. Because WWF trademarks were protected, the belt featured "WWF" lettering in a generic font rather than the official block logo. The company never sanctioned it and never intended for it to be on television.

Instead, it became Nelson's marketing weapon. He carried it to independent shows and displayed it at autograph signings. Its massive size and striking design made it instantly recognizable and helped cement his King of the Ring legacy long after his WWF run had ended.

When I asked where the belt is today, he told me he sold it to a private collector for thousands of dollars. But the belt was only part of his story.

Nine months after our January 2009 shoot interview wrapped, I saw Nelson again — this time with the DVDs now released so he could sign covers for fans. But what happened that weekend would become one of the most meaningful moments of my life in wrestling.

Fifteen years after King of the Ring in Philadelphia, everything came full circle in the city of Brotherly Love.

THE NIGHT before Signamania in September 2009, Nelson invited me to his hotel room to hang out. What I didn't know when I walked in was that Mo and Oscar had flown in that same night and were staying in the same hotel.

It was the first time the three of them had seen each other in over a decade — ahead of their public reunion signing the next morning in Levittown, PA.

I brought Nelson a box of our shoot interview DVDs so he could take them home and give copies to family and friends. We stayed up all night. It was nearly three in the morning, and I had roughly a three-hour ride back to New Jersey, but I wasn't leaving.

I KNEW I WAS LISTENING, watching, and witnessing something special. The reunion of Men on a Mission, with an audience of one. **Me.**

NELSON JOKED that I was the only one who witnessed this reunion and that we gotta do an on-camera shoot of all three of us. But the stories I heard firsthand that night could never have been filmed. Let's just put it that way.

One story, however, found closure.

.   .   .

OSCAR LOOKED at Nelson and said, *"You hurt me when Vince asked if I should manage you when you turned heel. And you said you didn't think it would work. And then I was released."*

Nelson walked over to Oscar, sitting in the chair, and gave him a hug that lasted over a minute—or felt like it did.

Nelson apologized. Oscar broke down in tears.

I took a photo of Nelson and Bobby Horne (known to fans more famously as Mo) together that night — the first time they had stood side by side in over a decade.

They talked about everything. Mo remembered how difficult Shawn Michaels was to deal with in 1995.

Oscar talked about being ribbed and tortured the most by Luna Vachon and Bam Bam Bigelow. Yet he never quit. Oscar recalled meeting Vince McMahon, who said he loved Oscar's rapping and told him to come to the office. Men on a Mission was born.

They even addressed the old legend that they accidentally won the tag team titles due to a botched finish. That story, they confirmed, was false.

VINCE WANTED them to win the belts to show that "anything can happen in the WWF." The Quebecers won them back on a European tour. The title change was never shown on television.

I asked Nelson about *the infamous urban legend that he was scheduled to be the THIRD Man* — the story that he was scheduled to join Hall and Nash in WCW as the third member of the NWO.

He laughed and said that if he were contacted about being the "third man," he would have been game, as he put it. He was not under contract with the WWF when the NWO was forming, but more importantly, he was not asked.

WHAT HE SAID WAS TRUE: Yokozuna, Undertaker, and others early in his career were getting injured while they worked with him. He felt horrible about it. Undertaker, as locker room leader, had to pull him aside and tell him to work more safely. Nelson credited Taker and Kevin Nash as the men who had the power to get him fired — but chose not to. Also confirmed by the 500 lb giant, Nelson, was that he was never promised the WWF Championship.

Nelson Frazier — known to fans as Mabel, Viscera, and Big Daddy V — passed away on February 18, 2014, just four days after his 43rd birthday.

Bobby Horne — our Mo — left us on October 19, 2025.

ONE KING OF THE RING. One night in Philadelphia.

And somehow, it all circles back there, fifteen years after the spotlight faded — Men on a Mission found something far more important than a crown. Not in front of a crowd. But quietly inside a hotel room, where their reunion was witnessed for an audience of one.

CHAPTER 31
ICONIC ENTRANCES THEMES RECYCLED

BEFORE A PUNCH IS THROWN, before a promo is cut, before a bell is rung, the music hits.

That first note tells the crowd who's coming.

It sets the mood. It creates anticipation. It turns a wrestler into a larger-than-life character before they even step through the curtain.

Some songs become inseparable from the wrestlers who used them.

But like many of wrestling's greatest legends, the truth is more complicated. Because many of those iconic songs didn't originally belong to the men who made them famous, in wrestling, thunder is often borrowed.

BEFORE "REAL AMERICAN" ever blasted through WWF arenas, Hulk Hogan sometimes came to the ring to one of the most recognizable songs in movie history: "Eye of the Tiger," the anthem from Rocky III. The connection was perfect.

In 1982, Hogan appeared in the film as the towering pro wrestler Thunderlips, introducing him to mainstream audiences years before Hulkamania ran wild.

So when Hogan walked out to that music, he wasn't just a wrestler. He was a movie star, a crossover attraction, a superhero. Fans knew the song. They knew the movie. They knew Thunderlips.

But licensing movie music was expensive.

WWF needed something they owned, something permanent, something they could build an empire around.

THAT'S WHEN "REAL AMERICAN" entered the picture. Written by Rick Derringer in 1985, the song was created for Mike Rotunda and Barry Windham, The U.S. Express.

They came to the ring waving American flags while the anthem blared through the speakers.

For a brief moment, the song belonged to them. Then Windham left the company, the team faded, and the music was shelved. Too powerful to waste. Too perfect to forget.

When Hogan arrived as the face of the new WWF, Vince McMahon needed an anthem that felt like Rocky, Top Gun, and a Fourth of July parade rolled into one.

"Real American" was reborn, and from that moment on, it belonged to Hulk Hogan.

———

THE ULTIMATE WARRIOR'S theme followed a similar path.

Before the face paint, before the ropes shook, before the war drums ever echoed through arenas, the song belonged to The Rockers.

Shawn Michaels and Marty Jannetty used the fast-paced, pounding track during their 1988 run with the WWF.

It fit their style perfectly—energetic, explosive, chaotic.

Dingo Warrior on the C-town house show markets was transformed into The Ultimate Warrior on television with an iconic entrance theme that belonged to the Rockers for a short time.

Then the song found its most famous home. When WWF began grooming Warrior as their next monster babyface, the music was reassigned once again. When that theme hit, the building shook. Warrior didn't walk—he sprinted. He shook the ropes. He stared into the camera. He breathed fire. The drums didn't just introduce him. They unleashed him.

New instrumental music was given to the Rockers afterward. And ironically, when The Rockers split in 1992, their music didn't disappear.

In 1993, the Rock 'n' Roll Express—Ricky Morton and Robert Gibson—arrived in the WWF for a short run, and ran to the ring using The Rockers' theme.

It was a strange full-circle moment.

The Rockers had been inspired by the Rock 'n' Roll Express for years, and now the originals were walking to the ring to the soundtrack of their protégés—a passing of the torch through music.

Another forgotten case came from one of WWF's most electric tag teams of the late 1980s, High Energy. Owen Hart and Koko B. Ware went to the ring to one of the most upbeat, high-tempo themes the company ever produced.

The song fit their style—flashy, athletic, and fun. When High Energy disbanded, their music didn't disappear.

It went to The Heavenly Bodies. The same theme that once introduced two babyfaces now played for one of the most arrogant, obnoxious heel teams of the early 1990s.

Same song. Completely different energy.

Proof that in wrestling, presentation can rewrite perception.

———

THEN THERE WAS the case of The Patriot.

In 1997, Del Wilkes arrived in the WWF as the masked, flag-waving Patriot. His entrance music was a pounding, orchestral march that felt like a national anthem turned into a war cry.

The Patriots' run was brief. The character faded.

But the music stayed.

Two years later, in 1999, WWF signed an Olympic gold medalist. Kurt Angle debuted not just as another rookie, but as an American hero, a legitimate athlete, a real-life champion.

When his music hit, it was The Patriot's theme. The same anthem, the same march, the same patriotic power—now belonging to one of the most outstanding performers in wrestling history. Once again, borrowed thunder became legendary.

. . .

THEN THERE WAS one of the most fun examples of all—Ernest "The Cat" Miller.

In WCW, The Cat wasn't just a wrestler—he was a vibe.

A karate expert with charisma for days, he danced to the ring, high-fived fans, and turned every entrance into a party.

And when Miller was with the WWE in 2002-2004, his theme music—"Somebody call my momma!"—had the crowd in sync. It was funky and fitting to the character that once danced with James Brown on a WCW pay-per-view.

Years later, when WWE was searching for a theme for a dancing, funk-loving monster named Brodus Clay, they went back to the well. They brought back "Somebody Call My Momma." Same song. Same energy. Same party.

Only now it belonged to the Funkasaurus.

These weren't isolated cases. In the old WWF, theme music was treated like ring gear. If someone left, their music stayed. If a new star needed a push, they were given the best song available. Vince McMahon believed presentation created stars, and sometimes a great song was more important than a great gimmick.

Hogan could have walked out to anything, but "Eye of the Tiger" made him a movie star and "Real American" made him a superhero.

Warrior could have used any fast rock song, but those war drums made him feel unstoppable.

Kurt Angle could have debuted to anything, but that anthem made him feel like destiny.

Brodus Clay could have danced to anything, but "Somebody Call My Momma" made him unforgettable. The Rock 'n'

Roll Express could have used anything, but walking to The Rockers' theme was wrestling poetry.

TODAY, fans hear those themes and immediately think of the men who made them famous. They hear "Real American" and see Hogan ripping his shirt. They hear Warrior's drums and see him sprinting to the ring. They hear Angle's march and think of Olympic gold. They hear "Somebody Call My Momma" and start dancing.

BUT BEHIND EVERY iconic entrance is a forgotten first owner. A tag team that waved the flags first. A high-flying duo that danced to the beat. A legendary team that borrowed from their successors. A masked patriot who passed the torch. A karate master who started the party.

It's another reminder that in wrestling, legends are often built from recycled parts. Old ideas become new stars. Old songs become new anthems. Old thunder becomes borrowed thunder.

And when the music hits, history rewrites itself.

CHAPTER 32
THE WBF EXPERIMENT

"*It's the ICOPRO you sent us.*" - Steve Keirn

COMFORT AND SECURITY weren't reserved for the men grinding through twenty-eight days a month on the road —working hurt, working sick, living out of rental cars and airport terminals.

They were reserved for the muscle men, whose guarantees were funded by the blood, sweat, and broken bodies of the same wrestlers flying coach and earning based on where they were placed on cards and how much the houses drew.

Guaranteed money. First-class flights. Five-star hotels.

Everyone knows the story of the WBF's ultimately failure, but few people outside the organization truly know how it all began or why.

In the vast portfolio of Vince McMahon's business ventures, few failures loom as strangely — or as quietly — as the World Bodybuilding Federation.

Launched in 1990 and dissolved less than two years later, the WBF was McMahon's attempt to force the wrestling "sports entertainment" model onto competitive bodybuilding.

Drawing on his national expansion strategy from several years earlier, Vince planned a hostile takeover aimed squarely at the International Federation of Bodybuilders, the empire controlled by Joe Weider and his brother, Ben Weider, guardians of the sport's crown jewel, Mr. Olympia.

This wasn't just a failed league. It was corporate warfare, aggressive branding, federal scrutiny, and ego colliding at exactly the wrong time.

BEFORE THE WBF was publicly announced, Bodybuilding Lifestyles — McMahon's glossy in-house magazine — quietly embedded itself inside the IFBB ecosystem. In 1990, at the Mr. Olympia, the magazine bought booth space and appeared as an official sponsor.

In the middle of bodybuilding's most prestigious event, Tom Platz took the stage to speak on behalf of the magazine. Then, in pure pro-wrestling fashion, he dropped the swerve: the creation of the World Bodybuilding Federation, a direct competitor to the IFBB, announced on its biggest night.

Behind the scenes, IFBB competitors were quietly approached and offered contracts during the show itself.

It was an ambush.

McMahon needed bodies, and he needed them fast. Thirteen IFBB pros defected, rebranded not as athletes but as WBF Bodystars — a deliberate echo of WWF Superstars.

The contracts were staggering by bodybuilding standards: guaranteed deals reportedly ranging from $85,000 to $350,000 annually, first-class flights, and security that was never offered to the wrestlers.

These weren't wrestlers pretending to pose. They were bodybuilders forced into kayfabe.

EVERY COMPETITOR RECEIVED A GIMMICK, a persona, and a role. WBF pay-per-views featured an "Entertainment Round," complete with pre-taped skits that were continued live on stage. Physiques weren't just judged — characters were performed.

Competitors like Mike Quinn were repackaged with exaggerated personas. The emphasis shifted away from anatomical precision toward crowd response and "personality." Judges recoiled. Fans bristled. What McMahon called evolution, the sport saw as contamination.

THE WBF WAS NEVER the endgame.

It was the billboard. The real engine was ICOPRO — the Integrated Conditioning Program. McMahon wasn't selling contests; he was building a vertically integrated lifestyle brand.

The Bodystars became walking advertisements. Every magazine spread, pay-per-view broadcast, and appearance funneled attention toward powders and bars marketed as the source of WBF physiques.

In reality, it placed a massive target on McMahon's back — just as the federal government was tightening its grip on steroids and supplements.

The formation of the WBF coincided almost perfectly with the arrest and conviction of George Zahorian, the WWF doctor accused of illegally distributing anabolic steroids. Federal investigators began circling McMahon himself.

Suddenly, running a bodybuilding federation was radioactive.

The WBF pivoted publicly, declaring itself drug-free and implementing testing in 1992. The optics were disastrous. Bodybuilding was inseparable from chemical enhancement in the public imagination, and now the federation built on freakish excess was insisting it was clean.

Reports later surfaced that as many as ten of the thirteen WBF competitors failed drug tests — yet their suspensions conveniently expired just before the 1992 pay-per-view.

THE 1992 LONG BEACH championship was a visual disaster. Competitors were noticeably smaller, flatter, and depleted — not just from drug testing, but from a strict ketogenic diet encouraged by WBF medical staff. The freak factor was gone.

Back-to-back champion Gary Strydom retained his size better than most others, fueling whispers of selective enforcement. Others looked like shadows of their former selves. Fans felt misled.

THE BROADCAST DIDN'T HELP. Hosting duties were handed to Bobby Heenan and a comedy writer named Lex Luger — not the wrestler — creating an awkward, flippant tone that undercut the athletes' preparation. The pay-per-view buyrate collapsed. The live gate was weak.

The experiment was finished.

To legitimize the WBF with mainstream audiences, McMahon courted Lou Ferrigno, famous for The Incredible Hulk. Ferrigno signed a lucrative deal meant to mark his return to competitive bodybuilding.

He never competed.

Ferrigno walked away in 1992 and instead returned to Mr. Olympia, choosing legacy over spectacle. For the WBF, losing its biggest mainstream name was another quiet admission that star power couldn't save a collapsing fantasy.

WEEKS LATER, McMahon called WBF president Bernie Arkimovich and reportedly told him it was over because the federal government was coming down hard on them.

ON JULY 15, 1992, the WBF was dissolved immediately. Bodybuilding Lifestyles ceased publication.

Contracts were paid out or quietly settled.

The Bodystars were left stranded — exiles who had publicly defected from the IFBB. Initially, the WBF had been taken seriously enough that the IFBB raised prize money in response. But after the collapse, McMahon contacted the Weiders not to threaten them — *but to surrender*, which was unlike McMahon at all. After paying a hefty fine, the former WBF athletes were allowed back.

THE RETURN WAS AT ONCE MORE bizarre and theatrical. At the 1993 Night of Champions, the ex-

Bodystars were "resurrected" from coffins in a surreal skit — a symbolic burial and rebirth that felt more ritual than reconciliation.

You can't make this stuff up.

ICOPRO DIDN'T DIE IMMEDIATELY.

BANNERS REMAINED HANGING in WWF arenas for years because the advertising had already been paid for.

Wrestlers cut promos in front of branding for a dead supplement. In his autobiography, Bret Hart noted the absurdity. The product was gone. The federation was erased. The signage remained.

Steve Keirn later laughed about it with me. *"Vince would ask me how I was getting so big while they were testing us for steroids. I'd tell him, it's the ICOPRO you sent us. I had boxes of those things, Andrew."*

THE WBF COST Vince McMahon and the WWF millions. And when the experiment collapsed, the fallout didn't come with an announcement. It came quietly, through tightened budgets and fewer opportunities, and a locker room that understood exactly where the money had gone.

That's where the resentment truly took hold.

The men wrestling twenty-eight days a month didn't have guaranteed contracts. They were paid per night. Miss a date and miss a paycheck.

Then they watched guaranteed money, first-class accommodations, and television time flow to muscle men who weren't carrying the house—and who weren't risking their bodies in the ring.

WHEN THE WBF FAILED, the loss didn't vanish. It landed where losses always landed—in the locker room. Everyone felt it.

That didn't make Vince reckless. It made him consistent.

McMahon believed—correctly more often than not—that spectacle, personality, and scale could turn niche worlds into mainstream entertainment.

Wrestling worked because it already had a culture built on loyalty, tradition, and emotional investment. Bodybuilding didn't. The WBF tried to manufacture belonging instead of earning it, and the wrestlers—who lived inside a real grind every night—saw the difference immediately.

A decade later, Vince would gamble again with the XFL, repeating the same core assumption: that branding and presentation could substitute for culture. The failure wasn't a lack of vision. It was timing, context, and the absurdity of trying to force passion where none existed.

THE WBF WASN'T DOOMED because Vince lacked guts. It was doomed because its cost was real, and it was paid by the WWF superstars, who had no guarantees, no protection, and no margin for error, but were not always treated as such. They flew coach, rented cars, worked hard, worked sick, and hoped nothing went wrong because there was no safety net waiting for them.

CHAPTER 33

VINCE'S CHAMPION

"You're going to have a great match, whether you like it or not." - Bret "the Hitman" Hart.

WHEN VINCE TOLD BRET, *"You're my champion. You're in charge,"* something shifted permanently.

"That's the way I was for the rest of my career, Andrew. From '93 on, nobody told me how to wrestle. Period." The only exception he acknowledged was The Undertaker. And even that wasn't control — it was collaboration. *"Because of his gimmick, you had to blend his ideas with yours."* The supernatural aura. The pacing. The Frankenstein cadence. That required adjustment. Bret welcomed ideas. *"You can give me ideas. We'll find a place for them."* If Steve Austin had a spot he liked, Bret would incorporate it — but within the larger design. The match still had architecture.

There was still escalation. But after 1992? The blueprint belonged to "The Hitman."

. . .

THE MATCH at WrestleMania VIII against Roddy Piper is the perfect example of how Bret operated.

He knew he was going over months in advance. Roddy losing to anyone was a big deal. Piper never put Hogan over—there was always a disqualification or countout finish in their series of bouts in the 1980s.

The Mountie's loss was already a setup piece. But it wasn't until a week before WrestleMania that he and Roddy had actually mapped it out.

THEY SCHEDULED A DINNER IN MONCTON, New Brunswick. Bret admitted he was nervous. *"What if we don't see eye to eye?"*

Two strong personalities. Two clear visions. One championship match. Roddy said, *"What do you want to do?"*

Bret deferred first. And, Roddy laid out his vision. Bret listened. *"It was Roddy's finish. And, it was the same match I had pictured in my head."*

THE SLEEPER. The kick-off the ropes. The roll-through. A finish Roddy had been saving for decades. *"He said he'd been saving it in his back pocket,"* Roddy told Bret something profound that night.

He wanted to find one wrestler at the end of his career who could beat him — and elevate him in the process. The Piper match was in 1992, before the full shift.

. . .

AFTER BRET BECAME the World champion, he wasn't asking what others wanted to do, although he listened to their ideas. He didn't immediately dismiss opponents, but, in the end, he was *telling* them what they were doing. Because he understood something now. The champion sets the tone and dictates the rhythm.

———

BLOOD, **Structure, and the Feeling of Sabotage**

THE REMATCH with Davey Boy Smith at WWE In Your House 5: Seasons Beatings wasn't just another title defense from their classic at Summerslam in Wembley Stadium in 1992. In London that August night, the hometown Bulldog was a babyface, as Bret.

This rematch was different from the start. Davey had turned heel. He cut his hair. The presentation shifted. On paper, that should have added tension. But Bret felt something else building beneath the surface. *"Davey was a great wrestler. But he was not a good heel."* It wasn't cruelty in the statement — it was a diagnosis. *"His idea of being a heel was to do a suplex and a powerslam. I said, Davey, those are babyface moves."*

Bret understood that a heel doesn't just execute offense — he manipulates tempo. And because Davey was the heel, tradition dictated that Davey should call the match.

THAT'S where Bret felt trapped. *"I had to let Davey call the match because he was the heel. But he didn't know how to call a match as a heel."*

. . .

AND HERE IS where Bret used a word carefully.

"It felt like sabotage." Not sabotage from Davey personally.

The champion was placed into a match where the psychology engine depended on someone who wasn't built for that role. At a time when Bret already felt momentum being chipped away, this felt intentional. *"It was almost like they picked it to be a dud."*

He saw the larger picture: Shawn and Nash gaining influence in booking conversations. Other angles are receiving priority. His title reign was not framed with the gravity he believed it deserved.

"NO ONE EVEN CARED THAT *I won the title from Kevin Nash. I didn't even do a promo."* Bret was referring to his match with Diesel at the Survivor Series the previous month. So Bret adjusted. Mid-match, when Davey suplexed him over the top rope, and he crashed to the floor, Bret made a decision.

He cut himself. "I'm not a juice guy." But Bret understood escalation and the drama it added. *"There are certain situations where blood can enhance the match."*

The blood changed everything. Suddenly, Davey wasn't just working holds — he was hurting himself. Suddenly, the match had a narrative arc that the psychology alone hadn't delivered. That was the missing ingredient. Without the blood, Bret believes the match would have been remembered as technically competent but emotionally flat — a pale shadow of Wembley. With it, it became visceral. He didn't blade to shock. He bladed to save structure.

· · ·

THE CHAMPION Who Refused to Be Flattened

One of the criticisms Bret has heard over the years is that he *"got himself over."* That he protected his own image too fiercely. That he was territorial about his position.

"YOU'VE GOT AN OUT. That's the most important thing. You've got an out." The idea was simple: Nash doesn't get tapped out clean in the Sharpshooter. He loses because of a momentary lapse — a split-second miscalculation.

A SMALL PACKAGE. A guard dropped for one second —an upset.

"This is as good a way as I can think of for you to lose the belt and still keep your momentum." Nash was sulking at the time. He didn't feel it. Years later, he would tell Bret that it was the best match of his career. And fans still bring it up to him at signings.

BRET STILL TALKS about one sequence in that match with pride — not ego, but craft. Nash sets up for the Jackknife. Bret kicks his legs backward, catches the top rope with his boots, forcing Nash to reset. Nash tries again. Bret bites his hand and rolls free.

"IT'S SO DESPERATE. *It's like, what does a guy do when he's fighting uphill against someone that big?"* That's storytelling.

No one had seen it before. It wasn't borrowed or recycled. Another example of that creativity was the table sequence — a spot Bret devised after watching too many predictable table crashes in wrestling. He hated the telegraphing. *"Everybody knows the guy on the table is going to move."*

HE PROPOSED that Nash launch him backward through the table — violently, unexpectedly. Then Nash would hesitate — a flicker of remorse — before rolling Bret back into the ring. That hesitation would cost him. Small package. One. Two. Three. The hesitation wasn't weakness.

It was humanity. And that humanity created the opening. Bret pitched it to Vince. Vince loved it. In fact, Vince loved it so much that the next day he called Bret and enthusiastically laid out the same finish, as if it had just occurred to him. Bret laughed about it. It didn't matter who "owned" the idea. What mattered was that it worked.

Bret takes pride in originality. The rope-cable spot tying Nash's leg to the post — messy but inventive. At the same time, another tension was building. After defeating Kevin Nash for the WWF Championship, Bret expected an ascent. Instead, there was no sustained framing of him as the new standard-bearer. Nash powerbombed him quickly after the title change.

FOR ALL THE pride Bret takes in the Survivor Series match with Kevin Nash, there was a physical cost that rarely gets discussed. The match itself went beautifully. The pacing. The desperation spots. The small package is finished. It all worked.

. . .

BRET HAS SPOKEN OPENLY about what happened next. *"He gave me two or three really reckless powerbombs after the end of that match, if you go back and watch,"* Bret says. *"He didn't do it right. I think he was pissed off."* And those post-match powerbombs had consequences. In the weeks that followed, Nash would go for the Jackknife frequently — sometimes unexpectedly. *"Every night he'd go for the powerbomb."* At first, Bret believed Nash felt he was resisting his finisher out of stubbornness. He was protecting his body. *"No. You hurt me with your finish, and I can't take it anymore."* The damage lingered. "I couldn't even take a deep breath." He describes it like being hit in the back with a baseball bat. He couldn't even safely execute things like the flying head mare—a simple move easily executed by one of the best, but not when you're injured.

"I had trouble taking a breath." It was accumulated trauma. Then, as champion Interference finishes, television momentum stalled. Bret began noticing something alarming: *"I haven't won a match clean since I became champion."* Heading into WrestleMania XII, discussions surfaced about leaving him laid out again before the Iron Man match. This time, Bret did not bend. *"You can't send me into the main event of WrestleMania looking weak."*

HE CONFRONTED The Undertaker and Nash directly at the In Your House in Louisville, a month before Mania's Iron Man match with Shawn. Taker and Diesel believed their match and angle were equally important. Bret disagreed. *"I'm the champion. My match is more important. You can't just leave me laying again. I haven't done anything for two months. You've got to give me some light."*

· · ·

THE DISAGREEMENT ESCALATED to Vince's room. Arguments were laid out. Vince sided with Bret. And Bret has never softened on that memory. *"I was right. And they were wrong."* Not because he won the argument. But because the psychology demanded it.

"YOU CAN PUT that match right on par with Wembley. They're probably the two best matches Davey ever had." And Bret loves that In Your House match. "It was one of my greatest stories."

Because he turned what he believed was structural sabotage into something unforgettable, Bret believed the match was positioned in a way that would make him look flat heading into WrestleMania. *"They gave me zero momentum going in. They put the belt on me, and all they wanted to do was beat me with Shawn."*

IN BRET'S MIND, if they weren't going to build him up, he would build himself up. "I needed some momentum. They weren't going to give it to me, so I had to get it myself." That's the difference between a champion and a placeholder.

NOW CONTRAST that with SummerSlam 1992 at Wembley. That morning, Bret approached Vince. *"Do you want me to go over the match and tell you the finish?"*

VINCE STOPPED HIM. *"Don't tell me. I just want to watch."*

That was the trust Vince didn't give many people post-Attitude Era, when angles and matches were heavily scripted and produced, unlike how it was for what Gorilla Monsoon labeled him: the "Excellence of Execution." But Bret was his champion. Bret had already promised Vince they would have one of the greatest matches of all time. And behind the curtain that day, Davey was in no condition to carry anything. *"He told me he hadn't lifted a weight in two months. He'd been on a coke binge."*

FOUR MINUTES INTO THE MATCH, Davey blew up. From that point forward, Bret carried him. *"I had to tell him word by word what was next."* If you rewatch Wembley, you can occasionally see Bret leaning in, quietly directing traffic. He was guiding the biggest match of Davey's career in real time. *"You're going to have a great match whether you like it or not."*

AND THEY DID. The finish at Wembley — the sunset flip counter — was Bret's architecture. A finish he had protected for years that he once gave to Brian Blair of the Killer Bees for a match, but he rejected it. Bret said he would never offer that finish to anyone else again. He, as Piper's finish to the Hitman earlier that year, was one of two different finishes that they protected well. At In Your House, the blood was Bret's adjustment.

WHAT MAKES this section so important is that it reframes the idea that Bret was difficult. He wasn't protecting his ego. Bret was protecting quality. When he believed something would improve the match, he did it. When he believed something would weaken the champion, he resisted it. And when he sensed that momentum was being cut off, he created it himself. *"I wasn't going to fall short."*

When Bret Hart looks back on that stretch of his career — late 1995 into early 1996 — he doesn't speak like a man defending ego. He speaks like an architect defending a structure. That distinction matters. After regaining the WWF Championship from Kevin Nash, Bret expected a lift. Instead, he felt erosion. There was no sustained framing of him as the new standard-bearer. No strong promotional runway. Nash powerbombed him almost immediately after the title change. Interference finished, followed by momentum that stalled before it could even form. Bret noticed something alarming. *"I hadn't won a match clean since I became champion."*

THAT   REALIZATION   CHANGED EVERYTHING. Because heading into WrestleMania XII against Shawn Michaels, there were discussions about leaving him laid out on television again. This time, Bret refused. *"You can't send me into the main event of WrestleMania looking weak."* The champion's match is the apex. If the audience doubts the champion, the entire main event collapses. The disagreement escalated to Vince. Vince sided with Bret. *"I was right. And they were wrong."*

AROUND THE SAME TIME, Bret found himself in a different kind of bind at WWE In Your House 5: Seasons Beatings in a rematch with Davey Boy Smith. On paper, it was the sequel to Wembley — a match already etched in history. But the dynamic had shifted. Davey had turned heel. His presentation changed. The chemistry had to change with it.

The match, in its early stages, was technically solid. There was a suplex across the ropes. Bret fell to the floor. It was fine. And that's precisely the problem. *"If it ended right there, I'd give it a three out of ten."* Bret believed the structure put him at a disadvantage. As the heel, Davey traditionally would call the match. But Bret didn't believe Davey had the instincts to generate sustained heat.

"DAVEY WAS A GREAT WRESTLER. *But he was a horrible heel. His idea of being a heel was to do a suplex and a powerslam. Those aren't heel moves. Those are babyface moves."*

AND THEN THE word Bret rarely throws around lightly: *"It felt like sabotage."* Not sabotage by Davey personally — sabotage in design. A champion is placed in a scenario where the psychology engine relies on someone who is unequipped for that role. Bret could feel the match plateauing. It would have been good. But not great. Not on the level of Wembley. And certainly not strong enough to restore his fading momentum. So he adjusted. When Davey suplexed him and he crashed to the floor, Bret made a decision.

"I KNEW *that if I could accidentally get blood, it would change the whole tempo."* Not for shock. For urgency. The blood instantly reframed Davey's offense. Now he wasn't just wrestling Bret — he was hurting him. The crowd shifted from watching to worrying. The match breathed differently.

. . .

"YOU CAN PUT *that match right side-by-side with Wembley.*"

Two completely different stories. Same opponent. Years apart. Both masterclasses — but built under entirely different pressures. That's the pattern in Bret's career. When the structure weakened, he reinforced it himself. The same philosophy was applied at Survivor Series 1995 against Kevin Nash. That match stretched over forty minutes. Anything goes. Psychological. Desperate. Nash didn't like the finish. He wanted it changed.

"YOU'VE GOT AN OUT. *That's the most important thing.*"

THE SMALL PACKAGE wasn't humiliating. It was a fluke—a split-second lapse. A champion catching a giant off guard. Nash lost without losing momentum. Years later, Nash would call it the best match of his career. Bret still talks about one moment in that match with pride — not ego, but craft. Nash sets up for the Jackknife. Bret kicks his legs backward, hooks the top rope with his boots, forcing Nash to reset. Nash tries again. Bret bites his hand, twists his arm, and boots him beautifully in the chest. It looks chaotic. It looks desperate.

"WHAT DOES *a guy do when he's fighting uphill against someone that big?*" That wasn't choreography. That was survival storytelling. But that match had a cost. After the bell, Nash delivered two or three reckless powerbombs. If you watch closely, Bret lands three-point each time — hips and hands absorbing the impact.

. . .

"HE DIDN'T DO IT RIGHT." Bret doesn't frame it as malice. He frames it as frustration. *"I think he was pissed off."* In the weeks that followed, Nash frequently attempted the powerbomb again. At first, Nash believed Bret was being difficult.

"No. You hurt me with your finish, and I can't take it anymore."

BRET CONTINUED, *"I couldn't even take a deep breath, like being hit in the back with a baseball bat."* Wrestling at that level has consequences. Even when the story is controlled, the body absorbs reality. Whether it was Davey's heat deficiency, Nash's powerbomb, or the erosion of championship momentum, Bret's response was consistent: protect the structure.

HE INNOVATED CONSTANTLY—THE table finish where Nash launches him backward through the wood — Bret's idea. The rope-cable spot tying Nash to the post — original. The turnbuckle climb battle with Curt Hennig at Madison Square Garden — two men fighting up the corner from opposite sides of the ring apron. *"I was always exploring. Trying to find new ways to do stuff."*

BRET HAS HEARD the criticism that he protected himself too fiercely. He rejects it calmly. *"I only put my foot down when I was right."* He wasn't avoiding losses. He was protecting momentum. Bret didn't bury opponents; he preserved them, even in defeat, as he did for Davey at

Summerslam. If the finish feels flat, the audience disengages. When Vince told him in 1992, *"You're my champion. You're in charge,"* Bret took that seriously. From that moment forward, he called the match.

AND WHEN MOMENTUM wasn't given, Bret Hart created it himself.

CHAPTER 34

THE ACCIDENTAL UNDEFEATED STREAK

"You watch it grow—that character—and it grows, and you see it come to life." - Bruce Pritchard.

FOR OVER TWO DECADES, The Undertaker's WrestleMania streak stood as wrestling's most sacred record — 21 victories, zero defeats, a legacy so perfect it felt supernatural.

But like most legends, it didn't start as one.

There was no plan, no storyline, no long-term design.

It was a coincidence — a pattern no one noticed until it became history.

And it all began in Toronto, on a night when The Undertaker raised his hands to the sky and silently told the world: *I'm 10 and 0.*

At *WrestleMania VII* in 1991, he defeated Jimmy "Superfly" Snuka. It was just another match. No one in the company thought of it as the beginning of anything, least of all The

Undertaker himself. In those early years, wins and losses didn't carry streak implications. He faced Jake "The Snake" Roberts, Giant Gonzalez, King Kong Bundy — monsters battling monsters.

Bruce Pritchard jokingly says, sitting in front of Undertaker: "I thought the streak should've ended with Giant González."

Undertaker cracked a smile and said, "I almost ended it with Giant González."

Each year, he won, but nobody was keeping score. Not yet.

It wasn't until *WrestleMania X8* in 2002 that the myth finally found its name.

The Undertaker faced Ric Flair that night — an old-school showdown between two men from different eras, performing under the bright lights of the SkyDome in Toronto.

Flair bled, Arn Anderson, the longtime Horsemen enforcer, even had a cameo, and The Undertaker didn't blink.

When it was over, he pinned "The Nature Boy".

Then, something unscripted happened.

As the crowd roared, The Undertaker rose and stood on the ring apron, extended both arms, and slowly lifted his fingers — first one hand with all five raised, then the other.

Ten fingers. Ten wins.

Ten WrestleManias.

10–0.

For the first time in his career, he acknowledged it — and the fans understood immediately. Someone in the crowd even had a 10-0 sign. They understood.

There was no commentary cue.

No pre-match hype package. No script. Jerry Lawler improvised and proclaimed, "he is 10-0!"

Even WWE officials backstage didn't realize the exact number until that night, except for Michael P.S. Hayes, who brought it up to Vince in a meeting.

As Bruce Prichard said on the Undertaker's podcast in January 2026:

"*It came up in a production meeting, and I believe it was **Michael Hayes** who said, 'Boss, hey, I think Undertaker's undefeated at WrestleMania—like, ten times in a row.'*"

The Dead Man responded:

"*I'm surprised I didn't get beaten right then—like, as soon as that was brought to light. Because once it was brought to life, the reaction was, 'Well, we've got to beat him.'*"

EVERY WRESTLEMANIA MATCH afterward carried a number — a countdown and a dare.

Commentators began referencing it in promos.

Opponents like Randy Orton, Batista, Edge, and Shawn Michaels began chasing it like the holy grail. Undertaker's matches at Wrestlemania had as much significance as being in the main event (and sometimes the two joined).

But it was born that night in Toronto, not in a booking meeting.

Undertaker himself later said in an interview:

"I never thought about it until someone pointed it out. It wasn't something we planned — it just became part of who I was. Once it had a life, I had to protect it."

And protect it he did.

Over the next decade, the streak grew from quiet trivia to prophecy. Every WrestleMania became Judgment Day.

———

EVERY CHALLENGER BECAME a name etched into history — another offering to wrestling's most unintentional altar.

That's what makes it poetic. The Undertaker's streak — one of wrestling's most iconic achievements — wasn't designed by writers or marketing.

It evolved on its own, in silence, match after match, until even the company couldn't ignore it.

It's rare in wrestling for something to organically grow into a legend without being planned, pushed, or rewritten.

When Brock Lesnar finally broke The Streak at *WrestleMania XXX* in 2014, the shock wasn't scripted either — it was real.

The silence that fell across the Mercedes-Benz Superdome wasn't disappointment.

IT WAS DISBELIEF — the kind reserved for when myths die before your eyes.

The Undertaker was concussed and had to be taken to the hospital. Vince McMahon left WrestleMania to accompany him, and in his Netflix documentary, he said he thought the loss of the streak was just too traumatic for Undertaker.

A decade earlier, Vince McMahon said on Steve Austin's podcast: *"No one wants to give back to the business more than The Undertaker—more than Mark Callaway. He understands when it's time to give back.*

And if you look down the roster at that time, who else could he possibly work with in the following year or the year after that? Who could benefit in the biggest possible way? When you really looked at the roster, there was only one person whose time was right. And Mark thought, 'This is it. It should be Brock' ".

WHEN PRESSED BY AUSTIN, Vince continued: *You have to make difficult decisions sometimes. And I believe I made the right call at the right time. Coming into the following WrestleMania, Brock Lesnar couldn't have been hotter— constantly reminding everyone that he broke The Undertaker's streak. Brock is a special attraction. You don't want him on television every week. When something is overexposed, it stops being special. Brock's presence needs to be rare. That's what makes it matter."*

Even after that loss, The Undertaker's legacy remained untouchable.

Because the streak was never about being 21–0.

IT WAS about a man who lived long enough to watch his own legend come to life — by accident, by fate, and by sheer endurance.

The Streak was never booked. It was discovered.

It didn't begin as a master plan or a sacred promise—it emerged quietly, almost by accident, until someone finally said it out loud. And once spoken, it could never be unheard. From that moment on, it stopped belonging to writers, bookers, or even the man who carried it.

It became something older and heavier than storyline—a modern wrestling myth, built on repetition, protection, and belief. Ending it was not about wins or losses; it was about whether wrestling still needed myths in an era obsessed with moments.

AND LIKE ALL MYTHS, it survived by repetition, and like all myths, it demanded a sacrifice to prove it was real. WrestleMania didn't lose its most famous streak that night—it consumed it, the way myths always do when they are no longer needed, only remembered.

What makes McMahon's account so revealing isn't the justification—it's the contradiction. In the same breath, he frames the decision as an act of generosity by The Undertaker, then reclaims sole ownership of it.

THE STREAK, once accidental and later sacred, ultimately ended not as a shared moment of legacy, but as a calculated business call—made in a production truck, filtered through timing, heat, and perceived roster value. Whether it was the right decision remains debatable. What isn't is this: the most protected myth in wrestling history ended the same way most things in WWE do—by one man deciding the moment had come.

CHAPTER 35

ULTIMATE WARRIOR DIED IN THE '90S

THE 1980S WERE a decade built on excess, power, and bright lights — and no one embodied that more than The Ultimate Warrior.

He looked carved out of lightning, sprinting to the ring in a blur of face paint, tassels, and chaos.

He didn't walk among mortals — he *raged* among them.

And then, without warning, he vanished.

That's when the strangest story in wrestling history began.

"The Ultimate Warrior Died."

When fans tuned in to *WWF Superstars* in the early 1990s, they noticed something odd. The Warrior's hair looked shorter. His face paint changed. His build seemed smaller.

He was louder, raspier — different.

Whispers spread:

"That's not the same guy."

"The real Warrior died."

"They replaced him with another wrestler."

I remember some kids at school trying to convince me that the Ultimate Warrior had died because their parents told them so. I was barely a teenager at the time, but I knew it was ridiculous then.

Even stories of a *funeral* that never happened.

Before social media, this was how folklore spread — through rumor, debate, and obsession.

And wrestling, with its blurred lines between fiction and reality, made the perfect breeding ground.

The myth exploded. People said the "new Warrior" was played by Kerry Von Erich or even by Rick Rude, wearing body paint.

Others claimed the "fake" version was left-handed, or that his eye color had changed.

One wild rumor insisted that he had *died lifting weights* — crushed by his own bench press — and that WWF secretly replaced him to protect the merch money.

There was no truth to any of it.

But in wrestling, truth is optional — mystery sells better.

WWF never publicly denied the rumor. They didn't have to.

Every time the crowd screamed, every time a kid wondered, the myth grew stronger. Even before his return in 1996, WWF announcers would play up the myth, remarking on his appearance and speculating on his weight, putting it at 400 pounds.

By 1995, the legend mutated again. WCW began teasing that Hulk Hogan would reveal *"The Ultimate Surprise."*

When the day came at a WCW pay-per-view entitled Uncensored in 1995, fans expected *The Ultimate Warrior* to burst through the curtain. I certainly did.

WHEN I INTERVIEWED Ultimate Warrior in 1997, it was the first question I asked: "Were you backstage at Uncensored '95?" His reply: "No." I tried to get more out of him, but he wanted to move on to another question.

Instead, they got The Renegade — a lookalike managed by Jimmy Hart, painted, muscled, and built to mimic the real thing.

For a few seconds, fans gasped — it *looked* like the myth was real.

Had WCW resurrected the Warrior?

As soon as The Renegade spoke, the illusion shattered.

He wasn't a Warrior.

He was *pretending* to be the rumor itself.

It was as if WCW had turned an urban legend into a living stunt. The rumor mill in the late '90s was hot with rumors circulating that Hulk Hogan had created the Renegade so he could get his "win back" from WrestleMania VI. It was ridiculous. However, Hogan did beat Warrior at Halloween Havoc '98. And he did get his win back.

They even used it in marketing — letting fans believe "The Ultimate One" had returned.

The hoax worked briefly, but the backlash was brutal.

And then came the darkest twist years later, when the man

behind The Renegade, Rick Wilson, took his own life — unable to escape the label of "fake Warrior."

It's as if the curse of the rumor claimed the one who tried to become it.

After leaving WWF, Warrior became more reclusive, occasionally making bizarre online videos in which he spoke in riddles, like his promos — about destiny, death, and immortality.

Fans shared the clips, calling him "the ghost talking to himself."

His ramblings about spirits and energy only fueled the "dead Warrior" myth again.

He'd show up at conventions, fans whispering, *"Is that really him?"*

On April 7, 2013, I saw the Ultimate Warrior at Wrestlecon in New Jersey — the same day as Wrestlemania 29.

I have a video of the Ultimate Warrior signing my vintage WWF pay-per-view posters, including this SummerSlam 1990, which was also signed by many others who have since passed away—Dusty Rhodes, Roddy Piper, Hulk Hogan, and others. Warrior was kind and took this time with everyone. I could not help but hug him. And, I am glad I did. It would be the first, last, and only time I met Jim Hellwig, aka The Ultimate Warrior.

My vintage Summerslam 1990 poster. One of my prized posters in my collection.

In April 2014, the myth came full circle. Warrior returned to WWE for the first time in nearly two decades — inducted into the Hall of Fame, reconciled with Vince McMahon and Hulk Hogan, and walked onto the stage at *WrestleMania XXX* one last time.

The next night on *Monday Night Raw*, wearing a trench coat and mask, Warrior delivered what sounded like a goodbye letter to the world.

He shook the ropes, as always, but his face was red, his breathing heavy. Something looked off. He died the following day. Watching that promo, it wasn't nostalgic anymore.

It was the Ultimate Warrior saying goodbye.

"NO WWE TALENT BECOMES A LEGEND ON THEIR OWN. EVERY MAN'S HEART ONE DAY BEATS ITS FINAL BEAT. HIS LUNGS BREATHE THEIR FINAL BREATH. AND IF WHAT THAT MAN DID IN HIS LIFE MAKES THE BLOOD PULSE THROUGH THE BODIES OF OTHERS— IF IT MAKES THEM BELIEVE IN SOMETHING LARGER THAN LIFE— THEN THAT MAN'S ESSENCE, HIS SPIRIT, WILL BE IMMORTALIZED BY THE STORYTELLERS. BY LOYALTY. BY MEMORY. YOU ARE THE LEGEND MAKERS OF THE ULTIMATE WARRIOR. IN THE BACK, I SEE MANY POTENTIAL LEGENDS. SOME OF THEM HAVE WARRIOR SPIRITS. AND YOU WILL DO THE SAME FOR THEM. YOU WILL DECIDE WHETHER THEY LIVE WITH PASSION AND INTENSITY— SO MUCH SO THAT YOU WILL TELL THEIR STORIES AND MAKE THEM LEGENDS AS WELL. I AM THE ULTIMATE WARRIOR. YOU ARE THE ULTIMATE WARRIOR FANS. AND THE SPIRIT OF THE ULTIMATE WARRIOR WILL RUN FOREVER!"

CHAPTER 36
RANDY SAVAGE
AND STEPHANIE

"Andrew, I have fifteen thousand reasons for this job interview to happen!" - Lanny Poffo.

FOR DECADES, one of the most talked-about—and most debated—urban legends in professional wrestling has circulated in locker rooms, rental cars, hotel bars, message boards, and podcasts. A story that has been repeated so many times that, in some circles, it has taken on the weight of fact—despite there being no confirmed proof, no verified firsthand account, and no public acknowledgment from anyone directly involved.

The rumor that Randy "Macho Man" Savage had a relationship with a younger Stephanie McMahon in the early '90s remains one of the most persistent—and most poisonous—urban legends in wrestling history. One concrete point often cited involves the Slim Jim sponsorship. Savage was inseparable from the brand, and when he left WWF, Slim Jim followed him out the door.

Fans still debate it on social media, podcasters still dance around it and ask other wrestlers their opinions, and interviewers still tease "the question."

The truth? Nobody really knows. But... I *nearly* found it.

WHEN RANDY SAVAGE abruptly left the WWF for WCW in late 1994, Vince McMahon announced it on television himself—something he had never done for a departing star.

On air, McMahon sounded emotional and visibly heartbroken. He thanked Randy for his years of service and wished him well. If you listen closely to that broadcast today, you can hear it.

Vince wasn't angry. He was hurt. The man who helped build Hulkamania was gone—and the tone in Vince's voice made fans feel like there was more to the story.

According to Lanny Poffo, Randy's brother, Vince genuinely wanted Randy to stay as an announcer, not a wrestler. But Randy felt he still had more to give in the ring.

The rumor mill, of course, had *other* ideas.

Fans began speculating that something had happened between Savage and a younger Stephanie McMahon years earlier. It was an accusation with no evidence, no witnesses, and no confirmation from anyone close to it. Still, the rumor spread.

People cited the supposed ban on Savage's name in WWE programming for years as evidence of Vince's supposed exile of Randy and his refusal to mention him by name.

WWE eventually made peace with top stars who had left on bad terms in the past, such as Ultimate Warrior, Hulk Hogan,

Bruno Sammartino, and even Bret Hart. They all came back, but Randy's relationship with the company stayed frozen longer until 2010.

Mattel released one of the first figures in their new toy partnership with WWE, with Randy Savage's defining moment from WrestleMania VII, with full gear and all.

A still photo of "Macho Man" Randy Savage with his first WWE action figure since Hasbro in the '90s, captured from fan video footage at the 2010 San Diego Comic-Con.

Randy even held it proudly and cut a promo for WWE. It looked as if Savage was near a WWE return. He even gave another promo on January 19, 2011, just four months before his passing, WWE All Stars, which released a video of what would be Randy Savage's last in-character promo.

———

I USED to talk to Lanny Poffo, Randy's brother—known to fans as "Leaping Lanny," who'd throw frisbees into the crowd while reciting poems before his matches. Later, as *The Genius*, he managed Mr. Perfect and the Beverly Brothers.

• • •

ONE MORNING IN 2009, while Lanny was in New York for a meet-and-greet, we met early in the hotel lobby for breakfast. Over small talk, I asked him about the rumor everyone wanted to know directly. I waited until I saw him in person, not on the phone.

He looked me straight in the eye without hesitation and said:

"I never had the balls to ask Randy that."

That line stuck with me—because it said everything.

Randy's own brother never asked him, according to Lanny, out of perhaps fear and respect. I honestly do not believe that, but I never pressed the issue. It was not Lanny's story to tell, even if he could confirm or deny it.

AFTER TALKING with Lanny on the phone throughout the next couple of months, I came close to securing a shoot interview with Randy, with Lanny's help. Lanny was my only hope.

Lanny was to receive $15,000 for his assistance.

He arranged a three-way call—the first, last, and only time I ever spoke directly to Randy Savage.

Before Lanny called, I asked him if he thought Randy would actually agree to an interview.

Lanny laughed and said, *"Andrew, I have fifteen thousand reasons for this shoot interview to happen!"*

I knew Lanny was doing everything he could to make it work.

Randy was quiet on the call, his tone calm but unreadable. His guard was up.

I told him I was a big fan of his as I worked up the courage to speak to him. Then, I hit him with it.

I OFFERED $125,000—THE second largest number I'd ever put on the table for a shoot interview. The highest was another story for another time.

The deal included one public appearance in New Jersey, where fans could meet Randy and have their items signed. Randy had no problem with my coming to Florida. Lanny told me Randy was too well-off and did not need to do appearances. I really wanted to bring him to New Jersey and make a weekend out of it.

I tried for three public appearances, but Randy agreed to one signing where he would sign in two separate blocks with a break in between. I knew if I secured Randy and was the first and only to get him for a public, the line would be too massive to handle in one setting or even just two to three hours. I would book Lanny with him, which I was already planning to do. Randy also said he appreciated that I thought of Lanny, and this could work.

The deal verbally was near complete—until Randy requested something that stopped me dead in my tracks—the dealbreaker.

FINAL CUT.

I COULDN'T AGREE to give Randy the final cut with the control to edit and cut the interview any way he wishes.

· · ·

HOW COULD A "SHOOT" interview be credible if the talent could erase footage of the questions everyone wanted answered, or tell other stories he later changed his mind about, especially if I am paying $125,000 for a then-DVD-style shoot interview?

I knew I needed to address that question once and for all to get people to buy the DVD if this investment was going to be successful.

I told Randy about the rumor—the one question everyone wanted to know, almost pleading with him.

Randy paused.

I thought he hung up the phone. I said, *"Hello?"*

"Go on and say it," Randy said calmly but in his Macho Man tone. He sounds like he did on television, by the way.

And, so I did. I asked about the Stephanie McMahon rumor and if he could address it on camera. I asked if he would be open to finally confirm, one way or another, his take on the widespread stories and rumors—whether they had any truth to them.

I want to end the rumor and be the guy who made it happen. And then I brought the phone closer to my ear.

He didn't give me anything—just silence.

Like a man holding his cards close, waiting for you to blink first. I learned right there that Randy Savage was a pro. Lanny felt the vibe and changed the subject.

But that quiet moment still gives me chills when I think about it—the pause so long it raised the hairs on the back of my neck.

That conversation happened on May 18, 2009. I remember it to this day because it was my friend Jay's birthday. I also graduated from college on May 18, 2003. The date has a lot of significance to me.

That interview could have ended the myth, but it never happened. I knew Lanny had done all he could—Randy was close to agreeing, but it was the final cut stipulation that killed it. I was more heartbroken when I learned Lanny had passed away due to Congestive Heart Failure on February 2, 2023.

Lanny was 68. The last time we spoke was sometime in 2022, when I reached out to find out when he would be in town so I could organize a private signing. He was living in Ecuador and having the time of his life.

I'll remember Lanny best for having *fifteen thousand reasons* for Randy to do the shoot interview with me. Lanny was indeed a poetic genius. Days after that three-way call between Lanny, Randy, and me, Lanny told me we'd try again down the line. I asked if perhaps I had screwed up this deal or if Randy was upset at me. Lanny said no, and I hope he wasn't trying to make me feel better. He said we would try again.

Unfortunately, Randy passed away on May 20, 2011, exactly two years and two days from the date I spoke to the "Macho Man" Randy Savage for the first, last, and only time.

Stephanie McMahon has never publicly commented on the rumor—and likely never will. But as they say in this business, *never say never*, right? Silence fuels the myth. Maybe there's nothing to say.

Maybe because, like her father, she understands that mystery—true or false—is part of wrestling's power. And maybe, in the most McMahon way possible, she knows that saying nothing keeps fans talking forever.

I did speak to Stephanie.

Not Stephanie McMahon, but Stephanie Bellars, who was the on-screen and off-screen girlfriend of Randy Savage while in WCW in 1999-2000 as the character "Georguos George." Before we began, I made it clear that nothing would be presented as fact—only as what she experienced and what she was told. She agreed immediately. *"Nobody really knows for sure,"* she told me. *"You're just going by what you were told. That's what I was told."* What she shared wasn't something she claimed to witness firsthand. It was something she said that came directly from Randy himself. *"Whether it's true or not... that's on him. I'm just telling you what he told me."* She explained she never even knew there was a rumor. *"I never heard it from anyone else. I heard it from him."*

According to Bellars, the conversation happened unexpectedly during a private moment. *"It just came up out of nowhere. We weren't even talking about anything like that."* She described being in the ocean at night when he brought it up. *"Randy told me they had connecting hotel rooms, and her room was next to his. She knocked, and he opened the door, and she came in. That's what he told me."* She was clear about her limits. *"I don't know when it happened. I know what he told me."* The next day, he backtracked according to Bellars. *"He asked me, 'Did I tell you anything?' I said, 'You told me enough.'"* Even then, she didn't know what to make of it. *"I believe what he told me, but I don't know what really happened."*

Bellars described Savage as someone she never viewed as predatory. *"I never got a bad feeling from him. It felt like he saw himself as younger than he really was."* But their relationship didn't end because of the rumor—it ended because of something personal. *"We broke up because of my sister,"* she said. According to Bellars, Savage suggested a living arrangement involving her and her sister that she found unacceptable. *"He thought it was a solution. I didn't see it that way."* At first, she thought it might have been a one-time situation. *"I thought maybe it was just because he wasn't in the right state."* But when he repeated it the next day, she realized it wasn't. *"That's when I knew it wasn't just a one-time thing."*

She ended the relationship with Randy.

She described that period as chaotic. *"There were moments where things got out of control. It started affecting people mentally."* She recalled her sister acting confused, doing things that didn't make sense. *"A lot was going on. It became constant."* She knew she had to leave. *"I couldn't live like that anymore."* She also described discovering what she believed were cameras connected to her home. *"He always seemed to know what I was doing. He would call and make comments that made it feel like he had been watching."* At first, she didn't understand it. *"I didn't know in the beginning."* But over time, she said it became clear something wasn't right. She described feeling isolated during wrestling events. *"There were times I was kept away from everyone else. People later told me they didn't even know I had a voice."* Even simple interactions became an issue. *"I felt like I was living in a bubble."* She also described a violent altercation. *"It was like two lions going at each other. No words—just fighting."* She said the scene was chaotic, with damage, and no one stepping in to stop it. *"Nobody stopped it. It was like a war."*

Bellars also described weekly visits to Savage's parents' home, where his father, Angelo, would administer steroid injections. She would sit downstairs while they were upstairs. *"We went there every week."* She said those visits created tension. *"There was always pressure on him."* The ride home was difficult. *"He would be hitting the steering wheel, yelling. I told him, 'You're going to have a heart attack.'"*

She also spoke about his relationship with his brother, Lanny Poffo. *"Randy wanted things done his way. Lanny was more of a free spirit. That caused tension."* She added that Lanny had said he was sometimes afraid of his older brother. An interesting detail involved the "Gorgeous George" name.

Savage acquired the rights during his WCW run. Initially, it was intended for Lanny Poffo, who even dyed his hair blonde in preparation, and reportedly was paid to stay home for an extended period while not being used. Eventually, the role went to Bellars. After the relationship ended, her life changed. Savage himself introduced her to Doyle from the Misfits. *"He's actually the one who introduced us."* They formed a relationship, married, and had a child together. *"We built a life and a family."*

IN THE END, Bellars returned to the same point. *"I only know what he told me. I didn't hear it from anyone else. Nobody really knows for sure."* Stephanie McMahon has never addressed the rumor publicly. Neither has Vince McMahon. And Randy Savage never answered it. I still think about that call. What if I had agreed to the final cut? Would we have gotten the truth? Or would it have been edited out? Randy Savage lived—and left—the business on his own terms. And maybe that's the only truth we'll ever have. Because in the end, the most powerful part of this story isn't what was said. It's what wasn't.

The same silence that made the rumor immortal also became one of wrestling's biggest urban tales and perhaps, for now, still unanswered.

CHAPTER 37

ROYAL RUMBLE'S MOST INFAMOUS RIB

"Crap in the crown!" - ...

EVERY WRESTLING LOCKER room has a rib and a story that refuses to die. But only one involves defecation, a crown, and thirty years of misplaced blame.

At the 1993 Royal Rumble, Jerry "The King" Lawler's crown was defiled while he was actively wrestling in the match.

The act was so grotesque, so personal, and so perfectly emblematic of the locker-room anarchy that it instantly became folklore. It didn't just *happen*—it metastasized, spreading like a disease.

And as most stories passed between wrestlers and fans, it eventually acquired a convenient villain.

Over time, the story took on a neat, modern scapegoat: The Kliq. But at the time of Royal Rumble '93, the Kliq—as fans later understood it—did not exist.

Triple H would not join the WWF until 1995.

Kevin Nash would not debut until the Spring of 1993 as Shawn Michaels' bodyguard—months after the '93 Rumble.

Shawn Michaels was the Intercontinental champion and in the early stages of his singles run.

The "Kliq did it" narrative is a retroactive rewrite—fans projecting later politics backward onto a locker room that hadn't yet consolidated power.

———

LAWLER ENTERED the Rumble at number seven and lasted roughly fourteen minutes.

If the crown was defiled while Lawler was in the ring—and every version of the story insists it was—then whoever did it had to be someone who was still backstage during Lawler's stretch.

And in that match, two key names weren't just *available*— they were positioned *perfectly* (pun intended).

Mr. Perfect entered at number ten.

Skinner entered at number eleven.

So while Lawler was already out there working, Curt Hennig and Steve Keirn were still in the back, still waiting, still with access to whatever a wrestler left behind when he went to the ring—like, for instance, a crown sitting in a bag.

Which is exactly why a rib like this had to be executed by the kind of people who already knew the rhythm backstage—who knew what they could get away with, and when.

In Bobby "The Brain" Heenan's book, Heenan said it was Steve Keirn (Skinner). And he didn't frame it as a rumor. He presented it as a locker-room fact. Keirn—working as Skinner—was the one who defecated in Lawler's crown.

For years, that was the story that circulated with the kind of certainty that only comes from wrestlers telling other wrestlers something they think will never leave the room.

BUT FOR THIS BOOK, the story stops being something people *say* and becomes something the person who did it actually *explains.*

The crowning, revealed by the guy who did it.

STEVE KEIRN, who wrestled as Skinner, told me Lawler was taking a lot of heat coming into the WWF at the time. Not casual heat—real heat. Lawler was the booker and promoter of Memphis, and a lot of those guys had long memories. Keirn named others who were part of that atmosphere, but asked me to leave them out of this book.

What matters is how the rib took shape, and who lit the fuse. Because, according to Keirn, this wasn't just one guy acting alone.

It was a rib born from a conversation—suggested by the man whose name belongs in the ribbing Hall of Fame, and who is covered in the next chapter. Mr. Fuji. Keirn said it plainly: *"Mr. Fuji loved me. He loved Curt. He's been my friend a long time."*

The way Keirn tells it, Lawler arrived and left his crown in his bag. The guys were debating what to do. Keirn thought the obvious play was too obvious—tired, predictable, the kind of "gotcha" that didn't have any staying power.

> *"Fuji looked at Curt and me after we were debating what to do,"* Keirn told me. *"I thought the padlock was stupid. Been done so many times. And Fuji said—'crap in the crown!'"*

That's the moment the story becomes more than an internet urban legend, because it explains its psychology.

A padlock is a nuisance. This was humiliation with intent—taking the literal emblem of "The King" and turning it into a toilet.

No investigation. No punishment. But Vince McMahon sent out a memo to the boys telling them that no more ribs are to be played on Lawler, and that no more defecating in Lawler's crown is allowed. Keirn confirms the memo, as well as another unnamed wrestler from that Royal Rumble in 1993.

Only pro wrestling could produce a sentence like that in official writing and then treat it as just another day at work.

No official reckoning that matched the act. That silence is not an accident—it's a snapshot of how the business operated then. The locker room didn't just tolerate things like this; it absorbed them and moved on.

Keirn's version also makes something else clear. This wasn't random. There was history here, the kind that makes a locker room rib feel "earned" to the people doing it—even when it's grotesque.

Keirn pointed out how long his relationship with Lawler had been and how blunt it could be. He gave me an example from years earlier—an ordinary life moment that still sounded like wrestling when he told it:

"Feb 7, 1984, my son was born, and I walked out on Lawler in Hendersonville. I told Lawler, 'I ain't going. Nobody listens to AM radio.' I'm celebrating my brand new son, he's my secondborn, Cory, who was born."

That's the tone of their world: family and business, love and resentment, life-changing events spoken about with the same rough edge as a locker-room argument. The relationship wasn't delicate. It didn't need to be. In that era, nothing was.

Keirn also confirmed the other piece that kept this legend alive long after the moment it stopped being a locker-room legend and became something you could buy in a bookstore.

Keirn told me Heenan "stooged" him out after twenty years. *"I told Bobby: Bobby, what the hell, man?"* Keirn said. *"Curt [Hennig] (Mr. Perfect) took the heat for years."*

Heenan said, *"I thought everyone knew already!"*

There's no way to tell this story without acknowledging what it says about that era. A locker room where power was informal, pranks were weapons, and humiliation passed for humor.

But wrestling changed. And so did Keirn.

In the years since, he has trained hundreds of performers who now headline major promotions worldwide—including Roman Reigns, Sheamus, Drew McIntyre, and countless others. And despite the history, Keirn later spoke to Lawler with real compassion—especially after the tragedy. When Lawler's son Brian Christopher passed away, Keirn told me he felt nothing but love for Brian and sorrow for Jerry Lawler:

> *"When he died, I saw Lawler with JR (Jim Ross) at a show, and I said, 'I really loved your son, man. He was a good man. When he smiled, I smiled. I am sorry for your loss."*

That doesn't sanitize the rib. And, it doesn't rewrite 1993 into something kinder than it was. It just reminds you that people aren't frozen in their worst impulses forever.

And maybe that's the most wrestling part of this whole story: the same business that can turn a man's crown into a toilet can also turn around years later and leave you standing face-to-face with grief, with no punchline left—only what's real.

CHAPTER 38
THE MASTER OF RIBS

BY THE TIME he walked into a locker room, the rules were already understood—spoken or not.

You didn't fall asleep. You didn't touch his food.

And you *never*, ever ribbed him back.

His reputation as the most feared prankster and ribber in professional wrestling wasn't born of one infamous incident, but of decades of accumulation, carried quietly from territory to territory and reinforced by the one thing he never did: deny a story.

Silence was his greatest ally.

What emerges from the men who knew him best—through

shoot interviews, podcasts, reunion panels, and firsthand testimony.

FROM DON MURACO, Larry Zbyszko, Tony Atlas, Savio Vega, the Bushwhackers, Kato, Tito Santana, Hillbilly Jim, S.D. Jones and others are not cartoon villains, but deeply intelligent, observant, old-school veterans who understood hierarchy, patience, and fear better than almost anyone in the business.

MR. FUJI DIDN'T RIB to be funny. Mr. Fuji ribbed to establish control.

"Fuji was funny as hell," Zbyszko said, *"but you had to know the rules. You didn't fall asleep."* Zbyszko recalled Fuji's infamous "hot foot" prank—taping a piece of clothing and briefly lighting it to wake someone up—calling it the worst rib he had personally witnessed Fuji pull. The rib itself wasn't what frightened people. *"If Fuji ribbed you and you laughed, it was over,"* Zbyszko explained. *"If you ribbed him back? Oh no. Then it was on. And you didn't want that."* Fuji, Zbyszko emphasized, always re-ribbed.

BUTCH OF THE BUSHWHACKERS, recounted an incident with his cousin Luke years ago. He said that during a match against the Powers of Pain in New Haven, Fuji slipped behind him on the floor and quietly attached a heavy metal padlock through the belt loop of his trousers. *"I didn't know it was there,"* Butch said.

Seconds later, he was thrown back into the ring and picked up for a slam. The padlock drove violently into his lower back, and he exited the ring instantly—no selling, no theatrics, pure instinct.

Years later, Butch laughed and said, "That's the only rib Fuji ever really got me with." The Bushwackers said they were very popular in the locker room and had seen much worse with the ribs, but this was the only time.

KATO of the Orient Express told a different story in an interview about his WWF run, particularly about his time when Pat Tanaka was injured, so the WWF paired Fuji with him as a replacement against The Rockers in San Antonio.

Kato realized he was watching something calculated. Fuji insisted on starting with Marty Jannetty, chopping him stiffly and beating him down before pausing to bow mockingly to the crowd.

On the second bow, Jannetty retaliated by pulling Fuji's tights down. Toilet paper spilled out, and the building erupted. "The place lost it," Kato recalled. What looked like Jannetty getting even had been Fuji's setup all along.

Fuji never reacted. He never acknowledged it. That silence, Kato said, was the real joke.

———

DON MURACO HAS RECOUNTED many ribs on his own podcast, which ran nearly 50 episodes from 2021 to 2022. During a brutal Buffalo winter, Muraco borrowed Moondog Spot's rental car to grab food. Fuji, who disliked Spot, noticed the opportunity and seized it.

Overnight, Fuji convinced a snowplow operator to completely bury the car, piling snow on top and hosing it down until it froze solid. *"The car was just gone,"* Muraco said.

POLICE REPORTS WERE FILED. Rental agencies were alerted, and weeks turned into months.

When the snow finally melted, the car was revealed exactly where it had been parked. Fuji never admitted anything. He didn't need to.

———

WHEN I SPOKE to Tony Atlas over dinner years ago, he loved to talk and share stories. Mr Fuji came up. Atlas said Fuji did not like Salvatore Bellomo. *"Brother, he ribbed him so bad!"* Atlas described combination locks attached to jackets to set off airport alarms, clothing chained together so Bellomo couldn't dress, and constant humiliation. *"Everybody knew it was Fuji,"* Atlas said. *"And nobody said a word."* Bellomo never retaliated. The locker-room code ensured silence.

Food became Fuji's favorite weapon because it required patience. Muraco, Savio Vega, and others have described how Fuji traveled everywhere with tuna sandwiches, and when wrestlers repeatedly stole them, he altered the contents. He never explained. He only smiled and said, *"This is what meat tastes like."* Stories circulated for decades about barbecues in Puerto Rico, New Jersey, and Hawaii—some involving laxatives, others involving shocking reveals after the meal.

———

HILLBILLY JIM RECOUNTED one of the most infamous stories during an interview with Hannibal, carefully naming witnesses while withholding the identity of the victim. *"Don Muraco was there,"* Jim said. *"And Fuji tells Muraco, 'Tonight is a special night. We are going to have teriyaki."*

According to Jim, Fuji instructed Muraco not to eat from one specific dish and quietly served him a different plate. An unnamed wrestler—described as someone who owed Fuji money and refused to pay—ate the meal enthusiastically and praised Fuji's cooking. *"You're a great cook, Fuji,"* Jim recalled the man saying.

Fuji then stood up, went into the kitchen, lifted the garbage can lid, and revealed what Jim described as the head of the man's dog. Within days, Jim noted, the man disappeared from the territory as the story circulated through the locker room.

———

ONE EXPLICIT, firsthand account of Fuji's ribs came from S.D. Jones told, publicly and on the record, during WrestleMania XX weekend at a Fan Slam convention in Totowa, New Jersey, promoted by Tommy Fierro.

S.D. Jones framed the story not as legend, but as lived experience. *"I kept telling Fuji, 'Brother, stay away from my stomach,"* Jones said, explaining that he had spent an entire day eating and drinking heavily with Fuji at Fuji's insistence. *"I wasn't feeling good. I said it over and over."* That night, Jones had a scheduled match involving Fuji. Back in the locker room, he politely warned Fuji again to go easy. Fuji smiled and told him not to worry.

During the match, Jones recalled, Fuji went straight after his stomach—multiple chops, followed by a bodyslam—then slowly walked over, stood above him, squatted, and dropped all of his weight directly onto Jones's abdomen. *"That was it,"* Jones said, acting out the moment as the room erupted in laughter.

The panelists beside him laughed hardest of all, recognizing exactly what had happened. This wasn't a rumor. It was the victim telling the story himself, publicly, decades later.

———

AT THE BREAKFAST of Champions panel during Wrestle Reunion 2011, with Fuji seated in the room, Savio Vega told Fuji stories directly to a live audience. *"Uncle (Mr. Fuji) knew every road,"* Savio said, describing Fuji's uncanny sense of direction. When Savio joked about Fuji's ribs, Fuji didn't deny them. He listened. He smiled. He said nothing.

———

NOT EVERYONE FEARED MR. FUJI. Tito Santana told me Fuji never ribbed him—not once. *"Mr. Fuji was a mentor to me,"* Santana explained. *"He helped me a lot during my Intercontinental run. He taught me a lot. I think that's why he never ribbed me."*

BY THE LATE 1980S, ribbing in the WWF—much of it attributed to Mr. Fuji—had escalated beyond what the company could ignore.

VINCE MCMAHON ORDERED a mandatory meeting in Connecticut at an undisclosed hotel, according to the Bushwackers.

The message was blunt and unprecedented: no more serious ribs. Any rib deemed excessive would result in heavy fines or termination. It wasn't aimed at one individual alone, but everyone in the room knew why the meeting was happening.

The culture didn't change overnight. Wrestlers would always rib. But the era of unchecked, dangerous pranks was officially over. Even the king of ribs had finally forced the office's hand.

MR. FUJI WAS INDUCTED into the WWE Hall of Fame in 2007 and fell asleep on stage. Maybe we all fell asleep on the master of the pranks and ribs. Because what remains is not just a collection of pranks, but a portrait of a locker room that governed itself through fear, respect, and silence—until it no longer could.

CHAPTER 39

O.J. SIMPSON AT WRESTLEMANIA

I don't believe O. J. Simpson is innocent! -
Roddy Piper

IN EARLY 1996, while America was still arguing about the verdict in the most televised trial in modern history, professional wrestling nearly tied itself directly to it. O. J. Simpson had been acquitted only months earlier. The country was split in half. Cameras followed him everywhere. Every public appearance drew reaction — applause from some, outrage from others, protests from many.

At the same time, the WWF was entering open warfare with WCW. Ratings mattered. Headlines mattered more. The company had been on the verge of financial collapse barely a year earlier. Sponsorships and corporate relationships weren't optional — they were oxygen.

If something generated mainstream buzz, it was worth at least discussing. And so, inside creative, a dangerous idea surfaced: put Roddy Piper in the ring at WrestleMania XII with O.J. Simpson.

The pitch reportedly originated in a creative meeting, with Vince Russo throwing the concept onto the table. Producer Bruce Prichard later acknowledged that the idea was serious enough to explore. Prichard personally called Piper and floated it.

Piper didn't hesitate. He was in. Early conversations even took place with Simpson's representatives, who were actively fielding offers. From a strictly business standpoint, the timing lined up. Piper was returning to television. Simpson was seeking income. WrestleMania needed attention.

On television, Piper began referencing Simpson in his promos — speaking about right and wrong in America and declaring he had returned to straighten things out. It wasn't random. The groundwork was being laid.

> *"You know, I started when I was 15 years old. I can feel the ring, I can put up posters, and I know how to tell the truth! I don't believe that Michael Jackson is innocent! I don't believe O. J. Simpson is innocent! And I don't believe Vader is innocent! And I think they all need to be taken care of! And how do you take care of 'em? The Prez walks in, because you know what? It's a heck of a lot easier to jump on me than it is to jump on the truth!"*

The match was reportedly slotted in the fourth position on the WrestleMania card — not the main event, but high enough to dominate headlines. The creative direction was simple: one night only. Piper wins decisively. The audience gets a sense of payoff. Internally, some believed letting Piper "handle" Simpson in the ring would feel like justice to a portion of the audience — that controversy could be converted into catharsis.

From a pay-per-view standpoint, it probably would have worked. It might have increased buys for one night.

But this was 1996. The WWF had barely stabilized financially. Simpson couldn't even go golfing without large groups of protesters surrounding the course. Every public appearance triggered outrage. Attaching that volatility to a national wrestling broadcast wouldn't have been simple storyline heat.

It would have been reputational damage. Between Hollywood contacts, advertisers, and corporate partners, it reportedly became clear: if the company went forward with it, sponsors would walk.

This wasn't a wrestling controversy.

This was corporate suicide.

The WWF at the time was willing to test almost anything. It aired skits mocking Ted Turner as Billionaire Ted. It parodied Hulk Hogan (The Huckster), Randy Savage (The Nacho Man), and Gene Okerlund (Scheme Gene). That was the creative climate — try it on, see if it fits, push the envelope. The Billionaire Ted sketches even wrapped up on the WrestleMania XII preshow in a quick, throwaway "let's move on" fashion.

But the O.J. Simpson match wasn't meant to be filler. It was planned as a special attraction with the Hot Rod.

And then the envelope pushed back.

Before contracts were signed and before any official announcement was made, the idea was scrapped.

The WWF didn't abandon shock.

It redirected it.

Instead of Simpson, Piper faced Goldust in the now-infamous Hollywood Backlot Brawl at WrestleMania XII — a pre-taped fight shot weeks earlier at Universal Studios.

Goldust had his own WrestleMania plans altered. He was originally scheduled to wrestle Razor Ramon, but Scott Hall reportedly felt uncomfortable with aspects of the Goldust character and was sent home. During the 1996 Slammy Awards, Shawn Michaels referenced Hall sitting at home without mentioning him by name.

The Backlot Brawl became the substitute spectacle.

Throughout the WrestleMania broadcast, the company cut repeatedly to what was presented as live footage of Piper chasing Goldust through the backlot — mirroring the now-infamous Bronco chase from the Simpson case. Goldust drove a gold Cadillac. Piper pursued him relentlessly. The segments aired throughout the night, building anticipation and blurring the line between taped and live production. The chase ultimately culminated as the second-to-last match before the Iron Man main event between Michaels and Bret Hart.

The fight itself was chaotic. Piper blasted Goldust with a fire hose, smashed the Cadillac window with a baseball bat — slicing his own hand in the process — and hurled Goldust into a steel dumpster that didn't budge, leaving him legitimately concussed. Later, at Goldust's request, Piper attempted to bust him open the hard way. The second punch broke Piper's hand.

The segment even included a white Bronco parody — close enough to the Simpson imagery that everyone understood the reference without it being spoken. As the fight spilled into the arena, Goldust stripped down to reveal women's undergarments beneath his ring gear, amplifying the character's provocative persona and adding another layer of shock to a night already leaning heavily into boundary-pushing imagery. By pivoting to Goldust, the WWF managed to keep its edge without igniting a corporate wildfire. The controversy stayed within the controlled chaos of wrestling.

But the O.J. story didn't die there. Years later, when Russo was head of creative in WCW, Simpson's name surfaced again. In a July 20, 2017 report for *The Sporting News*, Kevin Eck — then editor of *WCW Magazine* in 2000 — detailed how Russo pushed for WCW to pay Simpson millions to take a live lie detector test on pay-per-view. The idea was based on Simpson publicly stating he would take a polygraph test on pay-per-view for $3 million, supposedly to fund a reward to find the "real" killer. Simpson later indicated he would keep the money himself.

According to Eck, during a company meeting, Russo acknowledged that "Monday Nitro" ratings were struggling but insisted it wasn't a creative problem. The content was great, he argued — viewers weren't watching to realize it. WCW needed a publicity stunt. That's when he pitched the Simpson polygraph. Two different companies. Two different moments. Same lightning rod.

Neither plan materialized. The O.J. WrestleMania match lives on because it feels plausible. In 1996, wrestling was flirting with reality more than ever. Shock was a strategy. Attention was survival. For a moment, WrestleMania XII nearly became something far bigger — and far messier — than a wrestling show.

Instead, the company backed off the edge. And in this case, that restraint may have been the smartest move they could have made.

CHAPTER 40
STING MONEY

THERE ARE VERY few phrases that carry weight the moment they're spoken. Some words don't need explanation. Some terms don't need footnotes. They have meaning simply because of what they represent.

"Sting money."

It became the measuring stick. The gold standard. The number every top wrestler chased.

If you made Sting money, you had made it. You were a star. You had leverage. You had arrived.

Much like "Road Warrior pop" wasn't just a loud reaction — it was the measuring stick for how loud a building could get. In the locker room, you didn't say, "That was a huge reaction." You said, "That was a Road Warrior pop."

And you didn't say, "That's a strong deal." You said, "That's Sting money." Both phrases became industry shorthand.

To understand why "Sting money" carried that kind of weight, you have to understand what wrestling pay looked like before it existed. Before guaranteed contracts, wrestling was a gambler's business. You didn't sign multi-year security deals. You got booked for dates — sometimes ten dates at $150 a pop if you were lucky. You drove yourself. You paid for your own gas. You covered your own hotel and food expenses. If the town drew well, you did well. If it didn't, your paycheck reflected it immediately. If a territory collapsed, you packed your bags and hoped another promoter had space for you. There was no safety net. A contract often meant little more than a handshake.

Then Ted Turner entered the wrestling business, and it all started in World Championship Wrestling in the early 1990s. When WCW became a national promotion with real corporate backing, the model changed overnight.

Wrestlers could sign legitimate guaranteed contracts — paid whether the building sold out or not, paid if they were hurt, paid if creative plans changed. That kind of stability was revolutionary in a business built on uncertainty.

And at the center of that system stood Sting.

By the early 1990s, Sting was WCW's franchise player — their homegrown hero, their constant. While Ric Flair was the legend and Dusty Rhodes the architect, Sting was the future — the man the company was built around.

Open any WCW program, marketing piece, or arena guide from the late 1980s through the 1990s, and Sting was there: face paint, blond hair, colorful gear — later the black-and-white Crow: different looks, same role.

WCW was built around the Stinger.

Reportedly earning around $750,000 per year, fully guaranteed in the early 1990s, Sting's contract was life-changing money at a time when most wrestlers still depended heavily on the gate. It wasn't just big — it reset expectations.

Agents didn't ask about the pay scale. They asked, "What's Sting making?" If you were in that tier, you were protected. If you weren't, you were chasing it.

Eric Bischoff later confirmed that Sting and Lex Luger were already earning top-tier guaranteed deals before Nitro, before the nWo, before WCW was even profitable. There were tiers. "Sting money" was the top one.

When Kevin Nash and Scott Hall left the WWF for WCW in 1996, they signed multi-year guaranteed contracts reportedly at roughly the same level Sting had established years earlier, complete with favored-nations clauses. Adjusted for inflation, those deals would be roughly double in today's dollars.

The favored-nations protection meant that if someone new entered at a higher number, anyone already protected automatically rose to match it. When Bret Hart arrived in 1997, it lifted the entire top tier overnight. Later renegotiations with Goldberg had similar ripple effects.

By the late 1990s, WCW's payroll ballooned. Main-eventers made millions. Mid-carders made six figures. Even enhancement talent earned more than many top stars had made just a decade earlier. And it all traced back to that original benchmark — Sting's deal proving that a wrestler could be treated like a franchise investment rather than a traveling attraction.

When others left — when Flair jumped back and forth, when Dusty came and went — Sting stayed. And had he left during those fragile years between 1989 and 1992, many believe WCW might not have survived.

I asked that question directly.

On the afternoon of WrestleMania 35 at MetLife Stadium, at a Topps Transcendent VIP event limited to about fifty guests, Sting sat quietly in a small room wearing sunglasses — reserved and humble, exactly as you'd expect.

When it was time for Q&A, I didn't hesitate and asked him in front of the fifty of us and WWE and Topps staff, what fans had debated for decades—if he had jumped to the WWF between 1989 and 1992, would WCW have survived?

Before Sting could answer, Ric Flair, sitting next to him, jumped in and said, *"No way."*

Sting smiled and said little. He never needed to sell himself. The 16-time World champion and others did that for him.

That moment said everything. WCW without Sting wasn't WCW. That's why his contract became legendary.

Ironically, his greatest drawing power may have come when he wasn't even wrestling. In September 1996, Sting transformed from the colorful Surfer into the silent Crow. He stopped speaking. He stood in the rafters. And for over a year — from WarGames '96 to Starrcade '97 — he didn't wrestle a single match.

Yet he remained WCW's most popular star. Every building erupted when he appeared. Even while collecting guaranteed money, Sting remained the face of the company.

In a business known for broken promises and missed paydays, Sting had something almost no wrestler ever had.

Security.

Then the industry shifted again.

During the Attitude Era, contracts still included downside guarantees — often in the $500,000 to $1 million range for top stars — but the real money was in the upside. House show percentages, pay-per-view bonuses, and merchandise royalties could push earnings into astronomical territory if business were hot. No one embodied that better than Stone Cold Steve Austin.

When pay-per-view buy rates soared and "Austin 3:16" shirts became cultural staples, his income reportedly climbed into the seven-figure range. "Austin money" wasn't just a guarantee — it was what happened when the business exploded, and you were the face of it.

But in the 2010s, another transformation quietly took place.

With the launch of the WWE Network in 2014, traditional pay-per-view bonuses largely disappeared. Revenue models shifted from buy-rate-driven to subscription-based and, eventually, to billion-dollar media rights deals. House shows became less central to profitability. As predictable television money replaced volatile gate revenue, contracts evolved again.

The modern pivot can arguably be traced to Brock Lesnar's 2012 return to WWE. His contract reportedly centered on a set number of dates and a guaranteed amount of money. He wasn't grinding five nights a week on the road.

Lesnar was and still is a premium attraction, paid elite rates to appear at major events. It was less about upside bonuses and more about leverage and controlled workload.

"Brock money" represented something different: elite guarantees tied to limited appearances. Over time, that structure spread more broadly across top-tier contracts.

As pay-per-view bonuses faded and media rights revenue soared, flat guarantees became larger and more standardized.

So if "Sting money" defined the guaranteed era, and "Austin money" defined the explosive upside era, then "Brock money" defines the modern attraction era — high guarantees, controlled dates, premium positioning.

Professional wrestling's internal language has always reflected its peaks. "Road Warrior pop" marked the reaction ceiling. "Sting money" marked the guaranteed salary ceiling. "Austin money" marked the upside explosion. "Brock money" marks the era of leverage.

From ten dates at $150 a pop to seven-figure guarantees.

From hoping the gate was strong to negotiating how many dates you're willing to work. The business model varies, and the revenue streams changed. The contracts evolved.

But the shorthand remained. Because in wrestling, when something reaches the absolute top tier — whether it's sound or salary — it doesn't just become big.

It becomes a phrase.

And for a generation of wrestlers chasing security in an uncertain business, one phrase said it all:

"Is it Sting money?"

CHAPTER 41

STARRCADE 1997

"I Feel Like They Were Setting Me Up to Be the Fall Guy." – Nick Patrick

FOR YEARS, fans have argued about the moment that killed WCW.

Some point to the Fingerpoke of Doom. Others blame Bill Goldberg's first loss, Vince Russo's booking, or David Arquette's win over Goldberg for the World Heavyweight Championship. Those moments mattered—but they were accelerants, not the fire.

WCW ended in March 2001, but the countdown to WCW's demise began at their biggest show on **December 28, 1997**. That night—Starrcade 1997—WCW drew the largest buy rate in company history—roughly 700,000 buys and more than 17,500 fans at the MCI Center in Washington, D.C.

Fifteen months of storytelling led to one image: Hollywood Hogan standing across the ring from Sting's silent reckoning.

. . .

IT WAS the most organically built main event WCW ever produced. And WCW blinked.

The build was nearly flawless. After being falsely accused of joining the nWo at Fall Brawl 1996, Sting walked out on WCW and disappeared. He didn't wrestle for over a year. He said nothing. He watched from the rafters while an nWo Sting imposter destroyed his credibility.

WCW turned on him. Sting responded by becoming something else entirely—black-and-white, silent, patient.

By March 1997, he revealed his allegiance by attacking the nWo and pointing his bat directly at Hulk Hogan. The collision was inevitable.

Throughout 1997, WCW didn't cool off—it surged. Nitro dominated the ratings. Lex Luger reached peak popularity. Bill Goldberg began his undefeated streak. Bret Hart arrived fresh off the Montreal Screwjob.

At Starrcade, WCW even used Bret correctly—first. As special referee in the Eric Bischoff vs. Larry Zbyszko match, Bret teased joining the nWo, then turned, punching Bischoff and putting Scott Hall in the Sharpshooter.

The crowd erupted. WCW retained control of Nitro. Bret looked like a hero. Then came the match that mattered.

During a live Q&A at one Starrcast, Sting, speaking to Tony Shavione on stage, admitted a year-long plan existed—and that on the day of the show, it stopped being the plan.

"We had a plan... and that day, suddenly, it wasn't in motion like it was anymore," Sting said. *"Lots of changes. Lots of behind-the-scenes meetings. And I don't believe our match followed the buildup."*

He explained professionally and more diplomatically than anyone else that they didn't truly know the finish until they walked through the curtain.

"If we had just stayed with the game plan... everything would have been different."

What followed was confusion disguised as complexity.

NICK PATRICK ARRIVED KNOWING he was officiating the most important match in WCW history. Eric Bischoff initially told him the count would be normal.

Later, Hogan privately instructed Patrick to count slowly. Sting separately told him to count fast. The most critical step never happened.

"They never got us together," Patrick said. *"Not Hulk, Sting, Eric, and me. Not once. Ever."*

Patrick searched for Bischoff all day and couldn't find him. Hogan had his own locker room. Sting had his own understanding. Patrick was left alone to make the call.

So he split the difference.

"I really felt like they were setting me up," Patrick said. *"I thought if everything went south, it'd be easy to say Patrick didn't do what he was told."*

The count landed neither fast nor slow. Hogan celebrated. Bret Hart ran in. The finish was muddled. The moment was lost.

Then came the coronation that wasn't.

After fifteen months of silence, WCW handed Sting a

microphone. The locker room flooded the ring. The celebration should have sealed the era.

Instead, Sting looked into the camera and blurted a single word:

"Mamacita."

That was it. The mystique evaporated. The silent avenger became human, awkward, unclear. The character WCW had protected for over a year, cracked in seconds.

"That was the top moment for our business," Sting later said. *"And it didn't land the way it should have."*

ERIC BISCHOFF later defended the decision-making—but in doing so, revealed the real problem.

"There's a saying," he said. *"A camel is a horse created by committee. That's what that finish was."*

And then WCW made the worst possible move.

The very next night on Nitro, WCW gave away Sting versus Hogan for free—not as a celebration, but as damage control. The match didn't even finish. Fans were told to tune in later to Thunder, a new two-hour midweek live show that WCW added, a move Eric Bischoff opposed. Overexposure on weekly television would overexpose talent.

After paying for the biggest pay-per-view in company history, audiences were denied a finish twice in forty-eight hours.

Belief broke. From that point on, WCW borrowed momentum rather than creating it.

The Fingerpoke of Doom—where Hogan poked Kevin Nash —wasn't the cause. It was confirmation. The same Nitro featured Tony Schiavone spoiling Mick Foley's WWF title win —only to watch millions switch channels anyway.

WCW had already lost the audience's trust.

Goldberg's loss. Russo. Arquette. They didn't start the fire.

They were what happens after conviction is gone.

Meanwhile, WWF surged. Mike Tyson appeared at WrestleMania 14. The Attitude Era ignited. Momentum shifted permanently.

WCW didn't collapse overnight.

But on its biggest stage—when it needed clarity most—it chose uncertainty.

Starrcade 1997 was supposed to be WCW's coronation. Instead, it was the night the company proved it no longer knew how to land its own success.

Not with a bang but with confusion.

AND ONCE THAT trust was gone, everything that followed was just borrowed time.

CHAPTER 42

THE SABOTAGE OF BRET "HITMAN" HART

"Hogan was the puppet master pulling all the strings." - Bret Hart.

WHEN BRET HART arrived in WCW in December 1997, he was the hottest free agent in wrestling history. A year earlier, he had been heavily pursued and ultimately chose to stay and sign a 20-year contract with the WWF, becoming the highest-paid WWF superstar at the time. A year later, everything had changed.

Vince McMahon told Bret in August that he couldn't afford to pay him what he promised him and that he should negotiate with WCW. Bret was having his best year in the ring. His series of matches in 1997, from the iconic I Quit match against Steve Austin at WrestleMania 13 to SummerSlam with The Undertaker, and throughout the year with Shawn Michaels, The Patriot, Sid, Vader, and others, were some of his best.

But Bret had just gotten screwed for the title in Montreal and came into WCW with massive momentum. He had become the most talked-about wrestler in the world.

WCW signed him to a massive contract, reportedly worth $9–$10 million over three years. From a business standpoint, it made no sense to sabotage a man you just signed for $2.5–$3 million per year. Yet from the moment he arrived, his debut became a subject of debate among fans and insiders for one simple reason: WCW, whether intentional or not, buried The Hitman.

When I asked Bret who he wanted to work with when he arrived in WCW, there was no hesitation. *"For me, it was a natural to book me with Hogan."* Hulk Hogan. They had never truly worked a meaningful program in WWF during Bret's prime, and WCW was the perfect reset. Hogan was a heel. Bret could arrive as the wronged babyface. It wrote itself. *"I always thought I could give Hogan the match he never had,"* Bret told me. "A great working-style match with a technical kind of wrestler." There was no ego in it. No bitterness.

Just professional conviction. "I thought I could really do great stuff with Hogan. Maybe even catapult him even higher. I thought I could be good for him — and good for myself." Then he said something revealing. *"No one will ever know what kind of match me and Hogan could have had. But I would have had my heart in the right place. I wanted to deliver."* That's the key. He didn't go to WCW bitterly. He went motivated. *"I wanted to show everyone. I wanted to show Vince what they lost when they screwed me over."* And then something even more telling: *"I came in with kind of a clean slate. I was not very judgmental of WCW."*

After Montreal, Bret says he made a personal decision. *"I told myself I'll never take the wrestling business too seriously again. Whatever they want me to do in WCW — they just paid me an exorbitant fee — I'll do whatever they ask without complaining."* He was done with politics. *"No more politics for me. I don't give a shit what you do with me. Just use me to your best advantage. I'm ready to play ball."*

Instead, the phone call came with the first sign of dysfunction. Not for Hogan. Not for a debut feud or for a long-term build. They wanted him to referee—Eric Bischoff versus Larry Zbyszko, with control of Monday Nitro on the line. *"Referee?"* Bret said to me. *"It's really lame. It's an idea that's been done a million times before. It's not very original."* He knew instantly it didn't elevate him. *"You're not really getting any benefit out of me if you're just using me as a referee."* But he had made a promise to himself—no politics—so he did it.

What happened next is still debated. As discussed in the previous chapter, the plan was for referee Nick Patrick to execute a fast count to reinforce the corrupt Hogan narrative. Instead, a regular count. One. Two. Three. *"I remember jumping in the ring and going, 'It's a fast count!' — and it wasn't."* Bret didn't sugarcoat how it felt. *"I thought the whole thing sucked badly. I was embarrassed that that was my debut."* The hottest free agent in wrestling history, and his debut was a source of confusion.

A year into WCW, Bret says he finally understood what he hadn't seen clearly at first. *"I didn't really understand until maybe a year later that Hogan was calling all the shots."* He didn't mince words. *"Hogan was the puppet master pulling all the strings without anyone knowing it."* Bret described a contract structure where Eric Bischoff couldn't force Hogan into anything. *"He could approve or disapprove of anything anytime he wanted. And that was the end of it."*

He was blunt about Bischoff, too. *"Bischoff was pretending to be in charge and pretending to be a really smart, savvy booker like Vince was."* But behind the curtain? *"He had absolutely no business being a booker of anything. He had no idea. No brains for booking."* Then came the operational chaos. *"They would fly me down to TV on Monday night, and I'd spend the whole afternoon waiting to find out who I was wrestling."* And sometimes? *"They'd tell me at quarter to eight that I was off. You've flown down for nothing. You're flying home tomorrow."* Bret got paid, but he kept coming back to one thought: *"All that airfare, the hotel, my car rental — all paid for by Turner. And I just thought, what a waste of money."*

Bret's first WCW pay-per-view appearance came at Starrcade — WCW's WrestleMania. Starrcade began in 1983, a full year and a half before the birth of WrestleMania. One month after Montreal. The biggest show of the year. The most watched event in company history. And Bret Hart walked out as a referee. *"Referee? ... It's really lame."* The angle they placed him in was already overbooked, and instead of being positioned as the hottest star in the world, Bret was reduced to a prop.

"Why would you take me now — when I've come from WWE as hot as I am — and just beat me?" He made clear it wasn't about ego. He liked Booker T. *"I had a lot of respect for him. I looked forward to working with him."* But he couldn't understand the logic. *"Why would you pin me in the middle of the ring when I haven't been beaten in four or five years on TV by anybody? There's no booking. No rematch. No reason why we're wrestling."* Bischoff gave him the explanation, and it said everything about WCW's mindset: *"You just have to go out there and do a job for Booker T so I can prove to everybody that you're a businessman — that you're gonna cooperate."*

Bret's response was immediate. *"Are you really kidding me? What have I not cooperated on?"* Bret says Bischoff pushed a narrative that he didn't have fire anymore. *"He said I didn't have fire that I was brokenhearted. That I didn't have the right heart anymore."* Bret's reply was blunt: *"That is such horses**t. I showed up wanting to do business."*

He tried to pivot into what should have been obvious: put him with the best workers. *"I begged them to put me with Rey Mysterio and Eddie Guerrero. Every time I came up with anybody — Rey, Eddie, Sting — they'd give me the weakest reasons."* Bret would approach the wrestlers first, and they were open to it. *"They'd say, 'Oh, I'd love it.'"* Then Bret would go to Bischoff and get: *"You can't work with him because it's Friday... or it's Monday..."*

Bret said the excuses weren't even logical. And that's when confusion hardened into something else. ***"After a while, you start to realize that it's sabotage."*** That word wasn't mine. It was his. *"They brought me in to beat me up and pin me and get over anybody they could. To humiliate me and lower my value so I didn't mean anything."*

The greatest example was Toronto. When Bret returned to Canada for the first time since leaving the WWF, Maple Leaf Gardens was sold out. Twenty thousand inside. Five thousand more outside in subzero temperatures, chanting his name. *"Hitman! Hitman!"* Bret recalled hearing it and seeing the crowd awaiting his arrival. It should have been the greatest hit of the many misses of his WCW run. Instead, WCW tried to sabotage it, according to many fans, including Bret Hart.

Eric Bischoff wanted Bret to turn heel on his own country. The promo was written for him. *"What have you done for me lately? You (fans) guys haven't done s*** for me."* *"Kiss my ass,"* Bret recalled being told to say, and he knew instantly what it meant. Turning on his most loyal fanbase in his home country. Bret refused. It was Career suicide.

That same day, when Bret arrived at the building, he was told Bill Goldberg didn't want to do the finish that had been agreed on months earlier by Bret and Bill—the steel plate and the spear. But backstage politics got to Goldberg, according to Bret.

Goldberg reportedly was told the angle would kill his momentum, even though his streak had ended by the booker, Kevin Nash, six months earlier. Bret went directly to Goldberg and reminded him they had agreed to it months earlier. After much convincing, Bret says Goldberg calmed down and agreed.

Then Bischoff added another layer of insanity. After Bret knocks out Goldberg, Hulk Hogan's music would hit. Hogan would come to the ring. They would tease with a high-five, and Hogan would jump Bret and leave him lying there. No Hogan match. No Goldberg match. Just Hogan inserting himself into Bret's moment. Bret told Bischoff it was idiotic. Why bring Hogan out if there was no program? The answer told Bret everything: *"You have to clear it with Hogan."* That was who ran WCW. After the angle, Curt Hennig told Bret what happened backstage. Bischoff was running through the halls screaming at Goldberg to get to the ring faster — because Bret was *"killing him off."*

Even Bret's entrance gear was political. He wore a Hitman hockey jersey over a Toronto Maple Leafs jersey. He knew if Bischoff saw it, he'd make him change it — because WCW didn't want him getting too big a reaction. WCW had another chance to fix its mistake. They didn't take it. When Bret returned on Monday Nitro at the Georgia Dome, he spoke about his brother Owen. He spoke about loss. He spoke about his future. It was real. It was emotional. The audience was with him. It was the moment WCW could have rebuilt

Bret Hart as the heart of the company. They did nothing with it.

Then came Kansas City. Kemper Arena. The same city. The same building. Where Owen Hart had tragically died, after Owen's death, Bret pitched something deeply personal: a tribute match in that building against Chris Benoit. It made sense. Bret said the match was approved earlier in the week, but by the time he arrived in Kansas City, it had been scrubbed. *"They said it didn't make any sense to have a match between Benoit and me on Nitro."* It wasn't Bret who saved it. Bret told me it was Benoit. *"It was Benoit who went in and pleaded for the match."* Only then was it reinstated. The result became the highest-rated segment of Nitro that night, over twenty minutes, with Harley Race present in an official capacity—a match Bret remained proud of. And yet, in his words, *"They did everything they could to make sure it didn't happen."*

By the time WCW reached late 1998 and 1999, Bret's spot told the truth even louder than the promos. After five consecutive years headlining WWF pay-per-views and carrying the company to the top, he was moved down the card. Instead of being featured on Nitro, he was regularly booked on Thunder. Instead of main-event programs, he was working mid-card matches. Instead of chasing the World Heavyweight Championship, Bret Hart was wrestling for the United States Title. The Hitman headlined WrestleManias. He closed out shows and was more over in defeat than in victory, with the shining example—Wembley Stadium in front of 80,000 as he carried Davey Boy Smith to the greatest match he ever had at SummerSlam 1992. Now he was fighting for a secondary belt on the B-show. The message was clear: WCW didn't see Bret as the franchise. They saw him as just another name, even though they were paying him like a main event star.

Bret noticed the dysfunction everywhere. One night backstage, former wrestler-turned-agent Terry Taylor was running the show and made sure everyone knew it. He barked orders and threw his weight around, as Bret recalled. Bret watched the scene and leaned over to Chris Jericho. "So... the Red Rooster is running things here?" For Bret, it summed up the entire company.

For all the frustration, there were flashes of something different. Bret showed a side fans rarely saw in WWF—dry humor, sharp timing, perfect sarcasm. During a backstage promo, he repeatedly referred to Goldberg as *"Bill Goldberg."* When Mean Gene Okerlund tried to correct him, Bret waved it off. *"Tell him to say it to my face. Say it to my face, Bill Goldberg!"* Then there was the line that became immortal in another WCW Saturday Night backstage interview with Mean Gene: *"Who are you to doubt El Dandy?!"* Even the comedy landed because Bret's timing was real.

But WCW couldn't stop stepping on its own moments. One of the most confusing examples came when they opened Nitro with Bret standing in the ring, emotional, asking for forgiveness. He spoke for twenty minutes about regret and second chances. *"I just want a second chance. That's all."* It felt real. It felt vulnerable. It felt like a redemption story. And then later that same night, Bret turned on Roddy Piper to help Hulk Hogan. Another swerve. Another reset. Another story with no direction.

WCW didn't just waste Bret Hart. They broke him. They drained the spirit out of one of the greatest minds the business had ever known.

It's easy to blame Eric Bischoff because he was the face of management. But Bret kept coming back to the same conclusion: Bischoff didn't have the final say. Hulk Hogan did. Hogan's contract gave him creative control—not just over his own character, matches, and finishes, but over the direction of the entire show. If Hogan didn't like something, it could be changed. If Hogan didn't want someone getting too big, they could be cooled off. If Hogan wanted to insert himself, he could. If Hogan wanted something scrapped, it was gone.

Ric Flair remembers how, after Curt Hennig smashed his head inside the WarGames cage in 1997—a moment meant to launch a red-hot feud—Hogan walked out the next night wearing Flair's $5,000 robe and eventually cut the sleeves off without Flair's permission. The heat was gone. The story was gone. Hogan had become the focus and story.

The same power structure followed Bret everywhere—the Goldberg angle. Hogan wanted to be involved—the Toronto moment. Hogan had to be cleared—the main-event picture. Hogan controlled the gravity. Bret Hart was never allowed to matter more than Hogan.

Vince McMahon had said it before Bret ever signed. *"They wouldn't know what to do with a Bret Hart."* Bret believed he could have helped save the company if they had intended to do anything with him. *"I think I might have been able to save the company if they had any intention of actually doing anything with me."*

The cruel irony is that Bret was warned backstage that people were telling Goldberg, *"Bret is gonna kill you off. He's gonna ruin your career."* Yet it was Bret's career that ended. One kick. One concussion. One night that changed everything. The man accused of ruining others was the one who was destroyed.

Bret Hart didn't fail in WCW. WCW failed Bret Hart. And that failure became part of the story of WCW's demise.

Years later, Bret ran into Bischoff at a signing in England. Bischoff shook his hand and said, *"I just want you to know I don't have a bad thing to say about you."* Bret replied politely, *"I appreciate that."*

Five minutes later, Bret was brought on stage for a Q&A, and the first question from the crowd was the one Bischoff feared: What happened to you in WCW? Bret realized why Bischoff had approached him. *"He said that to me for the sole reason that he was hoping I'd go out there and say nice things about him instead of burying him like I always did."* Bret didn't soften it. *"I buried him like I always did."* Bischoff stood within earshot listening. Bret's explanation was simple. *"I'm always going to stick to my truths. Because it's the truth."*

Then Bret said the line that explains why this chapter will never fully die. *"He lied to me to my face for two years."* He didn't separate Bischoff from the structure that enabled him. He didn't separate Hogan from the control he wielded. *"Hogan basically put a line through my name the day I got there until the day I left."* Bret's view was clear: WCW didn't just mishandle him—they neutralized him. *"I'll never forgive how Bischoff and Hogan and those guys sabotaged me from the time I came in."*

That's why the WCW Bret Hart story isn't just a case study in bad booking. It's an autopsy of a power structure—where the booker didn't book, the boss didn't decide, and the hottest free agent in wrestling history walked into the biggest opportunity of his career only to realize the real main event was control.

CHAPTER 43

BRET HART AND BILL GOLDBERG

"I'm thinking, what kind of kick is he going to throw from that position?" - Bret Hart

WHEN GOLDBERG WAS INDUCTED into the WWE Hall of Fame, Bret Hart was in the building. Years had passed since the Goldberg kick. Years since the concussion ended his career. Time had created distance. But distance is not closure. Bret watched Goldberg walk to the podium. He listened to the speech. He heard the stories about dominance, intensity, undefeated streaks, aura, and power. What he didn't hear was acknowledgment.

> *"He was up there talking about how great he was. Never about the guys he hurt. He hurt me. He hurt Curt Hennig and Haku. So many guys who trusted him with their bodies."*

And when Bret sat in that room listening to the celebration, what struck him wasn't jealousy. It wasn't resentment over legacy. It was the absence of responsibility.

· · ·

"YOU NEVER ONCE HEARD HIM *say, 'I was reckless.' You never heard him say, 'I'm sorry to the guys I hurt.'"* Bret had defended Goldberg for years. *"It was an accident."*

What changed for Bret wasn't the kick itself. It was everything that followed. The night after the concussion, Bret wrestled Chris Benoit while already injured. He struggled through it. He paid for it physically in the weeks that followed.

Bret called Goldberg — not about the kick — but about Goldberg slicing his arm open in the windshield segment, where Goldberg couldn't break the car window with the object in his hand that was gimmicked to break the window with Bret Hart inside watching it unfold.

"I hope you're okay. I'm sorry you got hurt." Bret remembers telling Goldberg. But Goldberg never called him. *"He never once called me and said, 'Are you okay?'"* For Bret, that silence meant more than the kick. Years later, Bret saw Goldberg in Calgary during Stampede festivities.

But the distance grew. Then, at a Wrestlecon signing in Los Angeles one WrestleMania weekend, Goldberg approached Bret's table aggressively over comments Bret had made publicly. Security intervened before it escalated.

In Bret Hart's world, greatness in wrestling isn't just about drawing power or aura. It's about professionalism. It's about respect. And if you hurt someone, you acknowledge it. That's why he speaks the way he does now. When Bret Hart describes the kick that ended his career, he doesn't describe it as unlucky. He describes it as misunderstood.

"This should kick me from the ropes," Bret remembers coming off the ropes with barely two or three steps of space. Goldberg was standing sideways in the middle of the ring.

"I'm thinking, what kind of kick is he going to throw from that position?" And then it happened. Out of nowhere — a full-force side kick. A karate-style thrust. Every ounce of power behind it.

"Like he was actually trying to take my head off. He actually thought that's how wrestling works." In Bret's mind, that was the disconnect. Goldberg approached wrestling like combat. Like impact equaled realism. Like velocity equaled believability. But to Bret, realism is illusion — not force. *"You can't kick someone for real. That's how he was taught."* In Bret's view, that culture was enabled by WCW leadership.

HE DOESN'T HOLD back when he describes the people guiding that environment. *"Kevin Sullivan... Terry Taylor... [Eric] Bischoff... they had no business telling anybody how to work."* To Bret, they lacked nuance. They lacked psychology. They lacked understanding of pacing and safety. They were, in his words, out of their depth. Bret remembers being in Germany shortly after the injury, already concussed, struggling to think clearly, when Terry Taylor approached him with creative direction. Taylor wanted him to turn heel in Germany. *"I said, why would I turn heel in Germany?"* Taylor reportedly suggested he go out and challenge the crowd — "What have you done for me lately?" — as part of a character shift. Bret refused. *"I'm not doing that."* He was massively over.

When he returned backstage, Taylor apologized. *"He was almost in tears."* At that moment, for Bret, something crystallized. He was dealing with people who didn't understand audience psychology — yet were empowered to dictate it. *"That's what I was dealing with all the time."* Bret believes Vince McMahon would never have tolerated that level of creative confusion or inexperience. Even when Bret and Vince disagreed, there was structure. In WCW, Bret saw chaos. People with a limited understanding of wrestling psychology are telling veterans how to perform.

Bret acknowledged Dusty Rhodes as the only road agent or executive who knew what he was doing. Bret had a lot of respect for Dusty Rhodes. It was evident from how Bret spoke to me on the phone about him, compared to others. What hurt Bret almost as much as the injury was the isolation afterward.

GOLDBERG DIDN'T CALL. WCW cut his pay. Leadership deflected responsibility. He was concussed, emotionally unstable, financially uncertain — and creatively overruled. *These guys didn't know what they were doing.*

When Bret Hart talks about the kick that ended his career, what frustrates him most isn't just the injury. It's the misunderstanding behind it. Bret remembers coming off the ropes with barely two or three steps of space. Goldberg was standing sideways in the center of the ring.

"He actually thought that's how wrestling works. You throw somebody in the ropes, and you kick them full blast in the head — and that's my job to take it."

AND IN BRET'S VIEW, Goldberg never fully understood that trust.

"That's how he was taught." Which leads to something deeper — the environment around him. Bret has never softened his assessment of certain WCW leadership figures during that era. *"Guys like Kevin Sullivan and Terry Taylor*

— they were mental midgets telling guys like me how to work."

"I'M DONE WITH THAT GUY," said Bret. When Goldberg's kick ended Bret's career, Bret had nearly $12 million remaining on his WCW contract.

$2.8 million per year guaranteed.

Merchandise royalties were pushing it near $3 million annually with four years remaining. *"I never got a nickel."*

WCW cut his checks in half week by week until he was essentially unpaid. Then he was released. When WCW folded, and WWE bought the contracts, Goldberg was paid in full for the time he didn't work.

Turner paid Hogan and Goldberg in full for the remainder of their contracts. *"I got a thank you for your service letter, even though I had a 4-year contract worth roughly 3 million per year that would have set me up for the rest of my life. Gone in an instant."* Bret had to fight for five years in court against Lloyd's of London to collect partial compensation. *"I needed the money."* For Bret, wrestling is built on trust. You protect your opponent.

You protect their future. When that trust is broken, the cost isn't storyline. It's permanent. Bret doesn't raise his voice when he talks about Goldberg. He defended him for years. But over time, the absence of accountability mattered more than the accident itself.

CHAPTER 44

WHO WAS DRIVING THE HUMMER?

BY 1999, World Championship Wrestling had entered its strangest era. The company that once rewrote the business with the nWo had become a weekly exercise in shock value, half-finished ideas, and crash booking. No storyline better represents that collapse than the infamous White Hummer angle — a feud that began with sewage, escalated to vehicular assault, and ended with no explanation.

It wasn't just bad booking. It was chaos.

And it became one of wrestling's most infamous mysteries.

KEVIN NASH FOUND himself feuding with Randy Savage and his Team Madness entourage — Madusa, Mona, and Gorgeous George — in early 1999. What started as a normal rivalry quickly went off the rails in classic late-era WCW fashion.

One of the earliest segments saw Nash humiliate Savage by having a woman dump sewage on him. Yes. Actual sewage. The Macho Man wasn't about to let that slide.

Savage and the women of Team Madness lured Nash into the back of a limousine under pretenses. Once Nash was inside, Savage revealed himself as the driver. But instead of driving away, Savage stopped the limo in a parking lot and left Nash locked inside.

THEN CAME the moment that shocked wrestling fans.

A white Hummer smashed into the limo at full speed.

Nash staggered a while, dramatically punching out a car window — though not so injured that WCW couldn't still book him to work his scheduled match against Savage at the next pay-per-view, The Great American Bash.

Instead of following through with a clear reveal, WCW turned the Hummer into a year-long guessing game.

Savage promised to expose the driver. Sid interfered and looked suspicious.

Fake Stings appeared in Hummers. The real Sting got teased.

Hogan got accused. Bischoff got hinted at. But the reveal never came. The mastermind was never exposed. And the audience was left in confusion.

IRONICALLY, WWE ran its own mystery driver angle later that same year. In November 1999, Stone Cold Steve Austin was run over at the Survivor Series. The angle sidelined Austin for nearly a year while he recovered from real-life neck surgery.

.   .   .

WHEN AUSTIN RETURNED, the reveal came immediately. Rikishi was exposed as the driver. He got pushed toward the main event.

The execution wasn't perfect — Rikishi's run didn't last — but WWE at least finished the story. Later, they revealed that Triple H was the "mastermind" behind Rikishi running down Austin.

———

BEHIND THE SCENES, one rumor refused to die. Many fans believed the driver was initially planned to be actress Carmen Electra.

WCW had a long history of inserting celebrities into major storylines. Electra was a close friend of Kevin Nash in real life and was romantically linked to Dennis Rodman, who worked several WCW programs during the nWo era.

The idea of Electra as the mastermind may sound absurd — but in late-era WCW, it fit perfectly.

However, Eric Bischoff later disputed that version of events.

On his 83 Weeks podcast, Bischoff shut down the idea that WCW ever had a long-term plan for the Hummer angle.

According to him, there was never meant to be a secret driver just an escalation designed to rattle Kevin Nash heading into his match with Savage. In Bischoff's version, the Hummer was simply a storytelling device — a way to raise the stakes and make the feud feel personal and dangerous. There was no mystery to solve because there was never supposed to be one.

He did, however, confirm that Savage was meant to be the mastermind behind the attack — regardless of who was physically driving. The problem? WCW immediately started teasing a mystery. And once you tease a mystery, the audience expects answers. WCW couldn't resist piling on layers.

At The Great American Bash, Sid Vicious was revealed as Savage's new partner in crime — seemingly positioning him as the muscle behind the operation. Then, almost immediately, WCW walked it back and insisted the driver was still unknown.

Lex Luger accused Hulk Hogan and even produced a photo of Hogan sitting in a white Hummer. Never mind that the Hummer in the photo didn't match the one that hit Nash.

Then came the Sting reveal — except his Hummer was black, not white.

Finally, Eric Bischoff himself stepped out of a white Hummer on television. Some fans took it as the long-awaited answer. Others saw it as a wink — WCW acknowledging that there were a lot of white Hummers in the world and that the company was done pretending this story mattered.

WCW never clarified. They never closed the loop.

They just moved on. By 1999, WCW had become a company that no longer respected continuity. This urban tale is legendary because it represents the exact moment WCW forgot how to finish a story.

And somewhere in wrestling folklore that Hummer is still driving and waiting for a reveal that will never come.

CHAPTER 45
WWE MOLE SENT TO KILL WCW

"*Picking out Vince Russo's faults could be a full-time job for somebody*" - *Jim Cornette*.

IN WRESTLING, where fiction and reality constantly overlap, few figures blur the line like **Vince Russo** — the writer fans love to hate, the man credited with saving the WWF's *Attitude Era* and, some say, sinking WCW not long after. But there's one rumor that has followed him for decades:

Did the WWF secretly send Vince Russo to destroy WCW from the inside? It sounds far-fetched and a bit ridiculous.

But like all great wrestling legends, it started with just enough coincidence to feel possible.

By 1999, WCW was in chaos. Ratings were falling, storylines were looping, and the once-dominant company that beat *Raw* for 83 straight weeks was losing the war.

Enter Vince Russo.

. . .

AFTER LEAVING THE WWF — fresh off the success of *Stone Cold*, *The Rock*, *D-Generation X*, and the "Crash TV" formula — Russo was brought in by WCW executives desperate for the same magic.

He promised bold ideas, real emotion, and a creative revolution.

What WCW got instead was confusion, walkouts, and an avalanche of storylines that seemed to bury the product faster.

By the time Russo was done, fans weren't just mad.

They were convinced he had *done it on purpose.*

When Russo's booking began imploding in late 1999, conspiracy theories exploded online.

Fans noticed how many of his ideas seemed to backfire spectacularly:

David Arquette won the WCW World Title.

Vince Russo himself won the WCW World Title.

The "worked shoot" promos that broke kayfabe.

The infamous *Bash at the Beach 2000* incident, where Russo went into business for himself against Hulk Hogan.

The endless title changes, swerves, and overbooked chaos. It looked less like storytelling and more like sabotage.

The theory went like this:

After WCW embarrassed the WWF during the Monday Night Wars, Vince McMahon supposedly planted Russo inside WCW to finish the job — a creative Trojan horse sent to implode the competition from within.

. . .

ON THE SURFACE, it almost made sense.

Russo had just left the WWF. He took Ed Ferrera with him.

And shortly after his arrival, WCW's decline accelerated into free fall.

Fans didn't see a coincidence.

They saw a pattern. In truth, the "mole theory" doesn't hold up under scrutiny.

Russo was never secretly employed by the WWF.

He signed an official WCW contract, received Turner-issued paychecks, and clashed constantly with upper management — especially with Eric Bischoff, Terry Taylor, and Bill Busch.

If anything, he was *too eager* to prove himself as the creative genius behind the WWF's success.

Without Vince McMahon filtering or editing his ideas, Russo's writing went unchecked. What else went unchecked was missing out on the company stock that WWF offered employees when the company went public, just as Russo left New York.

Russo wasn't a mole — he was a mad scientist without a lab partner.

As Jim Cornette once put it, "Russo wasn't sent by Vince McMahon to destroy WCW. He just did it for free."

Even Russo himself has laughed off the conspiracy.

.   .   .

ON COUNTLESS PODCASTS AND INTERVIEWS, he's said the same thing:

"If Vince wanted me to destroy WCW, he would've paid me a lot more money."

If there's one night that cemented the conspiracy forever, it was *Bash at the Beach 2000*. Hulk Hogan refused to lose clean to Jeff Jarrett. Russo, furious, turned it into a shoot on live TV — having Jarrett lie down for Hogan, then cutting a promo burying him and declaring the title vacant.

The segment was chaos.

Fans didn't know what was real anymore.

Hogan left WCW and sued for defamation. Less than a year later, the company pulled the plug. It was no longer on life support.

To many, it looked like the perfect ending to the perfect sabotage.

But the truth was far less dramatic: ego, miscommunication, and corporate collapse collided.

Russo returned briefly to WWE creative in 2002 — but only for a matter of days.

He pitched radical ideas, including making the entire roster "start from scratch" through a single storyline reset. Vince McMahon rejected it, and Russo quietly left again.

If he were ever truly a "mole," that would've been the moment to expose it.

Instead, what fans saw was the same Russo — bold, creative, unpredictable, and self-destructive.

No, Vince Russo wasn't sent by WWE to destroy WCW.

But I've always felt he doesn't deserve the burden or shame of being labeled "the man who killed WCW."

The truth is, the company was already dying when he got there.

By the time Russo walked in the door, WCW was on life support.

When I reached out to Vince Russo to get his side, he said, ***"There are no questions to answer. If you look at the actual WCW numbers when I got there, I RAISED the ratings over the first three months before I went home. You can quote me on that because that's all I would say any way."***

It wasn't a matter of *if* it would die — just *when*.

Russo didn't pull the plug; he just happened to be outside the room when it was pulled from life support.

WWE was too far down the track.

That pony had already run the race, and WCW was never catching up.

Russo may have written some wild chapters in wrestling history, but he didn't write WCW's ending — he just happened to turn the page when it was already over.

CHAPTER 46

LLOYD'S OF LONDON INSURANCE

"I am an insurance policy. And you can never have enough insurance." - Rick Rude.

IN THE EARLY 1990S, a strange and highly profitable shadow economy quietly formed inside professional wrestling. It had nothing to do with merchandise, pay-per-views, or ticket sales.

It revolved around insurance — specifically, Lloyd's of London disability policies. What began as legitimate financial protection for dangerous careers quickly became one of the most controversial financial loopholes in wrestling history.

For a brief but infamous window of time, wrestlers were able to insure their bodies for massive lump-sum payouts if they suffered what was classified as a "career-ending" injury. On paper, the concept made sense. Wrestling was brutal. Careers were short. Bodies broke down.

. . .

RICK RUDE'S case became the most famous — and the most tragic. In 1994, Rude suffered a serious back injury while working against Sting. He filed a claim with Lloyd's of London, declaring the injury career-ending. The policy paid out a massive settlement, but it came with a devastating clause: once Rude accepted the money, he was legally forbidden from ever wrestling again. To return to the ring, he would have been required to repay every dollar of the settlement, well into six figures.

And years later, Rude desperately wanted to come back. Despite his injury, Rude believed he could still perform. He missed the business. He missed the locker room. He missed being a main-event player.

Rude returned to WWF television in 1997 — not as a wrestler, but as Shawn Michaels' "insurance policy." On television, he smirked and said, *I am an insurance policy. And you can never have enough insurance.*

Months later, following the Montreal Screwjob, Rude appeared live on Nitro the same night he was on a taped episode of Raw — shaving his beard to create the illusion of separation between the shows. Later, Rude approached his boss and close friend, Eric Bischoff, and asked for help. Rude wanted WCW to buy out the policy so he could wrestle again. Bischoff refused, and the decision shattered their relationship.

Rick Rude never wrestled again.

According to Bischoff on his "83 Weeks" podcast with Conrad Thompson, when Rude died in 1999 at age 40, that fracture remained. Bischoff later recalled arriving at Rude's funeral only to be asked to leave by Rude's sister. He left quietly and vowed never to attend another wrestler's funeral.

· · ·

CURT HENNIG'S situation was murkier. After SummerSlam 1991, Hennig stepped away from wrestling and transitioned into commentary — one of the most coveted jobs in the business. He reportedly carried a Lloyd's policy that would pay out around $300,000, but, in the end, according to Bret, he received about $50,000 for a career-ending injury.

Unlike Rude, however, Lloyd reportedly refused to pay Hennig's full claim. No clear public explanation was ever given. Without the payout, Hennig returned to the ring. In 1997, he debuted in WCW on Nitro — the same night Raven made his debut — and resumed full-time wrestling.

The myth that he "took the money and came back anyway" doesn't align cleanly with the timeline. Hennig received a fraction of what he tried to collect for his back injury.

TED DIBIASE REPRESENTS the cleanest example of the system functioning as designed. After SummerSlam 1993, DiBiase toured Japan with All Japan Pro Wrestling and suffered a herniated disc. The injury ended his in-ring career.

He cashed in his Lloyd's of London policy and retired. DiBiase never wrestled again after 1993. He transitioned into managing full-time.

IF THERE WAS a mastermind of the system, it may have been Road Warrior Animal. Animal reportedly convinced Lloyd's that he could continue wrestling while still collecting disability payments by limiting his physical involvement— primarily working tag matches and minimizing bumps. In other words, he was *"medically disabled"* while still performing. And it worked for a while.

THEN THERE WAS BRET HART.

Bret prided himself on being a craftsman — an artist — a professional in the purest sense of the word. If he could have continued wrestling, he absolutely would have.

When he signed with WCW, insurance protection was non-negotiable. In his WWF contract, he had negotiated comprehensive coverage. If he slipped while leaving the shower, he was covered. If he was injured boarding a plane, he was covered. Once he left his home to perform, he was protected. In WCW, that protection became harder to secure. *"No one would insure me."* Eventually, Lloyd's agreed — partially. Bret explained that the first year covered $1.5 million of his $3 million contract. The following year, it dropped to $1.25 million.

"They wouldn't give me any more than that." It wasn't ideal. But it was the only option available. At Starrcade 1999, a thrust kick from Bill Goldberg ended Bret's career. He finished the match. He tried to recover. He waited for symptoms to subside.

They didn't. He had years remaining on a contract worth roughly $2.8 million annually, plus merchandise royalties.

When the concussion ended his career in early 2000, WCW paid him weekly for six weeks.

Then the payments stopped. When he filed his Lloyd's claim, the insurance company fought back. They claimed Bret had a history of concussions that he failed to disclose.

They slowed the footage from matches with Steve Austin and Curt Hennig, frame by frame, in court.

Bret dismantled each claim. The Austin chair shot? Barely grazing contact.

The Hennig chair shot at Road Wild? Stopped short by over an inch. *"There was no contact with my head."*

Lloyds of London dragged the case out for five years.

"They fought me tooth and nail." Most wrestlers would have taken a reduced settlement. Bret refused. *"I was right."*

He eventually won — becoming, to his knowledge, the only wrestler to collect a full Lloyd's settlement.

Lloyd's reportedly stopped insuring professional wrestlers entirely by 2015.

Bret had paid premiums. He suffered a legitimate, documented injury. He fought for five years to collect what was contractually owed. *"I needed the money."* He had nearly $12 million remaining on his WCW contract when his career ended.

Goldberg's kick ended that.

The insurance company tried to avoid honoring it. Bret refused to fold.

THERE'S a cruel irony to the Lloyd's era. An industry built on illusion — choreographed violence, simulated impact — was forced to prove, in court, that certain impacts were not real injuries.

In some cases, policies were exploited. In others, they were denied. Some men walked away with settlements and never returned. Some returned without ever being paid.

And only one — Bret Hart — fought the system and won.

CHAPTER 47

THE POISON HAS ARRIVED

"History is written by the winners." - DDP

WHEN THE NWO returned to the World Wrestling Federation in February 2002, it was portrayed as poison. Vince McMahon framed it as a lethal dose injected into his own creation. The very men who once nearly put his company out of business were now standing inside his ring.

On television, it was chaos. In reality, the war was already over.

The collapse of World Championship Wrestling did not happen inside a squared circle. As Jim Ross later explained during a Q&A on Inside the Ropes, many of WCW's biggest stars were sitting at home collecting guaranteed Time Warner contracts worth seven figures a year.

One million dollars meant roughly $19,000 per week. Two million meant nearly $38,000 per week. Guaranteed. No travel. No injuries. No politics. Why rush back into a locker room that had just defeated you when the checks were still arriving?

The Invasion storyline of 2001 never had its full army. Fans imagined WWF versus WCW at full strength. Instead, they got a partial roster.

WHEN WCW NAMES began arriving in the WWF, the tone was not fantasy warfare. It was a hierarchy. When I interviewed Diamond Dallas Page, he did not speak with bitterness about his arrival in 2001. He spoke with realism. The war had just ended. They were "WCW guys."

The tension was real. He didn't refuse the stalker storyline with The Undertaker. He couldn't walk in dictating terms. He competed. He kept his head high. He told me he always believed his career would end in WWE.

He had blind faith that if he did the right thing and moved in a positive direction, something would eventually shift. Years later, when WWE called him about hosting "Mr. Nitro," he received a script that didn't sit right. He pushed back. He was told to change what he didn't like. That moment felt like trust returning. But in 2001, that trust wasn't there. There was positioning. And then DDP said the line that defines this era: *"History is written by the winners."*

THE CASE of Booker T is layered the same way. A five-time WCW World Champion, Booker entered the WWF during the Invasion and was treated dismissively by The Rock. It reinforced a message: this is WWE's house. At WrestleMania XIX, Booker challenged Triple H for the World Heavyweight Championship after winning a Battle Royal on Raw, where the following week, Triple H said that *"people like him"* were there to make *"people like me"* look good. The segment is still widely considered highly disrespectful by fans, especially given that Booker T never made his comeback or won the title. Instead, at WrestleMania, Triple H hits Booker with the Pedigree, but not before a long delay to score the pin in the middle of the ring. To some, it was creative direction. To others, that pause symbolized the closing of WCW's championship credibility on the grandest stage.

THEN CAME the nWo in 2002. On The Steve Austin Show, Stone Cold Steve Austin described the locker room vibe when Hulk Hogan, Scott Hall, and Kevin Nash returned as *"weird."* There was no welcoming atmosphere. Nash admitted the leverage they once held was gone. In WCW, they had creative influence. In WWF, they were part of a machine. He revealed that the original plan for WrestleMania X8 would have seen the nWo standing tall. That changed overnight when the Chicago crowd rejected Hogan as a heel. Hogan turned babyface. Hall lost clean to Austin. Nash did not wrestle.

The takeover narrative evaporated before it began. The build-up to Austin versus Hall crossed the line. Hall was duct-taped, locked in a beer cooler despite battling alcoholism, spray-painted with "3:16," and beaten decisively at WrestleMania even with Nash in his corner. Nash later admitted he was essentially insurance in case Hall faltered. The invader was not conquering.

He was being reduced. Creative instability followed.

WHILE VINCE MCMAHON and Stephanie McMahon were absent at one point, Shane McMahon found himself managing changes that the talent were pushing for. Vince was reportedly not pleased upon returning.

· · ·

ATTEMPTS TO PIVOT the group by adding Shawn Michaels and leaning into Kliq history were discussed but never solidified. Then Nash tore his quad. Hall was released. Bruce Prichard later described the entire run as "snakebit." A setback followed every attempt at momentum. By July 2002, Vince walked to the ring to nWo music only to declare it finished. Within months of purchasing WCW, the Invasion ended. The nWo dissolved.

WHEN GOLDBERG ARRIVED IN 2003, he brought one of the most protected presentations in wrestling history. In WCW, he was mystique and destruction personified. Then came the backstage segment with Goldust and a blonde wig. It was entertainment. It was harmless. But as that wig slid onto Goldberg's head, something else quietly slipped away. Years of aura and mystique that made him feel untouchable were humanized in seconds. Sometimes you don't have to beat a monster. You make the audience laugh at him. Once the crowd laughs, the fear rarely returns the same way.

YEARS LATER, when Sting finally debuted at WrestleMania 31 against Triple H in a match framed unmistakably as WCW versus WWE, the symbolism resurfaced.

STING LOST. And it made no sense except to remind everyone who won the Monday Night War yet again, in case anyone forgot.

AFTER THE MATCH, Triple H extended his hand — and patted Sting on the face. Not a firm shake of equals. A pat. Scott Hall later described telling Triple H it looked like a message: *"Welcome to the show... and you're my b**ch."*

TRIPLE H'S REPORTED RESPONSE? *"YEAH."* Hall didn't frame it as hatred. He framed it as a hierarchy. Sting wasn't being humiliated backstage. He was being positioned within WWE's structure.

LATER THAT SAME NIGHT, Triple H was central again in a segment with The Rock. Sting felt like a special attraction. Triple H felt permanent. Individually, every example can be defended—crowd reaction. Creative choice. Business loyalty. Injury. Timing. Collectively, the pattern is clear. Within a year of buying WCW, The Invasion concluded. WCW champions were repositioned. The nWo dissolved. The final holdout, Sting, later lost on the grandest stage.

WWF DID NOT JUST DEFEAT WCW. It absorbed it. And once the winner holds the pen, the story gets written accordingly. As Diamond Dallas Page told me, without bitterness and full clarity, *"History is written by the winners."*

CHAPTER 48

SOFTBALL, SQUIRRELS AND NO SHOWS

"We're live, pal!" - Jim Ross, 1995.

SID VICIOUS HAD many reputations in professional wrestling, but the most enduring one had nothing to do with powerbombs, championships, or promos.

Sid was infamous for disappearing. Sid would miss towns. Miss flights. Miss turns—Miss entire weekends.

He'd drift into softball tournaments, detour into nowhere, or vanish into what wrestlers came to call Sid Time — a parallel universe where schedules did not apply.

Eventually, promoters adapted. Some quietly began requiring insurance policies. Not written ones. Human ones. Enter Doug Gilbert — former wrestler and younger brother of the legendary "Hot Stuff" Eddie Gilbert. Following his in-ring career, Doug's job for the last decade wasn't to wrestle or to draw money. Doug's job was brutally simple:

Get Sid to the building.

If Doug Gilbert was traveling with Sid, promoters said you had about an eighty percent chance that Sid would actually arrive. Without Doug? All bets were off.

Sid Time expanded. Detours multiplied. Mystical, unexplained absences swallowed bookings whole. Doug became Sid's unofficial handler — driver, navigator, alarm clock, conscience, and accountability system.

Wrestlers joked Doug deserved half the booking fee just for getting Sid through the door.

They weren't wrong. Sid didn't vanish out of malice. He lived in his own orbit. Wrestling was important — but not central. The world, he proclaimed, was master and ruler of in promos, adjusted to Sid. Sid never adjusted to the world.

That same orbit produced some of the strangest stories in wrestling history. There was Sid's pet squirrel, which he reportedly brought with him and treated as a legitimate companion. In a business where wrestlers barely trusted each other, Sid trusted a squirrel.

There was the night Sid attacked Brian Pillman with a squeegee — not a weapon, not a chair, but a janitor's tool — because of course that's what Sid grabbed.

THEN THERE WERE THE PROMOS. Moments that live forever not because they were polished, but because they were unfiltered.

. . .

"WE'RE LIVE, PAL!"

Jim Ross's warning during a live *In Your House* pre-show in 1995, which somehow became immortal as seasoned vet and manager Ted Dibiase stood there as professional as he could be.

"HALF THE BRAIN YOU DO!"

A sentence that should not exist, yet somehow does during a promo with Scott Hall and Kevin Nash at WCW in 1999.

Sid wasn't bad at promos. *He was **Sid** at promos.* His mind moved faster than language, and the results were chaotic brilliance. You weren't always sure what he meant — but you were always sure it mattered. And despite all of it — the no-shows, the Sid Time, the squirrel, the squeegee, the verbal train wrecks — Sid remained employable. Because when he showed up, he felt real.

That's where Doug Gilbert mattered most post-retirement in the last several years. Doug didn't try to change Sid. He didn't tame him. He managed the chaos. He understood that Sid wasn't irresponsible — he was wired differently. Doug kept him focused just long enough for wrestling to capture the lightning. I saw a different side of Sid myself, away from the monster persona and the bloopers.

During a rare signing, Sid and I spoke privately about his son, Frank Eudy, who became a memorable and polarizing figure on *Big Brother*. I am a fan of the show and have watched every season of the reality hit TV show. The moment Frank came up, Sid softened. Not Psycho Sid. But Sid, the proud father.

He talked about Frank's size, strength, and athleticism — but he was also brutally honest. *"Everyone hated him because they feared him,"* Sid said. *"They knew if it came down to strength... Frank wins."*

It was surreal listening to one of wrestling's most intimidating figures casually break down reality-show politics — strategy, optics, alliances. Sid understood all of it. He didn't care to play those games himself. That same self-awareness surfaced in a smaller moment that stuck with me. Sid signed all my posters and original promos without hesitation — even one that read, *"Softball season never ends."*

He could've taken offense. Plenty of wrestlers would have. Instead, Sid smirked, laughed, and proudly signed it. I think our earlier conversation about Frank — and our shared appreciation for ZZ Top — put me over the top.

Sid Time didn't just exist in theory. I watched it unfold in real time in 2012 through Pro Wrestling Syndicate—an independent wrestling company in New Jersey, later rebranded WrestlePro, which just celebrated its 10th anniversary and is running strong throughout the country. They promoted shows in Alaska, and its co-founder, Pat Buck, trained some of the world's best talent, including MJF, Anthony Bowens, and many others.

WHEN SID NO-SHOWED IN RAHWAY, New Jersey, frustration boiled over. At the time, a decision was made that perfectly captured the absurdity of dealing with Sid. Sid's actual phone number was dialed and read out loud. It went straight to voicemail as fans chanted their thoughts.

Two days later, I decided to dial Sid's number myself. Sid answered, but I hung up immediately. Then came the most telling moment of the night. PWS offered a full refund to all attendees. Jay Lethal wrestled as his replacement and put on a helluva match. No one took the refund offer. The crowd stayed.

I wish Doug were with Sid that night. He didn't fight Sid's nature. Without Doug, Sid disappeared. With Doug, Sid was a solid bet to show up. And sometimes, in professional wrestling, that's the difference. Sid heard the whispers and knew the jokes. He recognized the legend. And when he trusted you, he could laugh at himself.

That's the part people miss because Sid wasn't stupid or oblivious. Sid was bizarre and, at times, intentional. There was genius in it, whether it was deliberate or not.

Sid's legacy was never quiet—it was loud, intense, and impossible to ignore. Yet in 2026, his induction into the WWE Hall of Fame Legacy Class felt far more subdued than the career he built. The morning after, on his Facebook, his other son, Gunnar Eudy, publicly expressed his disappointment, noting the lack of promotion, recognition, or even merchandise honoring his father. For a man who headlined the biggest stages and stood at the top of the industry, it didn't feel like a full tribute. It felt incomplete—like even in death, they still wouldn't fully put Sid over.

CHAPTER 49

THE MASS TRANSIT

BY THE END OF 1996, Extreme Championship Wrestling wasn't just an alternative. It was a threat. And we fans loved it. I was a huge ECW mark.

ECW had grown outside the system, without permission or protection. We didn't stumble onto ECW — we *found* them. Late-night syndication slots at two or three in the morning. Grainy UHF broadcasts. VHS tapes traded like contraband. The effort required to follow ECW became part of its identity, and that struggle forged loyalty no marketing budget could manufacture.

In wrestling terms, ECW was peaking. In business terms, it was about to be tested. The company was finally preparing to leap from an underground phenomenon to a legitimate national player. And we were Paul Heyman's foot soldiers. We signed petitions and flooded the inboxes of cable providers, including Viewers' Choice.

Pay-per-view wasn't a luxury — it was survival. Without it, ECW would always remain fragile, dependent on unstable television deals and fan passion alone.

. . .

THEN CAME MASS TRANSIT. On November 23, 1996, ECW collided head-on with the real world. Not the wrestling world — the corporate one.

Lawyers. Insurers. Standards-and-practices departments.

Media partners who didn't care about context, culture, or consent. They cared about risk. The incident itself was horrific, but what truly damaged ECW was how it reframed the company overnight. National outlets like *Inside Edition* didn't present the story as a tragic misunderstanding inside a niche subculture. They presented ECW as a reckless operation that allowed a teenager to nearly bleed to death in the ring.

From that moment forward, ECW lost control of its narrative.

Inside corporate boardrooms, ECW was no longer "edgy" or "alternative." It was unregulated, unpredictable, and potentially uninsurable.

At the center of that perception stood New Jack.

Within ECW, New Jack was authenticity incarnate — violent, unpredictable, and terrifying in a way no gimmick could replicate. Paul Heyman understood his value, but he also understood the cost. New Jack was a liability Heyman could not fully control.

After Mass Transit, ECW needed discipline and diplomacy. New Jack offered neither. He remained defiant, publicly and privately, insisting that Erich Kulas had lied about his age and training and had explicitly asked to be bladed. He never altered that stance — not in interviews, not in shoot tapes, not even in his final days.

His last tweet, posted one day before his death in May 2021, reiterated the same claim. That refusal to soften the story mattered. It reinforced the idea that ECW couldn't rein in its own performers — and that terrified media partners.

On Christmas Eve 1996, the primary PPV provider, Request TV, canceled ECW's scheduled debut. Other providers quickly expressed similar concerns. This wasn't just about one incident anymore. It was about ECW's entire presentation: excessive blood, violent unpredictability, controversial storylines, and performers who seemed untethered from oversight.

ECW was nearly finished. Paul Heyman fought back with everything he had. He proved that Kulas had misrepresented his age and training. He negotiated relentlessly. He convinced providers to reverse their decision — but the price was permanent scrutiny. From that point forward, ECW operated under a microscope.

Limits on excessive blood were imposed. Broadcast start times were pushed later into the night. Advanced scripts were required. Time cues had to be hit precisely. Every future television and pay-per-view deal came with heightened oversight. ECW survived — but it was no longer trusted.

The legal aftermath only added complexity. Despite the public outrage, New Jack was acquitted of all criminal and civil charges.

Evidence showed that Kulas had lied about his age and training and had explicitly requested to be bladed. The case highlighted just how difficult it was to litigate professional wrestling injuries, where consent, performance, and real danger exist in a legally gray space.

Legally, ECW and New Jack survived. Culturally, the damage was already done. Inside the ECW locker room, the incident caused quiet reflection. Some performers began questioning the environment they were working in — not the violence itself, but the lack of guardrails. Kulas had nearly died.

The realization that it could have happened to anyone lingered. ECW had always pushed limits, but Mass Transit forced wrestlers to confront what happened when there were none. Years later, the stigma still followed ECW.

When the company landed on TNN in 1999, it looked like validation — a national platform at last. In reality, it was probation. TNN tolerated ECW; it never fully embraced it. Standards departments watched closely. Advertisers hesitated. The shadow of Revere never disappeared.

And when WWE became available, the decision was swift and ruthless. TNN didn't just drop ECW — it paid WWE roughly $100 million to leave USA Network and move to what would become Spike TV. WWE was safe. WWE was scalable. WWE was controlled.

ECW was still seen as chaos waiting to happen. Once TNN pivoted, ECW had no oxygen. Without weekly television, the company lost momentum, leverage, and relevance.

ECW's World Champion Taz gave notice in the Fall of 1999 and headed to the WWF, a symbolic blow that signaled to the locker room that even the most loyal cornerstones no longer believed ECW could survive without stable television. Taz had been the face of the company — homegrown, protected, and synonymous with ECW's identity. When he left, it wasn't just a defection. It was a blow.

His replacement only underscored the chaos.

Mike Awesome, who won the ECW World Title from Taz, appeared on WCW Monday Nitro just weeks later, still ECW champion — a surreal moment that publicly exposed how powerless ECW had become.

A COMPANY once defined by rebellion was now watching its top title paraded on a rival's national television show, unable to stop it. The bleeding didn't stop there.

ECW's Tag Team Champions, The Dudley Boyz, followed shortly after, signing with WWE within weeks of each other. Like Taz, the Dudleys had been foundational to ECW's rise. Their departure stripped the company of another pillar — and confirmed to anyone paying attention that the endgame had begun. Without a network, without leverage, and without the ability to retain its champions, ECW didn't just lose talent.

It lost credibility. The Mass Transit Incident didn't kill ECW on November 23, 1996. But it became the cautionary tale that followed the company everywhere — a permanent reminder of what happens when an unregulated environment collides with corporate reality.

It forced changes across the independent wrestling scene, including stricter age verification and increased attention to safety protocols.

MASS TRANSIT MARKED the moment when ECW stopped being viewed as dangerous art and became an unacceptable risk — and once that line was crossed, the clock was already ticking.

CHAPTER 50

THE PEDIGREE THAT NEARLY KILLED

"I never thought about suing WWE." - Marty Garner.

IN 1995, Paul Levesque arrived in the World Wrestling Federation as a blue-blooded villain with an odd accent, an unusual name, and a future no one could yet imagine. He was new. Unproven. Still trying to establish himself in a company filled with established stars and larger-than-life personalities.

The man who would one day become Triple H — multiple-time world champion, WrestleMania main eventer, and eventually the creative architect of WWE — was just another young wrestler fighting for a spot.

And in May 1996, his entire career nearly ended before it ever truly began. What should have been a routine enhancement match on WWF Superstars became one of the most terrifying moments ever broadcast on WWE television.

ONE MISTIMED LANDING turned Triple H's Pedigree finisher into a near-tragedy. For a moment, it looked like Triple H's legacy might be defined not by championships, but by catastrophe. The wrestler taking the move believed he was receiving a Double Underhook Suplex—a maneuver in which the recipient is thrown backward and lands flat on their back.

Instead, Levesque drove him forward. Because the move was unfamiliar, the recipient failed to brace himself, either by extending his arms or by protecting his head. Rather than landing chest-first, he landed directly on the top of his head and neck. The impact compressed his cervical spine and sent a chill through everyone in the building.

THE PEDIGREE — which would go on to become one of the most protected finishers in wrestling history — was suddenly associated with one of the most dangerous accidents ever shown on WWF television. The man on the receiving end was enhancement talent, Marty Garner. Years later, Garner explained precisely how the misunderstanding happened during an appearance on the 'Two-Man Powertrip' podcast.

"[Triple H] was new up there, I'm new up there doing some jobs. He said, 'Can you take the Pedigree?' I said, 'Absolutely!' I had no idea what the Pedigree was. I was gonna kick. When he locked me in, and I kicked, it looked like a double-underhook piledriver. Triple H said, 'Geez, you alright?' I said, 'Bro, I'm good.' He goes, 'Oh my God,' and he pinned me. He goes to the back, and when I come through the curtain, he says, 'You sure you're okay?' 'Brother, I'm fine!' There was a rumor that I sued WWE, but I never thought about suing them. I was just happy to be there and do a TV match."

· · ·

DOCTORS LATER SAID Garner narrowly avoided paralysis.

The incident quickly escaped the wrestling bubble. The footage was replayed repeatedly on WWF programming, and anytime Triple H was on a talk show, and later dissected frame by frame on early internet wrestling forums. Soon, the story crossed over into mainstream media.

GARNER APPEARED on national daytime talk shows, including The Jenny Jones Show and The Montel Williams Show, where the clip was shown, and the realities of wrestling injuries were debated in front of millions of viewers. For a brief moment, Marty Garner became one of the most recognizable faces in wrestling — not for a championship or a rivalry, but for a near-tragedy caught on camera.

RUMORS SWIRLED for years that Garner had sued WWE and Triple H.

He never did. Despite the severity of the accident and the attention it generated, there was never any bad blood between the two men.

IN FACT, years later, Triple H acknowledged the moment with humor and respect. During a 2023 appearance on In the Weeds, Garner revealed that Triple H had signed a photo of the infamous botch — a picture that had circulated in wrestling magazines for years.

· · ·

"[THE BOTCHED PEDIGREE] *made for a good picture, and it showed up in a few magazines,*" Garner said. A few years later, it showed up again in a magazine. Triple H came up to him and said, *'This picture is making its rounds.' 'Yeah, it is,'* I replied.

"I NEVER GET *any autographs from anybody, I never get anybody to sign anything, but I did get Triple H to sign a picture of me in the air with him doing what looked like a double-underhook piledriver. I have a picture of that signed.*"

While the photo from the match is famous and widely circulated online and in wrestling magazines, Garner has mentioned in interviews that he owns the signed picture and keeps it as his only autograph. Still, he has not shared an image of the signed item itself.

One of wrestling's most infamous moments ended not with lawsuits or bitterness, but with mutual respect and the shared understanding of how close things came to ending far worse.

Garner's WWE run ended not long after the incident, though he continued wrestling. In 1999, he resurfaced in Extreme Championship Wrestling. He initially debuted as a manager under the name Ragin' Cajun before transitioning into an in-ring role as Puck Dupp, one-half of the hillbilly tag team The Dupps alongside Bo Dupp. The Dupps were deliberately obnoxious, over-the-top, and designed to generate heat. Their ECW run was short-lived, and by 2000, Garner had left the company.

Shortly afterward, he stepped away from wrestling entirely.

For nearly five years, he was out of the business.

.   .   .

IN 2004, Marty Garner found himself in an unlikely place.

A Hollywood movie set.

Garner worked as a production assistant on Walking Tall, one of Dwayne "The Rock" Johnson's early starring roles following his transition from wrestling to film.

The opportunity came together through an unusual connection in the video game industry.

"I was doing some stunts on a video game for Epic Games," Garner said. "This guy tells a guy in California, 'I want to bring him out here and do some stunts on my game.' I go out there, and the guy I was working for at the video game studio, he goes, 'Do you know The Rock?' 'Of course, I used to do some jobs at WWE, I was an enhancement guy.' 'I'm gonna call him and tell him you're with me. I just got his number.'"

That phone call led to Garner working behind the scenes on a primary Hollywood production with the same man who once headlined WrestleMania.

Marty Garner will forever be remembered for a single moment.

But behind that clip is a man who survived a near-paralyzing injury, rebuilt his life, and found a second act far from the ring.

The Pedigree would go on to become one of the most protected finishers in wrestling history.

Triple H would go on to become one of the most potent figures the business has ever seen.

But for one night in 1996, the future nearly disappeared before it ever arrived.

THE INTERRUPTIONS NEVER ASKED PERMISSION.

The screen would glitch. The broadcast would distort. Suddenly, viewers were staring at grainy black-and-white surveillance footage, as if someone had hijacked the truck in the parking lot.

Shane McMahon and the Mean Street Posse are allegedly exaggerating injuries.

Meat reportedly caught cheating on Terri Runnels. Val Venis is stuffing a sock into his tights. Locker-room vanity, immaturity, embarrassment — all exposed.

THEN THE SIGNAL would cut out. Three letters lingered. **GTV.** At first, it felt intentional — like the start of something clever. In the Attitude Era, nothing aired without a payoff. There was always a mastermind—a reveal. A confrontation awaits at the end.

· · ·

BUT AS WEEKS stretched into months in 1999, the mystery remained unanswered. Who was filming? Why were these moments being captured? What was the grand design?

Originally, the concept was reportedly intended to reintroduce Dustin Rhodes as Goldust. At the time, Rhodes had publicly distanced himself from the character — even burning the Goldust attire in a trash can. The hidden-camera gimmick was allegedly meant to position him as a born-again moral critic, exposing the excesses and hypocrisy of the Attitude Era. Early internal branding was reportedly labeled "GD TV," a not-so-subtle nod to Goldust before being simplified to GTV.

But resistance allegedly surfaced quickly. The USA Network was reportedly against bringing Goldust back in that direction. Creative momentum shifted. Then Dustin Rhodes departed WWE for WCW, removing the centerpiece of the entire angle.

INSTEAD OF SCRAPPING IT IMMEDIATELY, writers Vince Russo and Ed Ferrara reportedly kept the concept alive — even though its intended ending was gone. And that's when the angle reportedly began drifting.

With no wrestler attached to the reveal, Russo and Ferrara allegedly pitched a celebrity twist: comedian Tom Green. Green was a rising pop-culture figure at the time, known for absurd hidden-camera humor. The crossover potential seemed obvious — even the branding lined up conveniently.

GTV. Tom Green. On paper, it sounded like a marketing win.

But Vince McMahon was reportedly unimpressed after being shown Green's work. He allegedly didn't find it funny, and the idea was shut down before it gained traction.

A third possibility reportedly emerged: Headbanger Thrasher. Injured at the time, Glenn Ruth could have been reintroduced with a darker edge as the man manipulating footage from behind the curtain. There was even a tease tying him to storyline tension involving his partner, Mosh. That idea, too, reportedly faded.

By then, GTV had become something unusual — a storyline continuing to air without a defined destination. The interruptions grew less frequent as summer 1999 progressed. Eventually, they stopped altogether.

Then, in 2000, the signal unexpectedly returned. Brief surveillance clips — including a quiet backstage moment between Terri Runnels and The Kat — aired again. A few more hidden glimpses surfaced.

And then it disappeared. This time, permanently. No confession. No camera smashed in the ring. No mastermind stepping into the spotlight to explain months of voyeuristic chaos.

GTV was a 1999–2000 World Wrestling Federation hidden-camera storyline featuring grainy black-and-white footage of wrestlers in compromising or humorous backstage situations. It was reportedly intended to culminate with Goldust revealed as the architect behind the surveillance. Alternate ideas allegedly included Tom Green or Headbanger Thrasher before creative indecision and shifting priorities left the angle abandoned.

What remains is not the reveal — because there wasn't one.

What remains is the static.

And in wrestling, sometimes the most enduring legends aren't the stories that end with a bang. They're the ones that go dark.

CHAPTER 52

THE ARMSTRONG CURSE

BULLET BOB ARMSTRONG was the patriarch of one of professional wrestling's most respected families.

A hardened Southern veteran who bled in the Georgia, Alabama, Florida, and Mid-South territories, Bob Armstrong was known as a locker-room general, a trusted company man, and a trainer who helped shape future stars.

He never became a national headliner, but in the territory era, Bullet Bob was royalty. When his four sons followed him into the business, most assumed greatness was inevitable.

Instead, the Armstrong name became attached to one of wrestling's strangest and most enduring legends.

The Armstrong Curse was never meant to be real. It began as wrestling folklore—a tongue-in-cheek explanation for why the talented Armstrong brothers could never seem to win on camera, but behind the scenes, it was about "getting over."

The idea surfaced as early as 1996, but became far more prevalent in 1999 and 2000, when announcers openly referenced it on television. No matter how good Brad or Steve looked in the ring, something always went wrong—a missed opportunity.

At the same time, on the other side of the Monday Night Wars, the youngest Armstrong brother was thriving. In WWF, Brian Armstrong — now known to the world as Road Dogg Jesse James — had become one of the most popular stars of the Attitude Era as part of the New Age Outlaws and D-Generation X.

While WCW was portraying the Armstrong name as cursed, Road Dogg was selling out arenas and leading some of the loudest crowd chants in wrestling.

In a rare moment of cross-promotional acknowledgment, he turned the curse into a punchline, wearing a shirt that read, **"Look Mom, No Curse!"** — a playful jab at his brothers' WCW storyline and proof that at least one Armstrong had escaped the myth.

Road Dogg's success highlighted a truth the business has always known: personality sells. Brian Armstrong was not the best in-ring worker in his family. Brad was, by far. But wrestling has never been about pure technique alone. If it were, Dean Malenko would have headlined WrestleMania, and Hulk Hogan would have been opening the show.

The business rewards connection, charisma, and timing — and Brian had all three. His success proved that within the Armstrong family, personality was the true X-factor. Brad Armstrong, however, was widely considered the most naturally gifted of the brothers. A smooth technician, a high-level worker, and a dependable tag team performer, Brad was a WCW mainstay for years.

Among wrestlers, he was regarded as a hidden gem. Many in WCW remember Brad as endlessly charismatic behind the scenes — the kind of guy who could hold court in locker rooms and gyms, keeping the boys laughing for hours. But when the red light came on and the cameras rolled, that natural personality never quite translated on television.

No matter how good he was in the ring, no matter how magnetic he was backstage, the missing ingredient always seemed to be timing. The boys universally loved Brad. If you had a problem with Brad Armstrong, then you were the problem. He was the kind of wrestler everyone wanted to work with — safe, giving, unselfish, and professional to the core. He could step into the ring with anyone and make them look better than they really were.

Veterans trusted him. Young talent learned from him. Promoters relied on him.

He was more than just a "great hand." He was a polished, technically sound performer with natural timing, crisp execution, and an instinctive understanding of ring psychology.

Yet the very traits that made him invaluable behind the scenes may have worked against him on the booking sheet. He never complained. He never politicized. He went out every night and did his job — and did it better than most.

For all his talent, Brad Armstrong was never placed in the kinds of angles that turned good wrestlers into stars. There were no parking lot attacks. No straight-jacket whippings. No bloodbaths with Buzz Sawyer.

No savage betrayals. No moments designed to make fans feel rage on his behalf. He never had the chance to cut a truly fired-up promo because he was never given a situation that demanded one.

The closest he ever came was in 1992, when Brian Pillman turned heel and knocked him off his crutches. On paper, it was the perfect story. But it revolved around the Light Heavyweight Championship, a division already burdened by a jobber stigma, and by then, Brad had been devalued by years of laying down. The audience respected him, but they no longer believed in him.

By the late 1990s, WCW leaned fully into the curse. Between 1997 and 1998, Brad developed a heel turn built around blaming his string of losses on the Armstrong Curse itself. In 1999, he was repackaged as "B.A." and placed in Master P's No Limit Soldiers.

When the group disbanded, he entered a personal feud with Berlyn after Berlyn attacked his brother Scott. The storyline culminated at Halloween Havoc, where Brad defeated Berlyn in one of the few meaningful singles victories of his WCW run.

Soon after, he was given one final reinvention: Buzzkill, a Vince Russo creation modeled after Road Dogg's wildly successful Attitude Era persona. Even the entrance music mirrored the New Age Outlaws theme. To fans, it felt like an imitation. To Brad, it was another attempt to finally catch the break that had eluded him his entire career. The gimmick never connected, mainly because many fans had no idea the two were even brothers, and the comparison only reinforced the growing myth that no Armstrong except Road Dogg could ever truly get over.

Then came the injury that seemed to seal his fate. In early 2000, Armstrong was involved in a bizarre backstage accident at a WCW Saturday Night taping when he was run over, severely damaging his knee. The injury required surgery and sidelined him for months.

When his WCW contract expired in 2001, he quietly walked away from the business, disappearing for several years before resurfacing on the independent circuit in 2004.

In 2006, Brad was given one final opportunity on a national stage when he signed with World Wrestling Entertainment. He wrestled on ECW brand house shows, served as a trainer to younger talent, and briefly appeared as a guest commentator during a short-lived three-person booth experiment.

When the experiment ended, Armstrong returned to a behind-the-scenes producer role — once again respected, trusted, and valued, but never truly pushed.

On November 1, 2012, Brad Armstrong was found dead in his home in Marietta, Georgia. He had seen his physician the previous week for an undisclosed medical issue. He was fifty years old. WWE announced his passing later that day.

In 2005, fans were treated to a rare father-and-son moment when Bullet Bob teamed with Road Dogg in TNA Wrestling, a symbolic passing of the torch from the territory era to the Attitude Era. It was a reminder of just how deep the Armstrong roots ran in professional wrestling.

TODAY, Bullet Bob Armstrong is remembered as one of the great unsung patriarchs of the business, and his sons are among the most respected workers of their generation. The Armstrong Curse was never real. But in wrestling, perception becomes reality. And for one of the most talented families the business ever produced, bad timing, missed storytelling, and a system that rewarded charisma over craftsmanship somehow combined into a legend that refuses to die.

CHAPTER 53

THE NIGHT BROCK LESNAR MADE THE LIST

"Brock is a trained fighter, and he's a beast, but I'm not the type of person to back down from anybody." - Chris Jericho

IT WAS SUMMERSLAM 2016, and Brock Lesnar had just defeated Randy Orton in what was supposed to be a blockbuster main event at Brooklyn's Barclays Center. But instead of a traditional wrestling finish, the match ended in a shocking way.

Lesnar dropped Orton with a savage barrage of elbows to the head. These weren't work strikes. They were real. Orton was busted open hardway, blood streaming down his face as the referee stopped the match. The crowd sat in stunned silence. Backstage, the locker room was furious. To many watching behind the curtain, it looked like Brock Lesnar had gone into business for himself.

CHRIS JERICHO WAS one of those watching.

Jericho had been in the business long enough to know the difference between controlled violence and something that had crossed the line. From his perspective, Randy Orton had been legitimately hurt in a match that was supposed to be a carefully planned main event. Even worse, nobody seemed willing to give him a straight answer about whether the finish had even been approved.

When Brock Lesnar came back through the curtain, Jericho was waiting.

Jericho confronted Lesnar immediately, demanding to know who had signed off on the finish and why Orton had been split open with real elbows. Michael Hayes was present but offered no clear explanation. That only made Jericho angrier. The two men ended up chest to chest, nose to nose, neither willing to back down.

According to the Wrestling Observer Newsletter, the situation became so volatile that Brock Lesnar and Chris Jericho had to be broken up twice that night.

THE FIRST TIME, Triple H physically stepped in to separate them. The second time, Vince McMahon himself had to intervene to prevent the confrontation from turning into a real backstage fight. Reports later claimed the most intense moment came after Jericho spoke with Michael Hayes about what he believed had happened to Orton. When Brock found out, he allegedly shoved Jericho. That was the moment the altercation nearly exploded.

Earlier that night, Jericho had wrestled in the opening match of the SummerSlam main card, teaming with Kevin Owens as Jeri-KO against Enzo Amore and Big Cass. Enzo was backstage when the chaos unfolded, and he later confirmed just how real the situation was.

Appearing on *Busted Open Radio*, Enzo said, *"There was a real fight that took place that day in the middle of The Garden."* He described the scene as chaotic and surreal. *"It was very confusing,"* Enzo said. *"Because it was real."*

Enzo implied that Jericho was the instigator, storming into Gorilla Position furious and believing Brock had taken liberties with Orton. In Jericho's mind, Enzo explained, he wasn't just defending his friend. He was defending the business.

I asked Randy's legendary Dad, the Hall-of-Fame "Cowboy" Bob Orton, over sushi, what he was thinking watching Lesnar bust his son open. Orton said to me, *"I was really pissed off. And I still am. I wasn't happy about it."*

In the days that followed, Jericho addressed the confrontation himself on "You're Welcome! with Chael Sonnen."

"I thought the finish of that match was fierce and very violent," Jericho said. *"I didn't know if Randy was okay, and I was checking on Randy, my friend."*

Jericho made it clear that this wasn't about politics or ego. This was personal.

"Randy and I have always been pretty close," Jericho said. "I said something, and Brock said something, and the next thing you know, we're nose to nose, yelling at each other."

Jericho didn't shy away from the danger of the situation.

"Let's make no bones about this. Brock is a trained fighter, and he's a beast, but I'm not the type of person to back down from anybody."

Then, with his trademark humor, he added, *"I'm glad he didn't eat me."*

Eventually, the tension cooled when Randy Orton personally assured Jericho that the finish had been planned and that he had agreed to the brutality of the ending. Only then did Jericho stand down, satisfied that his friend had not been blindsided.

But by then, the damage had already been done. The confrontation had already become legend.

Years later, speaking to *Sports Illustrated*'s Justin Barrasso in October 2021, Jericho reflected on the incident with the same mindset that had carried him through decades in the business.

"WHEN YOU GET *into that moment, it is what it is,"* Jericho said. *"You either go for it, or you put your tail between your legs and hide, and I've never been that type of guy. I'm more of the type to die with boots on."*

In a business built on scripted violence and controlled chaos, SummerSlam 2016 nearly ended with something no one could script — a real fight between two of the most dangerous men in the industry.

And at the center of it all stood Chris Jericho.

Not the guy with the scarf. Not the rock star.

The Beast got himself on the list, and it took WWE's top brass to get him off.

CHAPTER 54
THE TITO LIFE

"I always gave it everything I had." -Tito Santana

IN PROFESSIONAL WRESTLING, where excess is often worn like a badge of honor, there exists a different kind of legend. Not one built on pyrotechnics, entourages, scandals, or chaos — but on respect, discipline, and longevity.

They call it *"The Tito Life."*

The phrase was made famous by Shawn Michaels during Tito Santana's induction into the WWE Hall of Fame in 2004. Michaels, a man whose own career embodied brilliance, turmoil, and survival, spoke of Tito as something rare in wrestling — a man who did it right.

Tito is a man who showed up, worked hard, protected his opponents, and went home to his family.

In a business that chewed people up and spit them out, Tito Santana walked away intact.

Tito Santana — born Merced Solis — wasn't just a beloved wrestler for decades. After leaving the ring, he quietly built a second career as a middle school Spanish teacher and coach in New Jersey, where he spent more than 20 years mentoring students before retiring in 2023.

No spotlight. No nostalgia tour. No clinging to fame.

Just service, discipline, and impact. To his students, he wasn't a former champion. He was Mr. Solis.

A teacher who believed in accountability.

A coach who demanded effort. A mentor who led by example.

That is what "The Tito Life" truly represents.

Tito was the definition of dependable. In an era when no-shows, burnout, and self-destruction were common, Tito was always there.

If the building needed a main event, Tito could deliver.

If a rookie needed a safe opponent, Tito was trusted.

If a town needed a hero, Tito was over. He rarely missed shows. He traveled every loop. He wrestled hurt. He carried young talent. He protected veterans. That reliability made him one of WWE's most consistent fan favorites across three different generations.

He was a two-time Intercontinental Champion, a Tag Team Champion, a Madison Square Garden mainstay, who wrestled on the first nine WrestleMania events, winning the very first match against "Playboy" Buddy Rose under a mask billed "the Executioner" in WrestleMania I.

He wasn't just part of the machine — he helped build it.

Tito was trusted to headline B shows as Intercontinental Champion. While Hulk Hogan anchored the A towns, Tito was the man sent to carry secondary markets.

He truly was the fightest workhorse champion that modern fans should really know more about. Tito wrestled 280+ times in 1986. Tito, usually, was kept off Hogan shows because the WWF machine trusted Tito as a top-tier babyface to carry the B-loop shows that were saturating and expanding around Hogan, who was the A+ show attraction and company champion.

A year later, in 1987, when Tom Zenk quit after he and Rick Martel as the Cam Am Connection were positioned to carry the tag team belts, the WWF put in their trusted and reliable guy, Tito Santana, and formed "Strike Force" with Rick Martel.

And the same rule applied. As Tag Team Champions, they carried loops, closed shows, and anchored cards.

Wherever the WWF went, if Tito Santana was on top, promoters could sleep easily. You could always count on Tito for a great match.

That reputation followed him everywhere.

Scott Hall once praised Tito not only for his work ethic but also for his influence. When Hall was creating the Razor Ramon character, he wanted a name that sounded strong and authentic. Tito suggested starting the last name with an "R" — just like Ramon. The idea stuck. Wrestling history followed.

When I asked Tito how he managed to survive and thrive in a business where drinking with the boys, partying with promoters, and being seen with the right people were often as important as what you did in the ring, he didn't hesitate.

"Andy, the thing is, I never wasted my money on drugs or out drinking."

I pressed him. I told him how many wrestlers have said that in those days, grabbing beers with the higher-ups — even the boss himself — was sometimes a fast track to better spots.

"I let my work in the ring do my talking," Tito said.

Then he told me a story that says everything about how Vince McMahon viewed him.

"One time Vince pulled Paul Orndorff and me after we had this match," Tito said. *"Vince told us it was one of the best matches he's ever seen."*

No schmoozing. No politics. Just two professionals delivering at the highest level — and earning praise directly from the boss.

When I asked Tito how he managed to last as long as he did in a business that chews up even the most gifted athletes, his answer was simple.

"I always gave it everything I had."

That philosophy defined every phase of his career. Tito never coasted. He didn't mail in house shows. He didn't save himself for television.

Whether it was Madison Square Garden or a small-town civic center, Tito wrestled like it mattered — because to him, it did.

One of the clearest examples of Vince McMahon's trust in Tito came at Survivor Series 1990. It was a strange night. The babyfaces were being wiped out.

One by one, the heroes were falling. By the time the dust settled, only three men remained standing to carry the company's banner into the Grand Finale.

Hulk Hogan. Ultimate Warrior.

And Tito Santana.

Tito had already survived his earlier match as the sole survivor of The Alliance against The Mercenaries. Then he was immediately sent back out for the closing segment.

"I remember it clearly," Tito told me. *"If you remember, Andy, I had just finished wrestling one match as the sole survivor, and then we were doing a promo with Hulk and Warrior. Warrior was pacing back and forth, and you couldn't see me. I was behind."*

It was classic Warrior — intensity, nerves, adrenaline spilling over. And Tito, calm as ever, was standing quietly in position. No theatrics. No ego. No need to be seen. Just ready.

When the bell rang for the Grand Finale, Tito didn't hesitate.

He sprinted into the ring and drilled The Warlord with a flying elbow, stunning the powerhouse and sending him over the top rope almost immediately.

One of the most physically imposing men in the company was gone in seconds.

It was vintage Tito.

Fast. Precise. Fearless.

Tito put on a strong showing before eventually being eliminated. Hogan and Warrior would stand tall as the ultimate survivors, but Tito belonged in that ring.

He belonged in that spotlight. And fans remember it to this day.

Because Survivor Series 1990 wasn't just about Hogan and Warrior.

It was about the company's most reliable soldier standing shoulder-to-shoulder with its two biggest icons.

Another detail perfectly sums up how trusted Tito Santana truly was.

He was the first man ever to pin The Undertaker in the WWF.

It happened on October 5, 1991, in Barcelona, Spain — less than a year after Undertaker's debut, when his aura was being guarded carefully as an unstoppable force. When it came time for someone to hand him his first pinfall loss, Vince chose Tito.

Not because Tito needed the win. Not because of politics. But because Tito was safe. Tito was reliable. Tito would protect the character.

When something important needed to be done, Tito Santana was the man they called.

Tito didn't last because he politicked. He didn't last because he partied. He lasted because he showed up. He didn't do pills. He didn't do drugs. He saved his money. He treated wrestling like a career, not a casino.

As Tito himself says, in this business, it's not what you make. It's what you save.

While many wrestlers from his era were forced to turn to crowdfunding campaigns to survive retirement, Tito never asked for a dime. Not once. He never needed to. He planned.

He saved. He built a second career.

He walked away with his dignity and independence intact.

No GoFundMe. No benefit shows. No desperation. Just a man who took care of business — then and now.

While researching this chapter, I tried to find someone — anyone — who would speak negatively about Tito Santana.

Not because I was looking for dirt, but because in a business built on jealousy, politics, and a dog-eat-dog mentality, someone who lasts decades without enemies is an anomaly.

I asked veterans. I spoke with insiders. I reached out to people from every era of his career.

No one said a bad word about him.

Not one.

Tito was never a heel — not on camera and not behind the scenes. He didn't stab people in the back. He didn't play politics. He didn't step on others to get ahead.

He showed up. He worked hard. He treated people right.

In a business that rewards selfishness and punishes kindness, Tito Santana built a career on respect — and walked away with it intact.

That may be the rarest achievement of all.

That's not just a great wrestling story.

That's **The Tito Life.**

CHAPTER 55

WRESTLERS COURT

LONG BEFORE WWE became a publicly traded corporation with HR departments and legal teams, the locker room ran on a different system of justice. They called it Wrestlers' Court.

Wrestlers' Court was part tribunal, part comedy roast, part fraternity hazing ritual.

. . .

COMMON OFFENSES LEADING TO WRESTLERS' Court included poor locker room etiquette, "schmoozing" with management, being "sloppy" in the ring, or disrespecting veterans. At the center of it all stood The Undertaker. It was designed to correct behavior, humble egos, and remind newcomers that the locker room had its own rules long before corporate structure arrived.

By universal agreement, Undertaker served as the judge. When Undertaker spoke, the room listened. His rulings were final.

The Godfather often served as bailiff. JBL frequently acted as prosecutor. And the jury was the entire locker room. John Bradshaw Layfield explained how cases even reached the court. If someone had heat, JBL would go directly to Undertaker to ask whether it should be handled privately or brought to court.

And once it did, there was no escaping it. Wrestlers' Court was never about company discipline. It was about locker room order.

Sometimes the punishment was lighthearted. Sometimes it wasn't very comfortable. Sometimes it crossed lines that would never be tolerated today. The most famous rule was also the simplest: the judge could always be bought.

Mark Henry once joked that anyone who took Wrestlers' Court too seriously had only themselves to blame. All you had to do was buy a bottle of Jack Daniel's and set it on Undertaker's table. Twenty-five dollars could make a sentence disappear.

But not everyone got off that easily.

. . .

THE MIZ LEARNED that lesson early.

Early in his WWE career, Miz was treated as an outsider. He was a reality TV star trying to break into a business that still ran on respect for territory and a locker-room hierarchy. One day, Miz made the fatal mistake of eating fried chicken over Chris Benoit's gear bag.

The locker room exploded.

Miz was summoned to Wrestlers' Court and sentenced to be kicked out of the locker room for six months. He had to find other places to shower, change, and use the restroom.

It was made clear that he had not yet earned his spot.

Years later, Miz would say he endured it because he refused to quit. The locker room wanted to see if he would break. He didn't.

Even writers weren't immune. Former WWE head writer Brian Gewirtz once found himself in Wrestlers' Court after Edge and Christian gifted him a Flash action figure. The locker room accused him of accepting bribes for TV time. Stone Cold Steve Austin led the charge, roasting Gewirtz in front of the entire roster.

Gewirtz later admitted he viewed the experience as a strange badge of honor. It meant the locker room considered him important enough to hold accountable.

Then there were the cases that became legend. Teddy Long once revealed he was taken to the Wrestlers' Court for selling viagra to Viscera and other wrestlers. JBL recalls how Teddy never liked to pay for anything, and he got the viagra pills for free and was selling them. Long asked Mae Young to be his lawyer. Mae agreed — and promptly mispronounced Viagra as "Niagra," which sealed his fate. Undertaker sentenced

Teddy to buy Ron Simmons and Bradshaw fried chicken and beer.

The Hardy Boyz once faced court over an airline seating dispute. Undertaker ultimately let them off but sentenced Michael Hayes to carry Kane's bags and buy him dinner for a week.

Enzo Amore, during a 2017 European tour, reportedly complained on a bus with other WWE wrestlers about the industry and his bank balance, using his phone. That crossed the line. Roman Reigns reportedly stepped in and told Enzo to get off the bus. Given Roman's calm demeanor and reputation, it must have been disruptive.

Ken Anderson, aka Mr. Kennedy, later recalled his own Wrestlers' Court experience when Tommy Dreamer was bailiff. One case involved a female talent whose bag was thrown into the trash by another female wrestler, who told her that's where it belonged, according to Anderson.

ONE OF THE MOST INFAMOUS WRESTLERS' Court sagas involved Chad and Tank Toland — later repackaged as Chad and James, The Dicks. They debuted with WWE from Ohio Valley Wrestling, WWE's developmental system, in 2005, and the office gave them a Chippendales-style male dancers gimmick.

The locker room immediately turned it into a joke.

Chad, determined to succeed, trained with a professional dancer on his own time and at his own expense, as Tank would reveal during the wrestler's court. Chris Benoit and some of the boys instigated much of the animosity between the tag partners. What followed was hazing. Chad was mocked, ridiculed, and humiliated in front of the entire roster. He cried while doing pushups and jumping jacks, recalls Tank.

The following night, supposedly, the locker room placed bets and eventually forced a real fight between the tag team partners.

Chad lost.

Bloodied and broken, he became the locker room's cautionary tale.

Both men were released soon after and never returned to WWE.

By 2016, many stars confirmed that the Wrestlers' Court no longer existed. WWE had become a corporate machine. The locker room culture had changed. Wrestlers were now employees, not road warriors enforcing their own code.

But for decades, Wrestlers' Court ruled the back hallways of wrestling. Depending on who you ask, it was justice — wrestling style. To some, it was an embarrassment. It had no rules, no appeals, and an unofficial authority that meted out ridicule and, often, hazing.

It thrived in an era when locker rooms governed themselves because no one else would, when peers and silence enforced respect as currency.

Over time, Wrestlers Court didn't fade because it was exposed —it faded because the industry changed.

HR departments replaced hazing, 'WWE Untold' replaced secrecy, and traditions that once passed for accountability could no longer survive daylight.

CHAPTER 56

BAD NEWS
FOR THE WWF

"As of tonight, I quit." - Bad News Brown

PROFESSIONAL WRESTLING IS BUILT on destiny. A chosen one. The moment when the company finally pulls the trigger and creates a champion. But sometimes destiny is promised and never delivered. Few stories in wrestling history are whispered with more bitterness than the tale of Bad News Brown — the man many believe was once promised the chance to become the first Black World Champion of the modern era. A promise that never came true.

Bad News Brown, born Allen Coage, was not a creation of the wrestling business. He was already a world-class fighter before he ever stepped into a ring. An Olympic-caliber judoka who represented the United States on the world stage, Coage carried himself with the confidence of a real warrior. When he entered wrestling, he brought something few performers ever had.

Legitimacy. By the late 1980s, Bad News Brown had become one of the most intimidating heels in the WWF. He did not smile or pander to the crowd. He sneered, scowled, and carried himself like a man who believed the world owed him something. Bad News began wearing a black glove. After victories, he would raise his fist in the air. To many fans, it looked like just another heel taunt. But to others, it meant something far more profound. It echoed one of the most potent political moments in sports history.

ON OCTOBER 16, 1968, at the Olympic Games in Mexico City, American sprinters Tommie Smith and John Carlos stood on the medal podium after winning gold and bronze in the 200 meters. As the U.S. national anthem played, both men raised black-gloved fists in a silent protest against racism and injustice. The image became immortal—a symbol of defiance, pride, protest, and power.

BAD NEWS BROWN knew exactly what he was referencing. And fans noticed. According to wrestling folklore, Vince McMahon privately told Brown that he wanted him to break wrestling's final racial barrier. That he would be the first Black World Champion. At the time, the idea was revolutionary. For decades, Black wrestlers had been denied the top prize in nearly every major promotion. We had Bobo Brazil as the U.S. champion and Tony Atlas & Rocky Johnson as the WWF tag team champions, but the World Champion had not yet been crowned.

NOT BECAUSE OF TALENT. But because of perception. Some promoters believed white audiences would accept black superstars, but not a black champion. Bad News Brown was supposed to prove them wrong. But wrestling history tells a different story. Bad News Brown never beat Hulk Hogan or Randy Savage to have that moment. He wrestled them respectively in main events in 1988 and 1989; he never headlined WrestleMania. He never got the moment that, apparently, among the boys, he was promised.

His consolation prize came on wrestling's biggest stage.

At WrestleMania IV in Atlantic City — the event that crowned Randy Savage as WWF Champion — Bad News Brown won the opening Battle Royal. It was a symbolic victory. A way to reward him without fully committing to what many believed he had earned.

For a brief moment, Bad News stood tall at the grandest show of them all. In 1988, he was positioned near the top of the card. He challenged Randy Savage during Savage's first reign as WWF Champion. He remained in the main-event orbit. He worked with Hulk Hogan. And in 1989, he received a featured payoff match on Saturday Night's Main Event — the rare network television stage reserved only for the company's biggest stars.

THAT NIGHT, Hogan hit the significant leg drop. Hogan posed. And Bad News Brown did the job. It was the only time many fans ever remember Bad News being asked to fall to Hogan's leg drop on television. The company protected him. They treated him as dangerous. They presented him as credible.

But they never gave him the belt. And that is the great tragedy of Bad News Brown. Before he ever stepped into a wrestling ring, Allen Coage was already one of the most accomplished heavyweight judokas in American history. He was a dominant force in the Amateur Athletic Union, capturing the AAU Heavyweight Championship five times in 1966, 1968, 1969, 1970, and 1975. In 1970, he became the AAU Grand Champion, the highest honor in American judo.

On the world stage, Coage represented the United States at the 1976 Olympic Games in Montreal, where he won the bronze medal in the heavyweight division. At the Pan American Games, he captured gold medals in 1967 and 1975.

This was not a wrestler learning how to throw punches. This was an Olympic-caliber fighter who chose wrestling. In the locker room, Bad News had a reputation as one of the toughest men in the business. Wrestlers knew not to test him. Promoters knew he could not be controlled like a bodybuilder or a pretty boy. He did not need wrestling.

Wrestling needed him. And yet the ultimate prize was never placed around his waist.

At a photo shoot, Vince McMahon spoke, according to Coage, in his only shoot interview conducted by RF Video before he passed away: *"You'll work with Hogan. You'll hold him up. Then you'll come back a year later — this time you've got the belt."* Then came the line that stayed with him: *"We've never had a Black world champion."*

It was framed as an opportunity. As history. And he believed it. Coage never denied Vince's brilliance. He understood what McMahon was building — cable expansion, pay-per-view growth, merchandising on a scale wrestling had never seen. But he also delivered a warning he would repeat years later: when you shake hands with him, count your fingers.

Bad News debuted strongly in 1988. He had legitimate Olympic credentials, a believable toughness, and a presence that didn't feel cartoonish. He won the WrestleMania IV battle royal. He was protected. He was positioned. Then the direction shifted. The world title talk disappeared. He did them without protest. If they told him to lose, he lost. But he could read the pattern. When he confronted Vince, the response was denial. *"What do you mean you're being jobbed?"* Then came the pivot: *"I wanted to put the strap on you. The office talked me out of it."*

Bad News told him your guys can't wipe their noses without you knowing. Vince explained there were concerns he was a shooter — that he might not return the belt to Hulk Hogan if asked. Coage dismissed it outright. If they didn't trust him, don't put it on him. Fire him if he doesn't comply. Make a new belt. The reasoning felt like camouflage.

The breaking point came not backstage but in a car during a California swing. His wife, who had never interfered in his career, finally spoke up. She told him she didn't like what she was seeing — the lies, the manipulation, the disrespect. When he stepped out of that car, he realized she was right.

The confrontation came in Huntsville. He arrived late on purpose — something he never did. He asked to see Vince. When McMahon tried to smooth things over, Coage cut him off. He told him he was tired of the promises, tired of the excuses. *"As of tonight, I quit."*

According to Coage, Vince didn't argue. He admitted he hadn't kept his word. Half the locker room was listening outside the door. They heard it. Broken promises weren't rare — he was simply the one who said it aloud.

His final pay-per-view appearance came at SummerSlam 1990 in Philadelphia against Jake Roberts, ending in disqualification after a chair shot. Days later, he wrestled what is widely recognized as his last WWF match — a house show bout against Koko B. Ware in Salt Lake City on August 31, 1990. After that, the schedule tells the story. The steel cage program continued. The towns remained booked. Jake's opponent stayed slotted. Only the name changed. Where Bad News had been penciled in, Akeem appeared as the substitute.

When Vince had told him, *"We've never had a Black world champion,"* it ignored history. In 1963, Bearcat Wright defeated Freddie Blassie for the WWA World Heavyweight Championship in Los Angeles during the civil rights era, becoming one of the first Black world champions in a major U.S. promotion. His reign ended when he was stripped of his title amid political fallout.

Nearly three decades later, in August 1992, Ron Simmons defeated Vader for the WCW World Heavyweight Championship and became the first Black world champion officially recognized within WWE's lineage language. His reign lasted five months before the belt returned to Vader, and Simmons never again challenged for the world title.

Bearcat Wright won it and was stripped of it. Ron Simmons won it and was cooled off. Bad News Brown was promised it and never given the chance. Different eras. Different companies. The same structure. Championships in professional wrestling are not simply rewards for talent. They are instruments of control — symbols handed to those who fit the image of the moment.

He could headline. He could sell. He could fight. But he could not cross the final line. During one of his stints in New Japan Pro Wrestling, Allen Coage found himself at the center of one of the most infamous backstage confrontations in wrestling history. Bad News told the story himself during a shoot interview with RF Video.

According to Coage, the incident occurred on a tour bus with the roster on board. Andre the Giant allegedly made an off-color remark that Bad News found deeply offensive. The exact wording has faded into folklore, but what followed became instant legend. Bad News demanded that the bus driver pull over.

Then he ordered Andre the Giant off the bus. The locker room froze. The Eighth Wonder of the World — a man who towered over everyone and intimidated generations of wrestlers — stood face to face with an Olympic judoka who feared no one.

According to Bad News, the confrontation nearly escalated into a physical altercation, but did not. And then something happened that stunned everyone. Andre the Giant apologized. Years later, Bad News Brown's daughter, Frances Coage, confirmed on Facebook that Andre did indeed apologize to her father for the remark. In a business built on ego and hierarchy, Andre the Giant rarely apologized to anyone. But he did to Allen Coage because Andre knew what everyone else knew. Bad News Brown was a shoot.

After wrestling, Coage quietly became a teacher. In Calgary, Alberta — one of wrestling's sacred cities — he partnered with Rick Bognar, best known as the fake Razor Ramon from the WWF in 1996. Together, they ran a wrestling school, passing on their knowledge to a new generation. Before his death, Bognar had begun working on a book about his career and his time running the Calgary school with Bad News.

It was never finished. But the legacy of Bad News Brown remains, as he was inducted into the 2026 Hall of Fame's Legacy class.

CHAPTER 57
SUPERFANS

"Being front row is like a drug." - K. Morris.

EVERY ERA of wrestling has its faces in the crowd — but some appear too often.

Always front row. Always hard cam. Always reacting at just the right moment.

Over time, fans stop asking who they are. They start asking why they're there. That's when the rumors begin.

Then the urban legends, tales, and whispers that certain superfans weren't just lucky—they were connected —are followed.

That they had an "in" with the company. Maybe even a job no one talked about. In wrestling, where kayfabe bleeds into reality, a familiar face in the front row can spark legends as big as anything in the ring. For decades, Vladimir was impossible to miss.

Front row. Center camera. TV tapings. Pay-per-views. His presence was so constant that fans invented explanations to make sense of it. Wrestlers knew who Vladimir and his friends were. Some swore he was a WWE employee. Others claimed he trained wrestlers.

The wildest version said he was once Vince McMahon's personal trainer — a secret role that earned him lifetime access.

The reality was far less conspiratorial, but no less impressive. WWE eventually leaned into the mystique, producing a documentary that revealed the truth. Its delayed release only fueled speculation.

In the end, the answer was simple: Vladimir is a devoted fan who built his life around wrestling.

Vladimir and I. (Dallas, TX) Wrestlemania weekend 2022.

THEN CAME THE MODERN VERSION—A man in a bright green T-shirt with a smiley face.

Always front row. Always visible. Fans dubbed him "Green Shirt Guy," and the theories exploded once again.

At some point, the roles blur. You're not just watching anymore.

YOU'RE BEING WATCHED. He laughs about it, but there's still something surreal underneath it. *"It's pretty cool,"* he says. *"Something I never would have imagined as a kid."*

It's not something he chased. It happened because he never stopped showing up.

"I've made friends with other fans. It's great seeing them in person." That's the part television can't capture. The conversations before the show, the familiar faces, and shared reactions. *"You can't beat the energy of the live crowd."*

That's what keeps him there. Not the camera. The feeling. Every era has its version of presence.

There are always stories that follow someone who becomes visible. One of the more recent ones circulating is that he was the fan struck by CM Punk, and that moment somehow led him to become a permanent fixture in the front row. Like most wrestling rumors, it sounds believable enough to spread —but it isn't true. *"There are a lot of stories out there,"* he says. *"That's one of the more recent ones, but none of them are true."*

What is true is much simpler. He's been a fan his entire life. As a kid in the 1980s, he convinced his father and grandfather to take him to shows, and from then on, he never really stopped going. At first, it was just being in the building, sitting wherever he could, occasionally landing a front-row seat when the opportunity came up. That part didn't feel unusual—it was just what fans did when they loved something enough to keep coming back.

After a few years of showing up in the same place, the same seat, at the same kind of shows, people began to notice. At first, it was small—quick acknowledgments during commercial breaks, brief conversations at house shows. Then it grew into something more visible. Talent started interacting with him during the actual broadcasts, not just between segments. Moments that weren't planned but weren't entirely accidental either.

He remembers specific ones. Logan Paul is calling him out on SmackDown. The following night at SummerSlam, Jelly Roll came over and said something to him before the match. And then there are the moments that stand out for a different reason—like before one of his final matches, when John Cena spotted him behind two security guards.

"At a pre-show hospitality event before his last match, John Cena spotted me behind two security guards and made a point to come over and greet me."

And at some point, something else shifted. Fans began recognizing him.

"They ask for autographs," he says, still sounding slightly surprised by it. *"They want pictures."*

It's not something he ever planned for. Not something he imagined as a kid sitting in the stands. But it's something he's come to enjoy. Not as attention—but as part of the experience.

Because for him, that's what it still is.

After all the shows, all the travel, all the time spent in the same seat, the reason hasn't really changed.

"It's the people," he says. Not just the wrestlers. The fans.

"I've made friends with other fans. It's great seeing them in person." That's the part you don't see on television. The conversations before the show. The familiar faces. The shared reactions. The energy that only exists in the building.

"You can't beat the energy of the live crowd."

And that's why he's still there. Not because the camera finds him.

Because he never stopped showing up.

FOR KERRY MORRIS, being front row didn't happen overnight, and it wasn't part of any arrangement. It unfolded slowly over decades, long before "superfan" was a recognized concept. His first live wrestling show came on December 17, 1989. Andre the Giant. The Ultimate Warrior. Dusty Rhodes.

For most fans, seeing even one of those names live would be enough. For Kerry, it was only the beginning.

His first front-row seat came on December 1, 1991, with Ric Flair and Roddy Piper headlining. Attendance increased gradually, becoming more consistent between 2004 and 2007. The turning point came at WrestleMania 26. From that moment forward, front row stopped being special — it became routine.

Life briefly slowed the pace — marriage, student loans, buying a house — but by 2015, Kerry was back at major events regularly. From WrestleMania 26 to today, he has been a constant presence at ringside.

With that proximity comes perspective. From the front row, Kerry says, you don't see everything — but you see enough. Entrances. Camera cues. Production tells.

He points to SummerSlam 2025 as an example: both nights, it was obvious something big was coming — not because of what aired, but because of where the cameraman was positioned.

When Stu, the longtime WWE camera operator, locks in on the ramp between segments, that's the signal. Someone's about to appear. Viewers at home never see that preparation. Front-row regulars do.

Recognition came gradually. Kevin Owens was the first wrestler to acknowledge Kerry openly. Drew McIntyre later surprised him by calling him by name, even though they had never been formally introduced.

ROMAN REIGNS WALKED over after a match, hugged Kerry, asked how he'd been, and casually mentioned Hawaii, where Kerry had just moved. That was the moment he realized what many front-row regulars eventually do: they're known — not as insiders, but as fixtures.

Despite persistent myths, Kerry has never attended an official WWE VIP party or sanctioned after-party. Like many regulars, he's stayed at talent hotels and ended up in lobby bars where wrestlers were drinking. The access is incidental, not invited.

That proximity occasionally reveals things fans aren't meant to see.

One moment that stuck with him involved Carmella giving Cash Wheeler a lap dance in a hotel lobby bar — which was surprising, given her public relationship with Big Cass at the time.

It was a reminder that the off-camera world doesn't always match the curated version fans are shown.

Asked which wrestlers' real-life demeanor contradicted their public persona, Morris says the Undertaker and Steve Austin are the nicest, most sincere people you could meet.

· · ·

EARLY PREMIUM SEATS were sold through in-house travel packages. Today, they're handled through On Location, WWE's premium experience partner, which tracks long-term customers and spending habits. Sometimes seats are locked in before a Ticketmaster presale. Sometimes months in advance.

WrestleMania 2026? Kerry paid $70,000.

And because he lives in Hawaii, the cost isn't just financial. It's time. Travel. Jet lag. Long flights he hates enduring.

"Being front row is like a drug," Kerry admits. Not every show — because then it becomes a chore — but the big ones. The moments that matter. It's the closest you can get without crossing the barricade.

Front Row Superfans at nearly every show, Green Shirt Guy & Kerry Morris

They aren't plants, insiders, or employees. They're the superfans who stayed, paid, returned — and eventually became part of the scenery.

CHAPTER 58

THE LIVES THE BOYS SAVED

"One of the most important things a person can be is of some use." - Perry Saturn.

SOMETIMES THE MOST incredible acts of heroism happen far away from the ring, with no cameras, no crowds, and no applause.

These are the stories fans rarely hear—the moments when wrestlers became real-life saviors.

SCOTT "BAM BAM" Bigelow was one of the most intimidating men to ever step into a wrestling ring. A 400-pound powerhouse with flames tattooed on his bald head and a full body suit covered in fire, Bigelow looked like a walking inferno.

In January 2000, Bigelow was staying at a motel in New Jersey when a fire broke out in the early morning hours. While others fled the building, Bigelow ran straight into it. Children were trapped inside.

Without hesitation, Bigelow charged through smoke and flames, carrying multiple children out to safety again and again. He suffered severe burns across his body and was hospitalized for weeks.

Parts of his famous flame tattoos were permanently damaged. The irony is impossible to ignore. A man whose entire wrestling persona was built around fire nearly lost his life fighting a real one.

———

PERRY SATURN WAS DRIVING his girlfriend to work in April 2014 when he witnessed something that alarmed him. Two men were attempting to force themselves on a woman. Without hesitation, Saturn intervened, and a fight broke out.

In the chaos, Saturn felt a sharp blow to the back of his head. At first, he thought he had been punched. Moments later, he realized he had been shot, the bullet entering the back of his neck and shoulder. The attackers fled, and the woman was saved.

But Saturn's injuries left him in constant pain. To cope, he turned to painkillers and eventually methamphetamine.

He lost his home. He disappeared for years. Friends searched for him, unsure if he was even alive.

It wasn't until 2010 that Saturn finally resurfaced. There was no award or recognition—just a man who chose to stand and paid a terrible price for doing the right thing.

Years later, the former Army Ranger would write, *"One of the most important things a person can be is of some use."*

• • •

DAVEY BOY SMITH JR. noticed a crowd gathered on a bridge in Calgary while driving in 2017, according to reports.

A young woman was hanging over the railing. Smith pulled over immediately. He approached slowly, speaking calmly, trying to keep her grounded.

The woman was distraught. She was crying and threatening to jump. When she began to lose her balance, Smith reacted on instinct, grabbing her and pulling her back over the railing to safety. Emergency responders arrived moments later.

A life was saved. There were no cameras and no headlines, just a wrestler doing the right thing when it mattered most.

———

MICK FOLEY MADE a career out of pain. He was thrown off cages, slammed onto concrete, wrapped in barbed wire, and covered in blood. But his most significant act of toughness came without a ring.

At a public appearance, a fan approached Foley and told him he was planning to take his own life. Security tried to intervene, but Foley refused. He sat with the man, listened, and spoke with him for hours. Foley shared his own struggles with depression. He spoke about family, hope, and the possibility that life could still change.

By the end of the conversation, the man agreed not to harm himself. He sought help. He lived. There were no cameras and no tribute video, just one human refusing to walk away from another.

———

ON MAY 17, 2020, Shad Gaspard, who WWE fans remember on-screen as Shad, one-half of Cryme Tyme, went swimming at Venice Beach with his ten-year-old son.

A powerful rip current pulled them both out to sea. Lifeguards rushed into the water. With the ocean overpowering him, Shad gave a simple command: ***"Save my son first."***

His son was pulled to safety. Shad disappeared beneath the waves. Days later, his body washed ashore and was identified by his tattoos.

Shad Gaspard died so his son could live. In 2022, WWE posthumously honored him with the Warrior Award. No championship could ever mean more.

THE REAL LEGACY of this business isn't measured in belts or banners — it's measured in moments no camera ever caught.

Bam Bam Bigelow ran into a burning building and carried children to safety.

Perry Saturn stepped in to stop a woman from being brutally assaulted and nearly paid for it with his life.

Mick Foley and Davey Boy Smith each intervened when a stranger needed help, not because they were asked, but because they couldn't walk away.

Long after the cheers fade and the legends blur, these are the stories that endure — the ones that never needed a spotlight to be heroic.

That's the legacy wrestling doesn't celebrate enough.

CHAPTER 59

WWF BUYING UFC

"When it was presented to me about buying the UFC, I didn't like the business model." - Vince

FOR YEARS, Shane McMahon's absence from WWE was misread as restlessness or ambition unmet. When Shane finally explained why he left, in conversations including an interview with Mick Foley several years ago, the answer was neither dramatic nor singular. It was cumulative.

Shane said the environment had stopped being collaborative.

HIS IDEAS WERE NO LONGER BEING EXPLORED. The freedom to contribute creatively—and to influence decisions financially—had narrowed to the point that pushing back carried consequences beyond work. What concerned him most wasn't losing arguments. It was what those arguments were doing to his relationship with Vince McMahon.

. . .

"IT STOPPED BEING A COLLABORATION," Shane said. *"It stopped being fun. And I wasn't going to allow a deteriorating business relationship to affect our personal lives. And that's exactly what was happening. I love him too much."*

THE UFC WAS NOT the reason Shane left WWE. It was one of many examples that showed him how little room there was for ideas that conflicted with Vince's worldview.

IN 1998, when SEG owned the UFC, which was banned in multiple states, losing cable clearance, and widely dismissed, Shane believed it represented the future of combat sports. According to Dave Meltzer, discussions progressed far enough that UFC executives believed WWE would acquire the company. The reported price was approximately $2 million.

SHANE WANTED WWE to own the UFC outright—no partnership, no merger. Had it happened, the UFC would have been a wholly owned McMahon asset, privately controlled and positioned to remain in the family for generations.

VINCE BACKED OUT. Vince told his son, Shane, *"If you want it so bad, buy it yourself."* Shane couldn't. He didn't have that capital in 1999.

The deal died. This wasn't about UFC specifically. It was about control. Years later, Paul Heyman described the dynamic bluntly in the Netflix documentary Mr. McMahon.

*   *   *

WHEN SHANE PUSHED an idea Vince fundamentally rejected, the disagreement could escalate fast—according to Heyman.

Vince ended it with four words: *"Not while I'm alive."*

Heyman recalled Vince handing Shane a knife and pointing to his own chest—telling him that if he wanted the decision badly enough, that's what it would take.

Otherwise, Shane could buy him out the way Vince had bought out his own father. He told the story not as a metaphor, but as an explanation.

That's the through-line Shane eventually recognized. Staying meant endless friction with a decision-maker who was also his father.

Winning arguments would cost him something he valued more than position. So he opted out.

The World Bodybuilding Federation failed first, causing Titan Sports to suffer multi-million-dollar losses due to guaranteed contracts, production, marketing, and the collapse of ICOPRO. The WBF is covered in detail in the next chapter.

Years later—after declining the UFC—Vince launched the XFL (2001), which folded after one season with reported losses of roughly $70 million.

In total, Vince spent far more than $2 million on ventures that failed—while rejecting a $2 million acquisition that later proved foundational to global combat sports.

In early 2000, the UFC was hanging on by a thread—bleeding money, struggling for mainstream respect, and one bad decision away from tapping out. Then came Dana White, a promoter with a relentless vision and zero patience for failure.

In 2001, the UFC was banned in most states and hemorrhaging cash. Dana White, a former amateur boxer, convinced casino owners and brothers, Lorenzo and Frank Fertitta, to buy the company for just $2 million. It was a gamble, but White saw potential where others, including Vince McMahon, saw failure.

Even if Vince hated the UFC and its business model, buying it just to shelf it may have been a better play.

Brothers Lorenzo and Frank Fertitta, with Dana White, bought the UFC in 2000 for $2 million and sold it in 2016 for $3.77 billion, according to ESPN.

ON MARCH 31, 2023, the day before WrestleMania 39, McMahon appeared on *CNBC's 'Halftime'* with Ari Emanuel, CEO of Endeavor, to form TKO Group Holdings, the WWE and UFC jointly.

ON SEPTEMBER 12, 2023, the deal, which combined the two entities into a $21.4 billion sports and entertainment company, made TKO a publicly traded company on the New York Stock Exchange.

THE UFC WAS VALUED at $12 billion at the time of the sale, while the WWE was valued at $9.3 billion.

VINCE SOLD A CONTROLLING stake for the first time in his career and remained Executive Chairman. Asked why now, Vince said building what Endeavor had already built with UFC would have taken him another ten years—and by then the market would have moved again. Selling control was, in his words, *the right time.*

This wasn't a reversal of belief. It was timing and leverage.

SHANE WANTED the UFC when it was cheap, risky, and unscripted—when ownership would have been total and kept in the family.

Vince rejected it, then absorbed tens of millions in losses elsewhere with the XFL. Two decades later, he merged with the UFC anyway—without sole ownership, without family control, and only after regulation and profitability were guaranteed.

UFC didn't cause Shane to leave. Being unheard did.

The UFC became the clearest symbol of ideas Vince rejected —and later embraced—on his own terms.

Shane didn't lose a fight. He refused to turn a family relationship into one.

AND IN THE END, the deal he once pushed for happened anyway—25 years later at 6,000 times the price, but the ultimate price was the loss of control.

CHAPTER 60
VANISHED AND
NEVER TO RETURN

"Dynimate Kid was a nasty man." -Outback Jack

NOT EVERYONE GETS A RETIREMENT SPEECH.

Some walk out of the arena and never come back. Wrestling is a business built on loud exits — farewell tours, Hall of Fame speeches, retirement runs, and one-last-match chants.

But for every legend who leaves the spotlight, some vanish into the shadows. They didn't die in the ring or announce their retirement.

And, there was no tribute video either. No Hall of Fame acceptance speech. They just disappeared — quietly, completely. And in the years since, their existences and exits from the business have become some of wrestling's strangest modern myths.

. . .

OUTBACK JACK WAS SUPPOSED **to be a star.**

Billed as a wild Australian brawler, he arrived in the WWF in 1987 with heavy promotion, television vignettes, and a push that suggested Vince McMahon saw real plans for him. That belief was confirmed when he was selected for LJN's Series 4 action figure line in 1987.

Less than six months later, he was gone. By the time kids were buying his figure off toy store pegs, Outback Jack had vanished from the company.

Behind the scenes, Jack walked into one of the most brutal locker rooms in wrestling history. In an online interview with Hannibal, Outback Jack spoke openly about Dynamite Kid, calling him a "nasty man" and describing a culture of harassment that went far beyond harmless ribbing.

At the time, WWF had plans to pair Outback Jack with Hillbilly Jim as a tag team, with discussions of a future WWF Tag Team Championship run. That plan angered the British Bulldogs, who were fiercely protective of their spot at the top of the division.

The Bulldogs were known for ruthless locker-room enforcement, and Outback Jack was singled out. The most infamous incident allegedly occurred during a television taping. According to many, including Jack himself, he was drugged and had one side of his head shaved while unconscious.

When he woke up, he had to shave the rest of his head to look presentable for his scheduled match. Instead of the rugged Australian brawler fans had been introduced to, Jack now looked like a brand-new marine. Management reportedly hated the look. The match went badly. The damage was done.

The bullying did not stop due to Outback's push, placement on the card, and his perceived ego. Jack was mocked for his accent, which makes it plausible when you realize the Bulldogs had a British accent. The pressure followed him from locker room to hotel to town after town. In his own words, Outback Jack said he couldn't take it anymore. By early 1988, he was gone.

The locker room failed him. Sometimes it isn't the ring that ends your career. It's the men waiting behind the curtain.

———

DOUG BASHAM WAS BEING GROOMED as a top heel in OVW under Jim Cornette, with plans to become one of the promotion's centerpiece talents.

Doug was the nephew of OVW Owner and Trainer Danny Davis, who Cornette said took care of him not due to nepotism but because Basham was good. Very good in fact.

Basham was heavily discussed during his time in OVW, not if but when he would be called up to WWE, and what the plans for him would be.

Then WWE called him up to Raw.

Without warning Cornette or OVW, WWE shaved Basham's head backstage to "see what he'd look like bald."

John Laurinaitis was the head of talent relations, and the culprit Cornette blamed.

Cornette called Laurinaitis to scream that his top heel just walked into the TV looking like a "40-year-old truck driver" and that Basham was "mind-raped out of the business" by the experience.

The company formed the Basham Brothers with Doug Basham, who would team with Daniel Hollie, with whom Doug actually worked against in OVW as Damaja. The Bashams were later aligned with Tough Enough 2 co-champion Shaniqua and portrayed with a bondage-based S&M gimmick. The "brothers" won the tag team titles and received a decent push. But Cornette thought he deserved better.

———

MUHAMMED HASSAN, played by Mark Copani, was being groomed as a top main-event heel in WWE. Many thought he was disrespectful, including Sgt. Slaughter, who told me in a 2009 shoot interview. Slaughter recalls other stars telling him not to worry and that they would handle the disrespect.

During his Iraqi sympathizer run in the early 1990s, Slaughter's life and family were threatened repeatedly. He believed Hassan could have been a much bigger star if he had embraced the push instead of fearing it.

As the son of Middle Eastern Arabic-speaking parents, I loved the gimmick. Hassan was a modern-day Iron Sheik, with more coherent promos, and his finisher was even the camel clutch. Just months after a WrestleMania moment with Hulk Hogan in Los Angeles and angles with top stars such as Shawn Michaels and Undertaker, a controversial segment on SmackDown aired the same day as the London terrorist bombings in 2005. It was taped a week before the attacks, and WWE and Hassan had no choice.

The backlash was immediate, unfair, and unjust. Sponsors threatened to walk away, and the backlash was immediate.

The timeline did not matter to most who wanted the character to die. The character was pulled from television. Copani was quietly released.

Instead of continuing his dream in pro wrestling, Copani walked away from wrestling entirely. He went back to school and became a teacher.

Copani is now a High school principal. One of the fastest-rising stars in WWE history vanished overnight.

———

BART GUNN WON WWE's real-fight Brawl for All tournament.

Instead of being rewarded, he was punished for knocking out Dr. Death Steve Williams, who was being positioned to work with Steve Austin at some point.

The company responded by placing Bart in a real boxing match against Butterbean at WrestleMania XV, where he was knocked out in less than thirty seconds.

He was set up. You can disagree with me.

You don't knock out the favorite in the tournament, as well as knocking out other wrestlers, win the thing, and then the machine has nothing for him.

Today, Bart works as an electrician and rarely, if at all, does autograph signings, even though fans often request them. Gunn enjoys riding motorcycles, barbecuing, and playing with his grandkids, according to WWE.com, when they covered his exile from the business.

———

AT ONE TIME, Monty Brown had everything in wrestling.

A look with charisma who got significant crowd reactions with one of the most explosive finishers ever — **The Pounce.** In TNA, he was positioned as the company's future. In WWE, under the ECW brand as Marcus Cor Von, he was again being groomed as a franchise player. Few wrestlers of his generation had the momentum that Monty Brown did.

Then he walked away. No farewell tour or retirement speech. Just silence. Behind the disappearance was tragedy. His departure from WWE in 2007 was due to "family issues," but details weren't disclosed publicly.

Brown quietly walked away from millions of dollars and a main-event push that was imminent. He never turned his story into a publicity tour. He disappeared into private life.

Some wrestlers leave the business in search of another spotlight.

Today, Monty lives quietly and serves as the director of Personal & Group Fitness Training at the Sagina Athletic Club. And in wrestling history, he remains one of the greatest "what if" stories the business has ever known.

CHAPTER 61
FUNERAL ATTENDANCE

THE WRESTLING BUSINESS is built on big personalities, sold-out arenas, and moments that last forever. But when it's all over, the reality can be very different. Careers are spent on the road, relationships come and go, and entire generations of wrestlers drift apart over time. Because of that, even some of the biggest names in the industry have had surprisingly quiet funerals.

One of the most talked-about recent examples is The Iron Sheik. According to Sergeant Slaughter, he was the only wrestler who attended Sheik's funeral. There's no official attendance list, and the service may have been private, but the statement itself says a lot. This was a former WWF Champion, a central figure in the early 1980s boom, and someone who helped set the stage for Hulkamania.

What makes it even more striking is how beloved he still was years later. At the WWE Hall of Fame in 2005, The Iron Sheik stole the show, getting the loudest reaction, after Hulk Hogan, of the night, and a massive crowd response.

It was a reminder of how much fans still connected with him—even decades after his peak. Yet by the time of his passing, the wrestling presence at his farewell—at least publicly—felt incredibly small.

Something similar came up when Gene Okerlund passed away in 2019.

"MEAN" Gene was one of the most recognizable voices in wrestling history, and you would expect a huge turnout. Instead, the wrestlers who were publicly known to be there included Diamond Dallas Page, Greg Gagne, Brian Blair, and Jim Brunzell, along with a couple of WWE executives.

DDP later spoke openly about how much that moment surprised him: *When Gene Okerlund died, I thought it was going to be a who's who—Hogan, Flair, everybody. But nobody showed up except for me. The only others there from the business were Kevin Dunn and Kerwin Silfies, Greg Gagne, Jim Brunzell, and Brian Blair. As far as the boys... that was it.*

He also recalled a meaningful moment with Greg Gagne that stayed with him, showing that even in a small gathering, the connections that did remain still mattered. At the same time, context matters. The service was reportedly private; many of Gene's closest peers had already passed away, and others may have chosen to pay their respects away from public view. Still, the perception of a quiet farewell has remained one of the most discussed examples in modern wrestling.

. . .

THE CASE of Sensational Sherri is often brought up, though the full details are less clear. Based on photos and later recollections, the wrestlers most often identified at her funeral were Booker T, Sharmell, Marty Jannetty, and Jake Roberts, who was known to be close with her. There's no confirmed full attendance list, but the perception remains that turnout from the wrestling world was limited for someone of her influence.

WITH JACK TUNNEY, things are even less documented. Tunney was the on-screen WWF President during the 1980s boom and played a major role in that era. When he passed away in 2004, there wasn't much public acknowledgment from WWE, and later accounts suggest there was little to no company presence at his funeral. However, there's no fully verified attendance record, so most of what's said comes from retrospective accounts.

THEN THERE'S PEDRO MORALES, one of the most important champions in WWE history. Morales was a trailblazer and one of the company's earliest megastars, especially in New York and Puerto Rico. From Puerto Rico to Shea Stadium, he was a major draw, even teaming with Bob Backlund to defeat The Wild Samoans—a reminder of just how big he was during his time. Yet when Morales passed away, reports painted a very different picture.

According to accounts attributed to wrestling coverage and Dave Meltzer, Backlund was reportedly the only pro wrestler in attendance and was very upset by the lack of turnout. Later clarification indicated that at least one other wrestling figure was present, but the overall attendance still appears extremely small, given Morales' legacy. Other names come up in similar conversations.

WHEN RICK RUDE passed away in 1999, his close friend Curt Hennig made his frustration clear: *"The thing that really burns me... is the people in that Atlanta area—the people Rick Rude made a lot of money for, the people that knew him—that didn't show up to his funeral. Stuff like that... It's really frustrating."* Hennig's words showed that this wasn't just fan perception—those inside the business noticed it too.

WAHOO MCDANIEL AND BUDDY ROGERS, similar stories have circulated over the years, suggesting lighter-than-expected attendance, though the details are harder to verify. There are also situations where it wasn't just about funeral attendance, but about the overall lack of acknowledgment.

WHEN ADRIAN ADONIS died in 1988 or when Mike Awesome passed in 2007, the industry response at the time felt minimal. That doesn't necessarily confirm who attended their funerals—but it reinforces the idea that wrestlers are sometimes quietly remembered rather than publicly honored. That's really what ties all of these stories together. It's not always about disrespect—it's about distance.

Time passes, people scatter, and the wrestling world keeps moving forward. Entire locker rooms change. Friendships fade. And sometimes, by the end, the circle is much smaller than anyone would expect. And maybe no one summed that up better than Hulk Hogan, reflecting on the business years later: "I mean... everybody's dead. I've got a store down in Clearwater Beach, and I'll look at a picture—there's six guys in it, and I'm the only one still alive. It's freaky. My parents are gone, my brother's gone, all my friends... I quit going to funerals. I've walked into too many hotel rooms where the guys had passed away. You look at other sports—maybe 10, 15, 20 guys... in wrestling, it's 350. I mean... everybody's dead." — Hulk Hogan.

It's a harsh way to put it, but it explains everything. By the time many of these funerals happen, entire generations are already gone. Others are scattered, out of the business, or no longer connected. Some can't bring themselves to keep going to funerals over and over again. A quiet farewell doesn't erase a legacy. The Iron Sheik still helped launch Hulkamania. Gene Okerlund is still the voice behind some of the most iconic interviews ever. Pedro Morales is still one of the greatest champions in WWE history. The crowds may not always be there at the end—but the moments they created never really leave

CHAPTER 62

THE LOST ROYAL RUMBLE OF 1987

"Pat, why don't you tell Dick Ebersol that stupid idea you had?" - Vince McMahon.

ON OCTOBER 4, 1987, the Royal Rumble quietly debuted at a WWF house show in St. Louis—and by nearly every measure, it failed. Initially.

THE EVENT DREW FEWER than 2,000 fans, a thin crowd in a building designed to hold 15,000+. Instead of the now-familiar 30 participants, this first version featured only wrestlers.

More critically, the architect of the concept, Pat Patterson, wasn't present. Without Patterson, the match unraveled.

The structure was unclear. Communication among agents and talent was poor. Wrestlers entered without a clear rhythm, and the staggered-entry format—so central to the Rumble's identity—felt confusing rather than suspenseful.

Patterson later explained the problem to CBS Sports in 2016: *"It didn't work because I wasn't there. The producer was mixed up, the talent was mixed up, and they didn't know how it was going to work."*

THE CROWD REACTION reflected that confusion—muted, uncertain, and disengaged. Even the finish failed to land. One Man Gang eliminated Junkyard Dog to win, but the moment had already been spoiled.

IN A BIZARRE TURN, earlier in the night, the ring announcer told fans that One Man Gang would be challenging Hulk Hogan on the next returned show in St. Louis, eliminating any sense of surprise.

Two elements now considered essential were also missing: a countdown clock and entrance music for most participants.

Without them, there was no anticipation—no tension between arrivals, no emotional buildup as the ring filled.

TO VINCE MCMAHON, the experiment looked dead on arrival. The concept was quietly shelved, written off as another idea that didn't translate beyond the drawing board.

And that might have been the end—if not for competition.

IN EARLY 1988, the WWF aired opposite on the USA Network, head-to-head with the scheduled NWA Bunkhouse Stampede pay-per-view.

McMahon suddenly needed something distinctive—something that would feel different from a standard card.

While planning the broadcast, McMahon presented NBC executive Dick Ebersol with a tentative lineup, which Ebersol found unimpressive.

McMahon turned to Patterson and said, *"Pat, why don't you tell Dick Ebersol that stupid idea you had?"*

Patterson did—and Ebersol immediately understood what McMahon had missed.

Unlike a traditional run-in, which is exciting but unexpected, the Royal Rumble promised guaranteed chaos at fixed intervals.

Ebersol loved it, and his endorsement was enough to convince McMahon to give the idea one more chance—this time, built specifically for television.

. . .

THE FIRST TELEVISED Royal Rumble aired on January 24, 1988, on the USA Network and corrected the flaws of the St. Louis test run.

THE FIELD EXPANDED to 20 participants, giving the match time to catch its breath.

Bret Hart and Tito Santana were hand-picked by Pat Patterson to start the Rumble match and establish pace and structure. In contrast, established names like Jake Roberts, Jim Duggan (eventual winner), and The Ultimate Warrior added credibility and star power. A countdown clock framed each entrance, and commentary sold the suspense. **The show drew an 8.2 rating, the highest cable rating for a wrestling broadcast at that time.**

The Royal Rumble wasn't just revived—it worked.

Today, the 1987 St. Louis match barely exists in official history. There is no confirmed record of all twelve participants. Even the winner struggled to recall it. One Man Gang later admitted, "I wish I could give you details about it, but I really don't remember it."

What began as a confused house-show experiment nearly disappeared forever. Instead, it evolved into one of WWE's Big Four events and the kickoff to WrestleMania each year.

The WWE has never promoted or acknowledged the match as a true Royal Rumble. In practice, it became a dress rehearsal—one WWE would rather leave behind.

CHAPTER 63

THE ROUGEAUS AND THE BULLDOGS

"Where does it end?" - Vince McMahon

THE JACQUES ROUGEAU–DYNAMITE Kid fight has been discussed for decades, but usually as a headline: a hallway punch, missing teeth, and a famous receipt of locker-room justice. Jacques has addressed it in interviews before, but what he shared publicly was the short version.

IN OUR LONG-FORM INTERVIEW, he did something he says he'd never done on record—he told it from the start, in order, with the details he carried for nearly thirty years: where the heat truly began, how the humiliation affected him, why he felt forced into a decision, what Vince McMahon said behind closed doors, and what the two weeks after the punch felt like when the Bulldogs had already given notice.

. . .

AS OF THIS 2026 PRINTING, Jacques describes it not as a story he's proud of, but as one he finally understands, and that has finally brought him closure.

WHAT FOLLOWS IS the chapter as I reconstructed it from Jacques' account—written cleanly and chronologically, while keeping his voice and key quotes intact.

"Andrew, people think it started in that hallway," Jacques told me. *"It didn't. It started before that."*

IT ALL BEGAN at SummerSlam 1988 at Madison Square Garden—the match that planted the first seed. He and Raymond worked the British Bulldogs in a 20-minute, no-time-limit draw. *"We knew we were gonna get beaten,"* Jacques said. *"They were the best team around. They were the World Tag Team Champions."* But Vince McMahon wanted the Rougeaus elevated.

"That's not what Vince wanted—he wanted us to level up to them," Jacques admitted. The draw felt like a win to him and Raymond. *"We were so happy that it must have shown on our faces."*

To the Bulldogs, Jacques believed, felt like an insult. *"I think there was a little bit of heat that started there,"* he said. *"They were worried about their position... everybody was fighting for the top."*

THE NEXT FLASHPOINT came on the road. Jacques described the grind—"25 days on the road"—and how rare family time was. In Syracuse, New York, he and Raymond found a flight home that same night—9:20 p.m. from Syracuse to Montreal—thanks to a monthly flight guide they carried. *"That means we get to sleep an extra night at home,"* he said. *"We were home about three days a month in those days."*

The Rougeaus were scheduled for the last match (number eight). The Bulldogs were scheduled third. Jacques checked the same guide for the Bulldogs. No flight could get them home to Calgary that night. So he went to the agent, Jay Strongbow, and asked to switch the matches: put the Bulldogs on last, the Rougeaus on third. *"They could do a hell of a job—there was no doubt,"* Jacques said. *"We were just gonna go ahead and jump in without taking a shower, go to the airport, and barely make that 35–40 minute flight."*

TO JACQUES, it was considerate. *"We would have done the same thing for them,"* he said. *"If they had an extra night at home, we would have gladly gone eight."* But he learned quickly that the Bulldogs took it differently.

Someone—Jacques believed it was Curt Hennig—warned him: *"The Bulldogs are not happy you switched the matches... I'd watch my stuff if I were you."* Before going out, he asked Hennig to keep an eye on his bag, passport, and essentials. When Jacques returned, Hennig didn't have to say anything. *"He looked at me right in the eyes... then he stared at my bag... stared at me... stared at my bag."* Jacques immediately understood they messed with his stuff.

He checked his bags quickly and didn't find anything missing. But on the adrenaline, as he left the building, he told Hennig something that—by Jacques' own telling—turned the heat into a fuse: *"I'm not gonna stand for this. When I get to TV next week, I'm gonna tell Vince [McMahon]. I'm gonna report this to Vince… we don't need this kind of stuff."*

THEN HE WENT HOME for three days—still unaware of what those words were about to cost him.

WHEN THE TOUR resumed in Miami, Jacques walked into a setup. Miami mattered to him because his father spent the winter there. *"Sometimes he'd pick us up… bring us to the show… we'd eat at his house… sleep at his house. It would break the trip."* That day, Jacques entered the dressing room and saw Curt Hennig positioned at a card table in the far corner. Jacques loved cards—*"I was a card maniac"*—a way to kill time on long tours.

But the table placement wasn't accidental. *"Curt was at the far end… his back to the wall,"* Jacques said, *"and the chair in front of him was back to the whole dressing room."* Jacques sat with his back to the room—unable to see anyone approach.

That's when the attack came. *"I got slapped on the side of my head so hard,"* Jacques said. Cards flew. He fell off the chair. When he got up dizzy, Dynamite was right there: *"You're gonna stooge on me. You're gonna report this to Vince."* Then, according to Jacques, Dynamite punched him in the face.

JACQUES STOPPED and clarified something he kept repeating throughout the interview because it defined how he experienced the whole thing. *"Let me make something clear. I'm not a fighter in real life. I'm an entertainer. I play the role of a bad guy and a tough guy… but I'm not. I'm an artist."*

In that moment, he didn't swing back. *"When he punched me, I was trying to talk my way out of this,"* Jacques said, *"but I was getting punched in the face... and he punched me hard enough that I fell to the ground."*

The image that haunted him wasn't the punch. It was where it happened. *"The funniest thing is my brother Raymond's not too far,"* he said, *"but he's on crutches... torn ligaments in his knee. So I'm getting beat up in front of Raymond."* Jacques couldn't even track how many shots. *"I can't remember how many... I never got into this with anybody to see how badly I got beaten up."* He remembers trying to rise. He remembers going down. He remembers Raymond saying only one thing over and over: *"Stay down. Stay down. Don't get up."*

AND JACQUES REMEMBERS ANOTHER THING: the wall behind Dynamite. *"Behind Dynamite, there was Davey Boy, there was the Hart Foundation, Bob Orton, and Don Muraco, a big clique."* Jacques wasn't fighting one man; he felt surrounded by an ecosystem.

WHEN JACQUES FINALLY STAYED DOWN, Raymond forced himself up on crutches. *"Hey, that's enough!"* Jacques believed Dynamite was kicking him while he lay there. Then, Dynamite turned and punched Raymond in the mouth. Raymond didn't flinch. *"You're gonna hit a guy on crutches?"* Raymond asked. Dynamite's reply burned into Jacques' memory: *"Nope. I'm gonna wait till you heal and then I'm gonna beat you up."* And then they left.

. . .

THE AFTERMATH that night was equally revealing. An agent came in later—Jacques believed it was Tony Garea, but was not 100% sure—panicked, asking if he was okay. The agent told him he didn't have to work; however, Jacques' pride took over. *"No, no, no—I'm gonna work tonight."* Raymond came out first, crutches clicking. Jacques followed, his face swollen so badly he felt deformed. *"I look like the Hunchback of Notre Dame, but in my face."* Because Raymond couldn't work, Jacques tried to wrestle the Hart Foundation alone. *"I think I did about eight minutes or nine minutes,"* he said, *"then I rolled out and told the referee to stop the match."*

They didn't shower. They grabbed their bags. Jacques' father had watched from the stands and had seen that something was wrong. In the car back, Jacques sat in the back seat and went silent. His father and Raymond spoke, but when their Dad tried speaking to him, *"I never answered,"* Jacques said. *"I never spoke again after that for quite a while."* At his father's house, Jacques went downstairs to a basement room and disappeared. The next morning, he packed in silence. *"I was traumatized,"* he said, *"mentally hurt very, very badly, more than physically. Embarrassed. My self-esteem had left me. I was broken."*

Then came the humiliation that branded the week. On the flight to Chicago, the plane landed to applause—WWF was hot, and the flight attendant welcomed the roster to a flight full of four hundred, according to Jacques.

Then she added a second announcement: *"We'd like to congratulate Jacques Rougeau on his boxing match last night."* Jacques described it as a nightmare. He saw the Bulldogs and other wrestlers grinning at him, waiting for his reaction. *"I put my head back down."*

In Milwaukee, he sat in the dressing room staring at the floor. *"I'm not looking at anybody in the face... my head is always down."* He kept telling himself: *"Keep going. Keep going. It's gonna get better."* Then Dynamite and the Bulldogs came in and played intimidation games—banging metal equipment trunks near him, hovering over him, making "jock itch" jokes that twisted his name. Jacques didn't call it funny. He called it what it was: intimidation and ridicule. "Please don't beat me anymore," his posture was saying, even if he didn't speak it.

AFTER THREE DAYS IN CHICAGO, Jacques finally spoke to Raymond in the car. It was the first time in days. *"I had enough,"* he said. *"I was so embarrassed and humiliated in front of the boys."* Then he said the line that changed the course of the story: *"Next month on TV, I'm gonna do my comeback."* Raymond was thrilled. That night, Raymond—on crutches—propped a mattress against the wall and started teaching Jacques how to jab and box at 11:30 p.m. Jacques never forgot the image of his injured brother trying to rebuild his pride in a hotel room.

SIX DAYS AFTER MIAMI, the night before TV (television taping scheduled) in Fort Wayne, Indiana, Jacques called his father. Jacques described his father as his hero—someone whose opinion mattered deeply.

Jacques wanted to make him proud again. *"Dad... I just wanna let you know I'm doing my comeback tomorrow."* His father's reply was blunt. He told Jacques go to the bank, get a roll of quarters, and when you hit him, hit him to kill him. Jacques described that as *"heavy."* He repeated that he wasn't a fighter at heart. *"I'm going against a big bully who's full of steroids, full of pills, full of everything.*" But he also described a deeper terror—becoming a coward in his father's eyes.

THEN CAME the detail fans never knew—the one that explains why Vince reacted the way he did later.

Call time was 10 a.m.

The bank opened at 10 a.m.

JACQUES AND RAYMOND went to the bank first. That meant they missed Vince's morning meeting, the first time they'd ever been absent. Jacques emphasized this hard: *"We were never late. We were always the first ones there, so professional and credible."* Vince didn't know they were at the bank. From Vince's perspective, they didn't show up and took it as disrespect because, as Jacques recalls, Vince and others believed the Rougeaus were quitting on their way out.

By the time Jacques and Raymond arrived, the locker room already had an earful from their boss Vince McMahon, tearing into everyone by the ring inside an empty arena before the television tapings that day— calling them out and warning his stars that the next fight would mean termination.

JACQUES AND RAYMOND arrived at approximately 10:45 am, according to Jacques' account, after the 10 am meeting. They approached the curtained dressing rooms. Raymond opened one curtain, closed it, and kept moving. Jacques peeked and saw why: Dynamite was inside with Dino Bravo and Davey Boy. Jacques looked at Raymond and said, *"In here."* He described it as choosing to enter the lion's den. He didn't know whether he wanted to confront his demons or run—but if he was going in, he was going in now. He walked past Dynamite, past Dino, and greeted Dino. Dino didn't even look at him. *"He was a friend of ours, Andrew. I felt betrayed."* Jacques said, *"he (Dino) didn't want to show the Bulldogs he was my friend."* Jacques described that as betrayal at the time, even if he later understood Dino's survival instincts. Then Raymond came in on crutches—and greeted Dino. Dino answered Raymond. Jacques' interpretation was blunt: Dino respected Raymond more because Raymond was dangerous in a different way. *"Raymond would have beaten Dino up... he would have pulled his eye out... torn him apart... You have no idea what kind of individual he is."* Jacques wasn't bragging; he was explaining the hierarchy: his father and his brother were respected shooters. Jacques—by his own description—was not.

JACQUES SAT DOWN and pulled out a book he'd bought at the airport—a revenge novel he couldn't remember. Then, as he and Raymond sat, the room emptied. The Bulldogs, Dino, and others left. "It's almost like nobody wanted to be identified in the same room with us."

AT 11 A.M., everyone went to the cafeteria before promos. Jacques and Raymond didn't. Jacques remembered his father's advice about fighting on an empty stomach. He sat ringside in a silent arena, waiting for the boys to eat and thinking, "Go ahead. Fill your stomach. Put the chances on my side."

· · ·

VINCE AND HULK HOGAN walked out, discussing the evening's finish and show planning. Vince passed right in front of Jacques. Jacques said nothing. He believed Vince expected him to speak—Vince, can I talk to you?—but Jacques stayed silent. Five minutes later, Vince circled back and said, *"Guys, I'd like to speak to you in a little bit."* Jacques nodded—*"Yes, sir."* Then Vince left.

That was the moment Jacques said he knew—without being told—that if they spoke to Vince first, Vince would warn them, and the window would close. Jacques looked at Raymond: *"We gotta do it NOW!"* It had to happen **before** the talk with Vince.

JACQUES DESCRIBED HIS FAITH HERE— HOW he talks to God daily and prays intensely during the week because he is afraid. He lost five pounds in one week. He couldn't eat without feeling nauseous. Jacques was shaking with nerves. Then the Rougeau brothers positioned themselves outside the cafeteria exit—a passageway seven feet wide, one way in and out. Raymond against one wall, Jacques against the other, about four feet between them. **And, a roll of quarters hidden in Jacques' right hand.**

ONE BY ONE, the pack thinned: Moraco and Orton. Bret and Anvil. Then Davey alone. Jacques watched the "wolf pack," as he called them, shrink and thought it reduced the chance they'd all swarm him if he missed. Then, just before Dynamite Kid, Pat Patterson walked into the setup.

. . .

"ANDREW, *you keep asking if Pat knew, and I am telling you, Pat Patterson had no clue and had nothing to do with it!*" Jacques emphasized this because fans, including myself, felt that Pat may have known. Jacques insisted Pat had no idea. Jacques was standing there, quarters in hand, terrified, he recalls. Pat greeted Jacques, who shot him a look that said, "*Not now.*" Pat turned to Raymond, and Raymond kept small talk to avoid giving anything away.

THEN JACQUES SAW Dynamite approaching from forty feet away, holding a cup of coffee. Jacques kept his head down, so Dynamite had to pass directly in front of him. At three feet, Jacques looked up and locked eyes with him for the first time in a week. Dynamite puffed his chest and smiled.

Jacques said calmly: "*How are you doing?*" And then Jacques' right hand came up. "*Bang. I hit him right in the mouth with everything I had with that roll of quarters.*"

DYNAMITE DROPPED TO ONE KNEE, clung to Jacques' waist—and then he heard Pat Patterson scream for help. Jacques described blood coming out "like a fountain," spraying like a horror movie, all over him. Jacques froze, staring. Raymond screamed at him to hit again. Jacques jabbed with his left. Bang. Bang.

BAD NEWS BROWN ARRIVED FIRST, according to Jacques, and grabbed Jacques by the throat, backing him up away from a bloodied Dynimate Kid. He didn't resist. Bad News was indeed Bad News for anyone who got in his way. He was a judo champion and competed in the

Olympics. Jacques said there were too many bodies now. Dynamite couldn't hit him. Bret and Davey came running— but it was too late.

IN A POOL OF BLOOD, Dynamite was still threatening, telling Jacques, *"I'm gonna f*** you up!"* Jacques stopped forty feet away, turned back, and walked toward him. Jacques said he didn't recognize himself. He told Dynamite, "Next time, I'm gonna put you in a wheelchair," which would be foretelling and tragic, as Dynamite Kid spent the final years of his life in a wheelchair due to severe spinal, back, and leg injuries.

Jacques described it as out-of-body, demons, trauma— something taking over that wasn't the man he thought he was. Then came the cinematic march to Vince's office. Jacques and Raymond walked against the traffic of wrestlers rushing toward the hallway. They passed Hulk's room. They passed Macho Man's room—Randy Savage opened the door, saw Jacques covered in blood from head to toe, and said, *"Ohhh, yeah,"* then shut the door.

Raymond knocked on Vince's door. Vince opened, *"Guys, later, okay?"*—the first time in four years Vince had ever been rude to them, according to Jacques, who then grabbed Raymond and stepped forward anyway: *"No. It's gonna be right now."*

HOGAN SAW Jacques covered in blood and said, *"I'm out of here, brother,"* and left. Vince's tone changed instantly. He let them in. Jacques cut Vince off before Vince could speak.

He said the line he never forgot: ***"If you wanna fire me, it's okay. Because for the last week I wasn't able to look at myself in the mirror, but now I'm gonna be able to go home and do so."***

Vince replied: *"I'm not firing anybody."*

Vince left briefly, then returned and said he would escort them to get their bags and take them out to the car. The Bulldogs were leaving that night on a red-eye for France.

Vince wanted to let it settle. Vince escorted Jacques and Raymond through the dressing room in front of everyone, brought them to the car, and they left.

THE NEXT DAY in New York at Madison Square Garden, Jacques said the isolation was total. The guys opened the dressing room door, saw the Rougeaus inside, and shut it —kept walking. *"Nobody wanted to dress with us,"* Jacques said, because anyone seen with them could be targeted or blocked by the Bulldogs.

Later, Dino Bravo came in and offered "good news and bad news." The Bulldogs had given notice; they were finishing in two weeks. At first, Jacques felt relief—then fear. "They're gonna kill me before they leave," he thought. "They're not gonna leave and lose face."

Jacques said this is where he took a strategic step. He wrote down a phone number on a piece of paper, then stopped Dino. He made Dino swear on his daughter's hand that he would never repeat what Jacques was about to say. Jacques admitted he did that because he knew Dino would tell them anyway.

. . .

JACQUES TOLD Dino Bravo that he had to call that number every night for the next two weeks, and if he missed one night, there would be a "hit" in Calgary—on Dynamite's family. Dino—known for mafia associations—took it seriously and warned the Bulldogs. For two weeks, Jacques and Raymond lived in fear. Jacques described parking back-to-back like a movie, walking into buildings together, walking out together, scanning for steel poles, constantly bracing for an ambush.

He said Bret even asked Dino what to do with the information, and Dino told him to keep working normally. The matches stayed normal. The arrival and departure were the terror. Jacques said they felt relieved after every day survived because there were still two weeks left to get through.

WHEN THE BULLDOGS returned before the final stretch, Vince arranged a private meeting room at the San Francisco airport. Jacques and Raymond arrived first; Vince seated them near the door. The Bulldogs entered, passed behind them, and then sat across from them. Vince spoke calmly: it should never have happened, and he posed the escalation question—"*you hit, he hit, where does it end?*"

Jacques believed Vince had heard the "hit" rumor and wanted no part of anything that could spill beyond wrestling, but agreed that Vince was right. Jacques said Dynamite was "broken" in that meeting—no posturing, unable to speak clearly because he had no teeth—and said he listened to Vince and, as instructed, they shook hands.

Jacques said he knew even then it wasn't truly over inside the Bulldogs' pride, but the meeting set boundaries.

. . .

THE TEETH MYTH Jacques addressed directly. He told me that, in a meeting, Dynamite demanded that Jacques pay for his teeth. Jacques' answer was blunt—he never paid. *"So I assume Vince paid. Vince McMahon was a fixer."* Jacques said. Jacques speculated Vince may have paid and allowed Dynamite to believe Jacques paid, because Vince could protect everyone's pride and keep the machine moving. But Jacques never wrote the check.

THE LAST NIGHT for the Bulldogs arrived at Survivor Series 1988 at Richfield Coliseum. What began on one pay-per-view came full circle on the next. Ten tag teams were involved. Vince gathered everyone to plan eliminations and wanted the Rougeaus out first.

DAVEY BOY STOOD up and volunteered to start with Jacques.

Jacques admitted he was terrified inside, but he did not show it. He looked Davey Boy in the eyes and said, *"Sure. What do you want to do?"* Davey laid out a dangerous press-and-throw sequence that Jacques feared could cripple him. Jacques cut him off before he finished and said, *"I love it."* It never happened, but he called their bluff. Bret Hart ended up pinning Raymond with the small package to eliminate the Rougues first, as planned.

Jacques said Pat Patterson had told them ahead of time that Vince wanted them to grab their bags after the match and leave immediately—no shower—so it would "ease things" and let certain people save face. Jacques said they wouldn't have left on their own, but they did because Vince asked. They left.

The Bulldogs left. And the two-week countdown ended without an ambush.

I ASKED Jacques in this chapter whether Dynamite's death on his 60th birthday, December 5, 2018, gave him any closure —not happiness—but closure. Jacques said it was the end of a bad era. Then Jacques told the part that most people never connect to the hallway: reconciliation.

Years later, at the Philadelphia Spectrum, Jacques, now wrestling as a single star repackaged as The Mountie, saw Davey Boy Smith's name on the sheet. Davey had his own issue with the Dynamite Kid, who was furious at Davey for trademarking the British Bulldog name, which will be covered in the next Urban Legend book for sure.

Jacques admitted he watched the door all night, tense. When Davey walked in, he stopped in front of Jacques and asked to talk in the showers. Jacques agreed—but inside, he said, he kept his distance. In the shower area, Davey stood at the far end, giving Jacques space. Davey extended his hand and said he wanted them to be friends.

Davey told Jacques, *"What you did to Dynamite, you were right."*

Jacques felt relief and caution at the same time—wondering if it was a setup—then took the handshake firmly, gripping in a way that kept him safe. Jacques told Davey he appreciated it and left. From that day on, Jacques said, they became genuine friends.

AT THE END of the story, Jacques returned to the core truth: he never wanted a fight. He never wanted a confrontation. He kept saying it because it defined his identity within the mythology. He wasn't his father. He wasn't Raymond. They were respected shooters. His father was his hero. Jacques called himself an artist. And the point of the story wasn't violence—it was dignity. For a week, he couldn't look in the mirror. After that hallway, he could.

THE BRITISH BULLDOGS were brilliant in the ring. They were intense, believable, and undeniably talented. Jacques made that clear before anything else. *"Before all that happened, they were my heroes,"* he said. *"They were incredible. They were so talented. They were so believable. They were so over."*

That truth is what makes this chapter layered rather than simple. Jacques' account does not just describe a fight; it reveals a culture where intimidation could quietly shape careers and silence people who wanted to survive, as we covered previously in this book with Outback Jack and how he was run out of the business, or how others tolerated it, like Terry Taylor, who had his clothes torn at the hands of the Bulldogs. How "ribs" sometimes crossed a line that should never have been crossed.

But what lingers here is not the blood. It is the mirror. When Jacques stood in Vince McMahon's office, still covered in blood, he said: *"If you want to fire us now, that's fine. For a week, I couldn't look at myself in the mirror — and now I can."* That wasn't anger. That wasn't pride. That was dignity.

The bullying did not end because the toughest man in the room snapped.

It ended because a man refused to keep living broken.

CHAPTER 64

TWO MINUTES AND THIRTY SECONDS

AS TOLD BY BRET "THE HITMAN" HART

"I am glad they caught my eyes rolling at him." - Bret Hart.

FEW MATCHES in wrestling history have reshaped the business the way Bret Hart vs. "Stone Cold" Steve Austin did at WrestleMania 13 in 1997. What began as a submission match became something far greater — the moment that ignited the Attitude Era. Austin, blood pouring down his face while trapped in Hart's Sharpshooter, refused to quit. Hart walked away the victor, but the audience saw Austin as the new anti-hero of wrestling. In a single match, the roles reversed: Bret Hart became the bitter villain, and Steve Austin became the most unlikely hero the industry had ever seen. **It is still the greatest double-turn in history.**

In 2025, WWE announced that the match would finally be inducted into the WWE Hall of Fame. For Bret Hart, however, the night would leave him with mixed feelings. When speaking about the experience afterward, Hart described the events of WrestleMania weekend in blunt and candid detail.

"Well, I will say that I was not very happy with that Hall of Fame. When Triple H came through town in November, he told me that when he saw me at the building, he said, "We're gonna do a thing with you at the Hall of Fame. You're gonna be the first guy to be inducted three times, and we're gonna induct your match with Steve as the greatest match of all time. And I'm like, sounds great. And then he told me, basically, that we're gonna give you $50,000 for coming to WrestleMania. As we got closer to WrestleMania, I kept calling and going back and forth, so I just want to confirm that they're gonna give me $50,000 to do this. They promised me $50,000 to do this. And then the day before I left, they say, Triple H says that he has no recollection of that conversation ever taking place, and that you're gonna get $10,000 or something like that. I think they said everybody gets $5,000, and that's the deal. They promised me $50,000." They ended up calling Bret back and agreeing to what he heard and felt was promised.

"And then when I got there on the night of the Hall of Fame, they put me in the dressing room with Shawn and Triple H in one room. Shawn and Triple H each had two valets, one carrying their bags and brushing and combing their hair, taking lint off their shoulders. It was almost embarrassing to watch. I think it was intentional that they wanted to show me that they're the bosses, like we're the kings around here, and you're just like a low-life servant on the bottom or something.

BUT THE BIGGEST *insult came when they told me I had two minutes, two and a half minutes. And if I said anything one word over two minutes and thirty seconds, they would cut my mic and drum me out with music. I'm watching all night, and everyone else is talking for five, six, eight minutes, sometimes ten minutes. And me, I was told not to talk for more than two minutes and thirty seconds. If you watch my speech, it's pretty short. I hardly even talked. And that was intentional.*

I was almost pissed off that they insulted me by telling me I only had two minutes and thirty seconds to talk. Then I went back to the dressing room, and Shawn Michaels and Triple H went out. Shawn Michaels, just introducing Triple H, talked for thirty minutes."

Bret continued.

*"Then Triple H came out, and it's like four in the morning on the East Coast, and he's talking for ninety minutes. That's when I was like, f*** you guys. You guys are a bunch of pieces of s***. The next day, if you watch, I roll my eyes at Triple H. I'm glad they caught me rolling my eyes at him. Some people made comments about it that it shows my true colors and my true feelings about that guy, which is fine with me, because I have no respect for them or that company. That's just the backstory to that day. I considered that whole day a slap in the face. I never got a ring, I never got anything. By the end of it, I kind of felt like chopped liver. So the next day, when Triple H came out, everyone saw me roll my eyes."*

The exchange standing next to Steve Austin on stage was, *"What are we, chopped liver?"* What I felt listening to Bret wasn't much anger, but rather disappointment. You can hear it in his voice. It's detachment. Something closed for him that weekend.

And when Bret Hart closes a door, he doesn't slam it. He simply walks away. *"I don't think I'll ever go to another WrestleMania again. I'm kind of done with WWE. I've washed my hands of them completely."*

CHAPTER 65
THE BOSS

" ..Bills had to be paid." - Dad

NO WRESTLER in history inspired more myths, locker-room fear, or global awe than André René Roussimoff.

Long before Hollywood, before *The Princess Bride*, before the undefeated streak and the body slam heard around the world, André was already something far rarer than a champion.

He was an attraction. Promoters didn't just book André — they built around him. Entire territories adjusted their calendars to secure a few dates. When André walked into a locker room, he wasn't treated like one of the boys.

He was the boss. But for all the awe he inspired inside arenas, the real world was never built for him. His size was his calling card — and his constant obstacle.

Long before I understood booking, politics, or territory wars, I understood car rides. My father, Fayez Khellah, drove a yellow cab out of Newark Airport — cab #507, a 1983 Mercury Colony Park station wagon.

While most taxis were too small, his wagon had space. So when dispatch needed a driver to accommodate the extra space, my Dad was next in line, thinking it could be someone with extra  luggage or a party of three or more to fit comfortably.

That's how he started driving wrestlers.

At times, it was a few of them at once — straight from Terminal C to Elizabeth, NJ, or sometimes the Meadowlands or Madison Square Garden. Those rides are how wrestling entered our house. That's how I fell in love with it.

But one ride was different.

Sometime in 1984 or 1985, Newark dispatch called for a car that could handle a very large passenger. When my dad pulled up, he saw him immediately — Andre the Giant — standing beside a young Haitian dispatcher my father knew well. She handed my dad a small note with the destination written on it. She didn't want to say it out loud as a small crowd was already forming.

Andre didn't talk much on that ride. He was polite, but quiet. My dad tried a light wrestling conversation. He got short answers, and Andre looked tired, so he didn't push.

Flying was an ordeal. Two first-class seats. Seatbelts barely reach. Airplane aisles are too narrow. On many planes, he couldn't even use the restroom. Hotels weren't much better — beds were too short, showers too tight.

Even taxis sometimes drove past him, unsure if he would fit.

But my dad's station wagon fit. Barely.

Polaroid of my Dad's taxicab years after he drove countless wrestlers, including Andre the Giant, Junkyard Dog, Tito Santana, Ricky Steamboat, and others.

The fare from Newark to Midtown Manhattan was $28. Andre handed him a fifty. When my dad reached for change, Andre told him to keep it.

My father pulled out a wallet-sized photo of my older brother, Johnny, and asked if he would sign it. Andre did — on the back. Years later, I teased my dad and said, *"Why didn't you use my picture?"* He laughed and said, *"You weren't even in Kindergarten."* My brother Johnny is three years older.

I once asked why he didn't save the fifty-dollar bill as a souvenir.

Dad looked at me like a kid who didn't understand real life and said, *"Bills had to be paid."*

My father didn't collect memorabilia. That was my obsession, not his. He once drove singer Ray Charles, and didn't even realize who he was until a Pepsi commercial came on TV and he said, *"I know this guy! I drove him with a lady."* We told him, *"Dad, that's Ray Charles."* He shrugged. *"Okay, so if he's famous, why doesn't he tip?!"*

But Andre tipped.

Years later, my father handed me something that became the centerpiece of my collection — André's final official WWF promotional photo autographed by the 8th Wonder of the World.

Over the years, I've been offered money for it. Real money. As high as $40,000. Every time, I listen. Every time, I shake my head. I could never pull the trigger. In 2014, I had the signature authenticated by PSA. It came back with a full letter. They even tried to buy it from me — offering promotions, grading

credits, incentives for future services. That's how strong it was.

But the moment that mattered most didn't come from an authentication company. In 2019, I showed it to André's daughter, Robin Christensen. She looked at it carefully and said, without hesitation: *"That is definitely my Dad's signature."*

Andre's daughter, Robin with me wearing her Dad's jacket. (New York on November 16, 2019)

That was it. No hologram or letter could mean more than that. The market can value it at six figures. PSA can put it on the letterhead. Collectors can circle.

It's a cab ride to Newark Airport. It's a fifty-dollar bill my father needed to pay real bills. It's a quiet giant in the back of a station wagon. And it's the reason I'm still a fan.

Not only did Robin graciously confirm her Dad's signature, but she also allowed me to wear André's actual jacket — the same one he wore countless times, the same one featured in magazines and press conferences alongside Hulk Hogan.

It hung heavy on my shoulders. Not just physically.

Historically.

I remember Bill Eadie (Ax of Demolition) telling me a different taxicab story with Andre in 2017.

"If they saw Andre, the taxi just sped up and kept going. When one finally stopped, I'd bend down like I was tying my shoelace, and Andre would try to sneak into the cab. The cab driver would complain [when the car dropped down] *and wanted to pull him out."*

ARNOLD SCHWARZENEGGER once went out to dinner with Andre and insisted on paying the bill. Arnold stood up and headed to the front desk. Andre grabbed him, lifted him off the floor, carried him back to the table, set him down, and said, "I pay!"

As impressive as the strength stories are, the stories his friends tell most often are about his drinking.

ANDRE MAY HAVE BEEN — without exaggeration — the greatest drinker who ever lived. On a flight from Chicago to Tokyo with Ric Flair, Andre drank all the vodka on the plane. When the crew ran out, there was no more alcohol left anywhere on board.

On a flight from Miami to Dayton, Hillbilly Jim and Andre ordered 56 miniature bottles of vodka. Andre drank 50 of them. Gerald Brisco confirmed that Andre would routinely drink six bottles of Portuguese wine before walking out to wrestle.

One night, when a bartender called last call, Andre ordered 40 vodka tonics. The bartender stayed open and kept pouring until Andre finished at five in the morning. During a month-long stay at a hotel in England, Andre ran up a bar tab totaling more than $40,000.

On an average day, Andre was consuming roughly 7,000 calories from alcohol alone. He once joked that it took two full bottles of vodka to feel warm.

During a Legends of Wrestling segment, Mike Graham said Andre once drank 156 beers in one sitting. Dusty Rhodes and Michael Hayes backed him up.

JOURNALIST AND FRIEND Bill Apter later recalled a night in New Orleans where Andre drank more than 125 beers while out with Harley Race.

Andre's closest friend and travel handler, Tim White, confirmed he was capable of those feats while chatting with him at WrestleMania weekend in Dallas, TX, in 2022.

Andre's friend Tim White. He passed away three months after this encounter.

My 'Friendly Tap' polo shirt broke the ice when White saw me wearing it. The 'Friendly Tap', for those who don't know, was his bar in Rhode Island that still exists today, and it hung memorabilia—some of which I own today.

It was the Undertaker who pointed it out to Tim while I was in line to meet the Dead Man.

Undertaker said, *"Tim is here,"* and pointed behind me at him. While in line, I get out and give Tim a hug. After I got out of the line, I saw him with my friend Danny Dec, and we chatted about his bar briefly before I asked, as a collector, if he had any Andre memorabilia. I took a shot, but he didn't have anything left.

When I remember most about what Tim said on the Andre documentary, *"He could drink an airplane dry before it got to take off,"* White said. *"He'd go into a restaurant and eat a dozen steaks and lobsters, especially if there were people around."*

BY HIS THIRTIES, Andre's size was destroying his body. His joints ached. His back deteriorated—every step hurt. The drinking wasn't just recreation. It was relief. By the time he was filming The Princess Bride, his back was so damaged that he could no longer safely lift Robin Wright. The production had to use a harness to support her weight. Actor and comedian Billy Crystal later wrote the film "My Giant" based on his real-life friendship with Andre.

One of the strangest myths that followed André was that he had two hearts. The rumor circulated for years as fans tried to explain how one human being could be so large and still function. The truth is, it was a hormonal disorder called acromegaly that we learned much later in life. His pituitary gland overproduced growth hormone, causing his bones and organs to continue growing long after puberty. The condition made him massive and, reportedly, according to doctors, it may have shortened his life.

Promoters learned quickly how to sell him. When Andre wrestled in Montreal, the building sold out. Fans didn't come to see his opponent. They came to see him. Booking him was difficult.

Almost anyone paired with him looked small. Even the biggest wrestlers appeared ordinary standing next to him. So promoters protected him with count-outs, disqualifications, tag matches, and battle royals. Andre wasn't there to be beaten.

Andre's strength became legendary long before weight rooms and performance centers.

BEHIND THE SCENES, Andre's real power had nothing to do with his size. It was his influence. King Kong Bundy learned early what it meant to fall out of Andre's favor. From my shoot interview with Bundy in 2010:

"Andre never liked me, Andy."

He shared a story of wrestling Andre before going to the WWF.

Bundy says he shook Andre's hand and said, *"It was a pleasure working with you, Boss. Thank you very much."*

As he turned away, Bundy patted Andre on the back and said, *"Well, I guess I'm ready for New York."*

Hulk Hogan later told Bundy that Andre had said the exact same words to him in Japan, further confirming that Andre did not like Bundy.

. . .

BIG JOHN STUDD understood the hierarchy. When a road agent asked how the locker room was doing, Bundy remembers Studd shouting out, *"Well, if Andre is happy, we're happy!"* Studd would even stay at a different hotel than Andre to protect kayfabe.

TITO SANTANA WAS one of the men Andre genuinely liked. He told me Andre upgraded Tito to first class so they could play pinochle on flights. *"If Andre liked you, he liked you. And if he didn't, boy, were you in trouble."*

Tito once drove Andre in his brand-new 1975 black Ford Granada. When Andre sat down, the bucket seat broke. They laughed. Tito told me, *"I felt bad for him. It wasn't easy for him on the road."*

One of the most famous stories told during the Andre 'A&E' produced documentary, Tim White, involves a group of men who harassed Andre at a bar. When they left, Andre followed them into the parking lot and flipped their car over, trapping them inside.

MEAN GENE OKERLUND once saw the man behind the legend. Flying from Denver to Minneapolis, Andre called him up to first class and ordered a Bloody Mary at eight in the morning.

"People think I have a great life... but I see them when they point at me. Little kids laugh and say, 'What kind of a man is he?'"

Gene said he watched Andre cry.

. . .

BRUNO SAMMARTINO MET Andre in New Zealand when Andre was twenty years old. *"He didn't like to be alone, so I used to keep him company a lot. At times, he struck me as a lonely man who needed company."*

RODDY PIPER CONSIDERED ANDRE FAMILY. *"Andre took me under his wing, as did many other old-timers. I was the only man who ever had Andre bleeding and carried out on a stretcher at Madison Square Garden. What do I think of Andre? I don't think I've ever met a finer human being."*

THERE WAS ALSO an urban legend that Andre ran the Fabulous Freebirds out of the WWF in 1984. The Freebirds arrived with major buzz and left quickly. Michael PS Hayes later clarified the story with Gerald Brisco and JBL on their podcast:

"Andre may not have wanted us there, but Vince was the one who fired us and said he couldn't trust us." Hayes also recalled a call from Booker George Scott.

"Vince doesn't trust you. So there's no way he's going to hire you back.' Andre may have said fire us, but Andre didn't officially fire us. Vince did." Hayes later pointed to a moment in Ohio when he met Vince outside a hotel bar and was falling asleep in front of him. That may have sealed it. Years later, Hayes returned to WWE and rebuilt that trust as an announcer, writer, and executive.

THE MYTHS around Andre grew larger than life. In July 1975, Washington Redskins coach and general manager

George Allen sent a scout to meet Andre and his promoters. Joe Theismann attended the meeting. The Greenville News reported Andre wrestled in Greenville on July 7, met the Redskins on July 8, wrestled in Albany on July 11, and wrestled at Madison Square Garden on July 12. Redskins personnel director Tim Temerario later said, *"The guy was making $200,000 a year. We couldn't touch it. Hell, he's making more than the entire Redskin backfield."*

ANOTHER MYTH CLAIMED Jerry Lawler pinned Andre. In reality, Lawler beat Andre by count-out. Bill Apter ran a magazine cover reading *"The Night a Midget Beat Andre the Giant."* And the headline caused major heat. Vince McMahon Sr. nearly banned both men from promoting Andre. A correction later ran: *"Andre the Giant: Wrestling's Only Undefeated Superstar."*

ANDRE'S final television appearance came on WCW's Clash of the Champions XX on January 27, 1993, during a celebration of 20 years of wrestling on TBS. Later that month, while attending his father's funeral in France, Andre passed away in his sleep at the age of 46. When WWE created its Hall of Fame, Andre the Giant was the first person ever inducted.

TO THE MEN who lived on the road with him, drank with him, feared him, loved him, and survived him, Andre the Giant was never just a wrestler.

To Robin, he was her Father. To the boys and those who knew Andre, he was and will always be *"Boss."*

ABOUT THE AUTHOR

Andrew has covered professional wrestling since 1996 and has interviewed hundreds of stars, promoters, executives, and other influential figures across wrestling and entertainment.

instagram.com/andrewkhellah

facebook.com/andrew.khellah

youtube.com/@getscreentimed